COLLECTOR'S ENCYCLOPEDIA OF
Milk Glass

Identification
& Value Guide

BETTY & BILL NEWBOUND

COLLECTOR BOOKS
A Division of Schroeder Publishing Co., Inc.

The current values in this book should be used only as a guide. They are not intended to set prices, which vary from one section of the country to another. Auction prices as well as dealer prices vary greatly and are affected by condition as well as demand. Neither the Authors nor the Publisher assumes responsibility for any losses that might be incurred as a result of consulting this guide.

Searching For A Publisher?

We are always looking for knowledgable people considered to be experts within their fields. If you feel that there is a real need for a book on your collectible subject and have a large comprehensive collection, contact Collector Books.

Photography: Bill Newbound

Cover Design: Sherry Kraus

Book Design: Karen Long

Cover Arrangement:

TOP (l to r): 6⅛" Robin on Pedestal Nest. Westmoreland, *$75.00 – 95.00;* Portieux, *$100.00 – 125.00;* Wavy Base Duck, 4¾" tall, 8½" long. Challinore/Taylor, *$125.00 – 135.00;* Westmoreland, *$85.00 – 100.00;* Lamp, 21" tall, *$350.00 – 370.00.*
BOTTOM (l to r): Rolling pin with wooden handles, 21" long, *$50.00 – 55.00;* blown glass rolling pin, 15" long, *$120.00 – 130.00;* compote, 9⅞ tall, *$30.00 – 35.00.*

Printed by IMAGE GRAPHICS, INC., Paducah, Kentucky

DEDICATION

This book is dedicated to Becky and Cindy (in alphabetical order) without whom there would be no book!

ACKNOWLEDGMENTS AND THANKS

A book like this one just could not be done without the help of many people. We had *lots* of help; everything from folks who trusted us with hundreds of their precious milk glass pieces for photographing and shared their carefully gathered research material with us, to young Andy Seabolt of Bristol, Tennessee, who spent his allowance money at a flea market so that he could present us with some milk glass saucers "for your book." (Who says there aren't any good kids any more?)

Many, many thanks to Cynthia Fahr and Rebecca Brandenburg; how can we ever thank you enough? Also to Ruby Morrison, Florence Champagne, Maureen McFarland, Katherine Lilly, Eileen & Louis Gandleman, Linda Douglas, Daphene and Bob Hansor, Russ and Virgie Johnson, Gene Harris Antique Auction Center and to Ed Lauckner, who loaned us stacks of old catalogs.

Our gratitude to Constance Taber Colby who graciously gave us permission to use excerpts from *Stillmeadow Daybook* and *Harvest of Yesterdays* written by her mother, Gladys Taber and published by J.B. Lippincott Company of Philadelphia and New York.

Thanks to Mr. Frank Fenton who gave permission to use the Fenton catalog pages contained herein and to Robert Gianni of L.E. Smith Glass Company for authorizing us to use pages from their 1963–64 catalog. Also to the U.S. Trotting Association for their help in tracking down information on Major Delmar, the horse pictured on the Forget-me-not edged plate shown in the plate section of this book.

And last but not least, thanks to Ellen — who started the whole thing so many years ago. We love you!

HELPING HANDS

Joining a club or visiting a museum help to add to the enjoyment of and knowledge about your glass collection.

National Milk Glass Collector's Society
$15.00 yearly dues. Opaque News quarterly newsletter; yearly convention.
Arlene Johnson, Treasurer
1113 Birchwood Dr.
Garland, TX 75043

Westmoreland Glass Collectors Newsletter
$16.00 per year. Monthly newsletter.
WGCN
P.O. Box 143
North Liberty, IA 52317

Westmoreland Glass Society Inc.
$15.00 yearly dues. Bi-monthly newsletter.
Harold Mayes
2712 Glenwood
Independence, MO 64052

National Westmoreland Glass Collector's Club
P.O. Box 372
Export, PA 15632

Westmoreland Glass Museum
1815 Trimble Ave.
Port Vue, PA 15133
Phone 412-678-7352
Owned by Phil and Hellen Rosso.

CONTENTS

PREFACE

What makes milk glass so appealing? Here we have a piece of glass that is white—just white. Admittedly, a bit of judicious hand painting, flowers, birds, etc., or a bit of gilt sometimes makes a piece more interesting, but mainly we have just plain white. Strangely enough, plain white chinaware does nothing for me—but the white glass is different! I think for one thing the artistry and inventiveness of the molds are always fascinating. Detail is usually wonderful and those old moldmakers surely knew their trade! I love the opal fire that shows around edges and even on the raised parts of many pieces. It is like seeing the living heart of the glass and makes it come alive somehow. Then, there's always been a fascination with white on white. I can remember my mother showing me the padded satin stitch embroidery she did when she was a young woman. All the stitches so close together, raised using a bit of cotton filling—always white on white and beautiful. But I think one of my fellow collectors put it best when she said "it's because you never know what you'll find next." And that's so true. When you're collecting dinnerware, for example, or a set of anything, you pretty much know what was made in your pattern, and although finding another piece to your set is pleasant, there are no surprises. But with milk glass, the next piece you may find hiding away in some dingy little shop may be an exceptional thing of beauty, or it may be a whimsical little item that will make you smile—or exclaim—or shriek, depending on your disposition. There have been times when I've done them all!

I must admit, some of the old Victorian decorators got a bit carried away with their paint and gilt! When I first started collecting, I just could not stand all the old paint slathered freely over everything and I would remove it. Then I learned better! *Do not* take off the old paint, because in many cases, that is one of the main elements that will prove the age of an item. Or, if you are like me, at least leave *some* of the paint; traces of decor can be even more esthetically pleasing than the original paint job. Decorating was done in two ways—what we now call "cold painted," which means the paint was not fired after being done, and permanent painting that was fired in the kilns. Washing cold painted or "touched up" items requires care; lukewarm water with no detergent. Also, when you wash pieces with set-in eyes or stones, keep in mind that these lovely additions were glued in and water may dislodge them. Try to wash carefully around the stones with a cloth rather than submerging that part of the piece in water. If your piece is *really* grungy, check to see if an eye or ring stone has come off before you dispose of the dishwater. Many a collector has seen irreplaceable stones go down the drain!

Now, there are some collectors who are content to just enjoy the beauty (or cuteness) of their pieces for what they are and just plain *don't care* who the manufacturer was or when the pieces were made. But, for the majority of collectors who do care about those things, we have done our best to find out the "who's and when's" of the pieces shown herein. The difficulty is those old manufacturers weren't making glass for collectors, all they cared about was the state of the current market and so old catalogs were destroyed and old molds made their way across the country or disappeared into the melting pots. Time further clouded the issue as old glasshouse workers died and took their memories with them. So please, readers, if you have information that we don't have, we would be happy to hear from you about it.

A SMIDGEN OF HISTORY

The concept of an opaque, milk-white glass is an ancient one. Milk glass was made as early as 1500 B.C. in Egypt and perhaps even earlier. The Chinese produced milk glass snuff bottles and vases by 140 B.C. and milk glass bottles and jars to contain spices and drugs have been found in Persian cities dating from about 635 A.D. The famous Portland vase which is dark cobalt blue glass with applied milk glass figures, dates to the first century A.D. Probably the first milk glass produced in this country was made at Jamestown, Virginia, about 1609. It was part of the fanciful beads produced to use in trading with the Indians.

In Italy about 1612, a book by Antonio Neri was published that contained a formula for making milk-white glass. The French produced milk glass from the mid 1820's—they called it Opaline—and it was very successful. In England and in Venice, milk glass was used as a substitute for porcelain, but the quality was poor and the decorations and colors garish. A very white, brittle product called "enamel glass" was produced from the 1760's in England Shapes were inspired by Chinese porcelain and were lavishly decorated with hand-painted flowers, transfer prints, and gold. It was referred to as "Bristol Glass."

By the mid 1800's, milk glass was extremely popular both in England and in the United States. America's milk glass manufacturers seemed to be concentrated in the East with Pennsylvania having Atterbury & Company's White House Flint Glass Works almost next door to Challinor, Hogan & Co. (later Challinor, Taylor Co.) and across from Ripley and Company's Tremont Glass Works. Nearby were S. McKee & Co., MeKee & Brothers, Fort Pitt Glass Works, Bakewell, Pears & Co. and a number of other glasshouses. Wouldn't you have loved to visit there in those times? Many of the glasshouse folks are interrelated and the youngsters often spread their wings and opened their own glasshouses.

The dolphin motif used for stems on candles, comports, etc., was an offshoot of the Empire style and introduced in the 1840's. The post Civil War era found quaint animals and birds popular in all types of pressed glass. By the turn of the century, the Spanish-American War was commemorated with covered dishes formed as ships and some with a bust of Admiral Dewey. After the laying of the Trans-Atlantic Cable, various patterns using the cable motif were popular. Drapery patterns resembling the festoons used in mourning were introduced on memorial pieces for Lincoln and Garfield. The whole history of our country can be followed in its glass. The peak years of milk glass popularity in the United States were 1895 – 1910, but of course, many companies continue to produce milk glass today.

TELLING OLD FROM NEW
THE MYTHS AND THE REALITIES

You will hear about dealers and collectors with sure-fire methods of telling old milk glass from new. "Old is opalescent at the edges," they say. Yes, a lot of it is, but a lot of it isn't! And much new milk glass has that same opalescence.

"Pressed old is three-mold"—nonsense! The number of mold pieces used has nothing to do with age. "Old has a seashell in the base"—again, this can be true of new glass as well as old. The "shell" is formed when the glass is poured too slowly, leaving a cooled heap on top of the mold (which of course is the bottom of the piece). It can also be caused when the mold is not warmed enough before pouring takes place. "Old is painted"—yes; and so is a lot of new! In fact, when I was enhancing and retouching some of the painted pieces in this book, in order to show the pattern more clearly in the photographs, I found that acrylic paint in the iridescent bronze looks just like the old, darkened gold paint used many years ago. "Black light will make old glass fluoresce." Well, new custard, for instance, fluoresces the same as old. Black light *will* make locating cracks and repairs easier, but lately a new epoxy glue has come on the market that even the black light will not detect.

So—what to do? First of all, do your homework. Read the books available on your collectible and the magazine articles. Join a club if you can; much invaluable information is contained in those newsletter pages. Request catalogs from the places known to sell reproductions and study them. Examine carefully the piece you are thinking of buying and look for marks. Sometimes they are hidden in unexpected places, such as inside the head of a covered hen dish. Visit the gift shops and other places where new glass is sold and familiarize yourself with what is being produced today. Pick it up—feel it—and do the same with old glass. Soon you will discover that your fingers have learned to tell old from new! Education and instinct will tell you what you need to know—depend on them!

—— What Is a Marriage and Do I Want One? ——

When two parts of an item such as a covered dish are put together, but do not belong together, collectors call it a "marriage." Sometimes the two parts are made by the same company, but the top may be on a split rib base, for instance, when it was originally produced only on a basket base. Two parts put together that were made by two different manufacturers is known as a "mixed marriage."

Often we will find covered dishes for sale where the lid fits very loosely—or doesn't quite fit on the base opening at all! This is undoubtedly a marriage. For instance, Challinor, Taylor lids will fit Westmoreland bases loosely; however, Westmoreland lids will not fit Challinor bases. Many Westmoreland covered hens were numbered on lids and base. These numbers should match to get a perfect fit. Also a lid and base should be the same color or shade of color, and you haven't lived until you try matching shades of white at a flea market on a sunny day!

Salt and pepper shakers are tricky little devils too! Often found without lids we have seen shakers labeled as ink bottles. One also runs across shakers with a small lamp burner attached and sold as a miniature lamp without its shade. Be careful, for many miniature lamps sold without shades are very likely a burner-added shaker. Then again, some covered pieces were originally made with two different lids or bases such as the Cannon on the Snare Drum, which has two bases, and the Boar's Head butter dish, which had a ribbed lid that fit onto the base just as the Boar's Head does. Of course, you all will have read the books and done your homework so that shouldn't bother you!

For some reason or other, lids for covered animal dishes seem more available than bases. I have quite a collection of "bottomless pets" myself! Some dealers will buy all the tops and bottoms they find and just put together whatever will more or less fit, willy-nilly! If the combination pleases you and above all if it's *cheap*, go ahead and buy it. But *don't* pay the price of a covered dish with the correct lid on the correct base. If you get it cheaply, someday you may find the right base/lid and have a wonderful piece for your collection!

My first piece of milk glass came to me as a birthday gift from a good friend way back in 1947. The piece was a Westmoreland Old Quilt celery vase; I still have it and the friend, after all these years! Probably twenty years passed before we really got into collecting as a hobby (or a disease, or a passion). Years filled with being a young working wife, with following Bill to Alaska for his Korean War stint, and then a mother and caring for our two girls. No time or money for collecting then! Still, my eyes traveled to the milk glass displayed on store shelves and now and then I splurged and bought a piece. Finally, Bill and I somehow began going to auctions and after that, we were hooked!

I've always considered collecting great therapy for whatever ails you. In fact, one day at a rummage sale, I heard one woman say to another, "Oh yes, I go every week—it's my mental health day." My favorite author, Gladys Taber, agrees with that. In *Stillmeadow Daybook*, she said: "This friend is a very wise woman. She is the one who started us on the milk glass in the beginning. We had a great deal of illness and sorrow in our families and life had a grey visage for us. 'Collect something,' said she, 'there is nothing like collecting to revive your interest in life; try milk glass.' And she helped us find our first small piece. From then on we were so busy scouring around that we got a lot of exercise and had less time to brood over our troubles."

Then, in *Harvest of Yesterdays*, Gladys wrote: "I suspect, as I think about it, that what one collects is not as important as the feeling of collecting. It is good to hunt patiently for something special and experience the triumph as the collection grows. Always the first object will lead to another and another." And…"So I was the one who found something. I absently lifted up an old, smelly piece of burlap. Dust and insects rained on me, and the odor of rats was stifling. But as I backed away, reaching for my handkerchief, I saw a white gleam in the midst of the debris. Even now as I look at it, I cannot really believe that white gleam was my swan compote, perfect, not even chipped! I picked

it up, cradling it in rather shaky hands. The swans seemed to be swimming around the bowl and they breathed. The color was that of very old glass, opaque yet lustrous. It was like moonlight on snow in a piny woods. ...I stood in a trance holding the compote against a thudding heart..." Don't we all know that "thudding heart" feeling? I've been lucky enough to have it many times in the past.

I have always felt, though, that you cannot be a collector by going into a shop or market, laying your money down and buying a whole collection at once. To collect means piece by piece—one at a time. Collecting means memories; it means "remember the flea market we visited and it was raining and we found the Atlas compote half-full of water." It means "remember the show where we set up and the lovely man across from us came over and *gave* me the big Westmoreland sleigh because he knew I loved it and couldn't afford to buy it." Collecting is also the periodic washing and rearranging of all the pieces, reflecting on where and how and with whom you found them. (Have you ever noticed that after you remove all the pieces from your cabinet and wash them, they never all fit back into the cabinet? I think they must swell up with the water!)

Collecting is learning: you find a piece you think is old—but is it? Is it this—or maybe that? You bring it home and hunt through your books; what a thrill when you find that it is indeed what you felt and hoped it was. What a good feeling it is to learn how a lovely piece was made; how it was decorated; who designed it; where it was made and when. How exciting to visit the glasshouses and see the process for yourself. How fascinating to find the human story behind a cherished piece. Who owned it before? How did it find its way to you?

Collecting is also giving: Perhaps you may give your whole collection to a local museum or historical society so that others can enjoy and marvel at the colors and sparkle and workmanship. That can be a great satisfaction. Or maybe your dear friend's daughter is getting married; "She loves old things," your friend says. Which of your treasures could you possibly live without, you wonder? Finally, you pick one, and the joy on her face when the package is opened and the love with which she displays it in her new home is also a great satisfaction. Helping a friend collect is another aspect of giving; "Look at the lovely pitcher (or hatpin or iron bank or whatever)—

wouldn't my friend love that!" The old Civil War book for the son-in-law; the ancient cast-iron steelyard for the husband; the lovely, feathery fan for the daughter; all giving.

Collecting is wonderful therapy for mind or body, as many of us will attest. Collecting for miserliness or for profit alone just doesn't hack it. You need to live all the joys to be a real collector!

WHERE ARE THE MOLDS?

Westmoreland Glass Company of Grapeville, PA, was, from 1890 – 1985, one of the most prolific producers of fine quality milk glass in the United States. When they closed in 1985, there were several sales and auctions held and the wonderful old molds owned by Westmoreland were scattered to the winds.

Imperial Glass Corporation of Bellaire, OH, (founded 1901), closed their doors in 1984. Before that time, they had purchased many of the old Cambridge Glass Company molds. When Imperial closed, much the same thing happened to their molds as happened to Westmoreland molds. They were purchased and are being used by a number of present-day glasshouses.

Since so many new pieces now on the market are made using Westmoreland and Imperial molds, we thought it might be a wise idea to give you some information on who purchased these molds at closing time. Our lists may not be complete and by this time some of the molds may have changed hands yet again, but every bit of information the collector can obtain is worthwhile.

Of course, mold switching from factory to factory is nothing new. In the photo sections of this book you will find the phrase "mold originally produced by" in many places. As an example, let's take Beaded Jewel or Lace and Dewdrop. Beaded Jewel was created by the George Duncan Glass Co. of Pittsburgh, PA, and made in clear glass only until Duncan went out of business in 1902. Co-

Operative Glass Co. of Beaver Falls, PA, purchased the molds and produced milk glass pieces under their "1902 Line" until 1929. The molds then went to The Phoenix Glass Co. of Monaca, PA. Phoenix made the pattern for several years in milk glass, plus they painted sections of the pieces in various colors, which makes it easier for collectors to recognize the Phoenix pieces. Mr. H. M. Tuska, a glass jobber, purchased the molds from Phoenix and then sold them to John Kemple in 1946. Kemple then made Lace and Dewdrop in milk glass, blue, and honey amber. After John Kemple's death in 1970, the molds went to the Wheaton Village glasshouse in Millville, NJ. They have produced a number of pieces in various colors.

Most molds have long histories such as outlined above, which often makes certain identification of the maker of an item very difficult and sometimes next to impossible. There are companies such as L.G. Wright, New Martinsville, WV, who do not make glass themselves but own thousands of molds from which they contract glass to be produced by various glasshouses. This tends to cloud the issue even further, as Wright purchased molds from sources all over the world—or simply copied them with or without subtle variations—or switched parts to make them item distinctive.

Thanks to Barbara Shaeffer's *Glass Review* magazine, however, we are able to share with you the following listings of Imperial and Westmoreland molds at the time of the closing auctions.

DISTRIBUTION OF IMPERIAL MOLDS:

MIRROR IMAGES—purchased:
  200 Candlewick molds
  7 Flower Frogs (Draped lady, etc.)

CAMBRIDGE COLLECTORS OF AMERICA—
      purchased:
  Swan punch bowl, base and cups
  #1119 Eagle bookends
  #1124 Pouter pigeon bookends
  #1128 Scotty dog bookends
  #1129 Lion bookends
  #511 Tombstone bookends
  Caprice heavy pressed goblet
  Caprice #13 coaster
  Caprice #17 cup and saucer
  Caprice #22 8½" plate
  Caprice #70 candlestick
  Caprice #73 reflector candle (incomplete)
  Caprice #98 3oz. ball shape oil
  Caprice #117 3 oz. oil
  Caprice #165 candy box with lid
  Caprice #178 90oz. Doulton jug
  Caprice #179 32 oz. Ball jug
  Caprice #201 ice bucket
  Caprice #202 cracker jar with lid
  Caprice #204 cigarette holder
  Caprice #205 cigarette holder
  Caprice #206 3" ashtray
  Caprice #207 cigarette box with lid
  #474 Punch bowl
  "Cascade" goblet, cup, saucer, cigarette box
      with lid
  "Cut Wild Rose" 5oz. cup
  "Gadroon" 6" bowl (ram's head)
  "Gadroon" 9" bowl (ram's head)
  "Gadroon" 10" urn with lid
  "Gadroon" 13" punch bowl (ram's head)
  "Gadroon" 3½" ashtray/coaster
  "Gadroon" 3½" and 4" ashtrays
  "Heirloom" 40, 41, 44, 45 cream and sugars
  "Marjorie" 15" punch bowl & cup
  "Mt. Vernon" wine, whiskey, cordial, and
      coaster
  #3011 "Statuesque" stem for 7" comport; stem
      for cocktail; stem for table goblet; 4" mint;
      paste molds ¾ blown tops
  #3400 Nut dish

Twist and rooster muddlers
#578 and #702 mini cornucopias
3" Ashtray; Canoe, Jefferson wine
3 Regency pattern stems

IMPERIAL GLASS COLLECTORS CLUB —
  purchased:
  3 square Candlewick ashtrays
  Robin mug
  #104 Mini pitcher
  Mini "Festival" pitcher
  #600 2½" pedestal salt

BOYD'S CRYSTAL ART GLASS—purchased:
  4 Parlour pup figurines
  Woodchuck figurine
  8" Ham bone ashtray
  Candlewick 400-176 square ashtray
  Candlewick 400-19 2¾" ashtray
  Candlewick 400-170 coaster with spoon rest
  Candlewick 400-96 5" tray
  Candlewick 400-64 nut dish
  Candlewick 400-264 candlebowl
  Candlewick 400-172, 173, 174 three piece
      heart ashtray set
  Candlewick 400-78 coaster (spoke center)
  Candlewick 400-42 two-handle fruit nappy
  Candlewick 400-118 "Between Places" ashtray
  Candlewick 400-134 cigarette box with lid
  Candlewick 400-134 rectangular ashtray
  Candlewick 400-34 4" jelly
  Candlewick 400-287 6" vase
  Candlewick 400-1776 Eagle ashtray and ciga-
      rette holder insert
  #530 Zodiac ashtray
  1950-20 Grape card holder
  #60 Honey jar (Beehive)
  4-pc. Child's lamb finial set
  Flower puff box
  Flower mirror
  Sleigh

WETZEL GLASS—Purchased: (out of business now).
      From Cambridge molds:
  Jenny Lind sugar and creamer
  Jenny Lind custard cup
  Martha #497 candlestick
  #3500 large sugar
  #1525 Salt dip

WETZEL GLASS — (continued)
  #399 Twin salts
  Virginia sugar and creamer
  Virginia custard cup
  Various salt shakers
      From Imperial molds:
  Various salt shakers
  Rose sugar and creamer
  Grape and Cable sugar and creamer
  Square sugar and creamer
  Nine cologne bottle molds

SUMMIT ART GLASS—purchased:
  12" covered rabbit
  Candlewick one-light candle (Iron Cross mark)
  Caprice ¼lb. butter
  Caprice #40 sugar and creamer
  Caprice 7" bowl
  Caprice 6" plate
  Caprice 3½" triangle ashtray
  Caprice 5 oz. wine, pressed
  Caprice 9 oz. tumbler, pressed, 10 oz. tumbler, pressed
  Caprice 2½ oz. wine, pressed
  Caprice 2½" master salt
  Everglades Buffalo Hunt bowl
  Everglades Large Tulip bowl
  Everglades Swan bowl
  Cut Wild Rose punch bowl
  18" blown mannequin head
      From Cambridge molds:
  7½" Buddha bookend
  #1115 10½" September Morn flower figure
  #50 8½" Dolphin candle
  #849 8½" Draped Lady (oval base)
  #1042 6½" Swan; #1043 - 8½" Swan
  #1044 10½" Swan Center bowl
  2" four-toe salt dip
  Caprice 3-toe shell card holder
  Caprice 3-toe master salt
  Caprice #300 zipper salt dip (IG mold)
  Covered Birdcage jar (IG mold)
  Nude lamp base

DISTRIBUTION OF WESTMORELAND MOLDS:

SUMMIT ART GLASS—purchased:
  #275 Jewel box

#80 Top hat
#555 Top hat
Straw hat
WWI soldier hat
#603 Egg cup
#42 Covered egg candy
#43 Clock candy container (mantle clock)
Safe candy container
#7 China cabinet candy container
#77 Player piano candy container
Lawn swing candy container
#26 two-handled picnic basket
#1031 Hatchet
#1205 2½" Curtain tieback; #207 3½" curtain tieback
#78 Large bulldog door stop
#1900 Slipper
#1933 Horn vase
Large butterfly
Banana weight - pear weight
Antique tire ashtray
#1211 Mini chamberstick
#304 Little Jo water set
#1 Duck individual salt
Small and medium butterflies
Sparrow
#5 Wren
#1078 Salt dip
#210 Salt dip, #216 salt dip, #217 salt dip
#1872 5½" Sleigh with Santa lid
#104 Hen on two-handle basket
#203 Salt
#1000 6" Covered turtle and ashtray
#335 6" Covered camel
#1107 Salt dip
#79 Round glove on base weight
#815 4½" Washboard
#700 Toy wine glass
Wren base
#1921 Lotus salt, #1079 Salt
#1857 Heart box
2½" Doghouse toothpick
9½" Sleigh
#1027 Bow card holder
#576 Three-swan toothpick
#594 Covered duck (orig Challinor-Taylor)
6" Wicker picnic basket
#909 Lacey Daisy mini berry set
#202, 209, 215, 216, 217 Salt dips

SUMMIT ART GLASS—(continued)
#300 Salt dip (English Hobnail)
Mantle clock, wash boiler, mailbox candy
   containers
#555 1-2" English Hobnail footed salt
#456 Ballerina mint dish
Figural pistol
#1932 10½" Elephant head bowl
#300, 1078, 200 Series salt dips
#909 Lacey salt
#1860 Turtle jar
#7 Chinese treasure chest
#1837 Ladle
#1022 Candle
#555 Nut dish
#1 12" Shell bowl, three footed
#1850 4" flower block
#1063 Starfish candle
#1045 Candle
#101 Spoonholder
#1982 Candle
6" Shell nappy
#10 Duck with base
#1957 Chocolate box with lid
#19 Pocket watch
#9 Chick with base
#71 Creamer
Turtle paperweight
Showcase and Wagon candy containers
#233 Treasure chest with lid
#1707 Flower pot and saucer
#909 Salt (Lacey Daisy)
#1039 Mini candle
#30 8" Plate
#1800 Soap dish and tumbler
#1803 Flower pot

VIKING GLASS—purchased:
#1049 Dolphin shell bowl
#1049 12" shell - Dolphin
#1049 9" Dolphin candles
#1049 4" Dolphin candles
#1933 Petal candles
#20 Love birds covered dish
#1048 Covered candy

JOHN J. BIONDICH (PLUM GLASS)—purchased:
Rose, #1967 7" Bowl, candle, honey and lid
Beaded Grape #1884 Individual cream and

sugar; 10½" plate; salt; parfait; ftd. bowl
and ftd. 5" bowl and lid; 6" plate; ftd. mayo;
8" ftd. salver; cup and saucer; 4" candle; 7"
ftd. bowl; 9" ftd. bowl; cigarette box and
lid; 9" vase; 5" ashtray.
#1928 10" Deep nappy (Leaf)
#1928 Maple Leaf candy; goblet; wine; 18"
   plate
#1701 Trinket box and lid
#666 Cheese plate
Bird
#555 Candy jar & lid (English Hobnail)
Small cardinal
Rabbit tray
Swallow figure
Medium swallow figure
#100-18" bowl
OA Stein
AB Stein
#200 Toothpick
#2 Salt
English Hobnail #555 nappy, 3½" ashtray
#1776 Colonial 5" and 6½" ashtrays
#1921 Candelabra
#1921 Lotus 4" bowl
#1873 Swan bottom
#1211 Candy and lid
#6 Peacock sugar, creamer, lid
#555 English Hobnail mayo, gingerale, 8" ash-
   tray, 4½" ashtray, footed iced tea, goblet,
   wine
#1923 6", 9", and 12" Leaf dishes

PELETIER GLASS COMPANY, OTTAWA, ILLINOIS—
   purchased:
#555 English Hobnail 10" deep bowl
#1881 11½" Oval bowl - Paneled Grape;
#1776 Colonial Berry sugar and creamer, but-
   ter with lid, 4" round nappy, 5" round nappy,
   handled olive, 9" round nappy, 1-qt. jug, tumbler, oval mayo 6" and plate, 7½" mayo plate,
   7½" mayo, 6" oil w/stopper
Colonial #1776 goblet, claret, sherbet, ftd.
   iced tea, brandy, cordial, 10" fruit bowl,
   ftd. sweetmeat, 10½" flat celery, 8" oval
   pickle, 10 " oval pickle
#77 American Hobnail candle, salver, goblet,
   butter complete, ftd. mayo, compote
#3 Bowl and foot

PELETIER GLASS COMPANY, OTTAWA, ILLINOIS—
    (continued)
    #3 Candle
    #1873 Swan lid
    #250 6" plate
    #1875 Ring and Petal bowl, bell, candle
    #1890 Lattice Edge bowl, candle
    #1881 Paneled Grape punch bowl, cheese
        cover
    #22 8½" Flat plate (Beaded Edge)
    #2/17 Plate
    #1881 Paneled Grape chocolate box and lid,
        parfait
    #100 18" Bowl, square vase
    #1058 12" Bell bowl (Della Robbia)
    #1058 Della Robbia candle
    #1879 Covered bowl (ribbed w/lace edge)
    #1891 bowl, spoke rim
    #1891 Candle
    #555 English Hobnail 9" candle
    #1921 9" Lotus bowl
    #1921 Lotus 3½" candle
    Fox lid for covered dish
    #299 Spooner (File & Fan)
    #61 Toothpick
    #1902 6" Blown vase
    #1943 Covered urn
    #1881 Paneled Grape window planter, oblong
        planter, square planter
    #1881 Paneled Grape marmalade w/lid, L.F.
        sherbet, ftd. compote
    #1921 Lotus 11½" oval bowl, ftd. mayo, vase/
        sugar/candy
    #1058 Della Robbia candy and lid

ALLERGHENY OPALESCENT GLASS COMPANY,
CONNELLSVILLE, PA—purchased:
    #1801 Bud vase
    #1800 Puff box

BLENKO GLASS COMPANY, MILTON, WV—
    purchased:
    #7 Robin top and base
    #1 Lion top
    #100 Rooster sherbet
    Lion goblet

BROOKE GLASS COMPANY, WELLSBURG, WV—
    purchased:
    #1971 Tiffany mini shade
    #753 Mini shade
    #101 6" plate
    English Hobnail 3½" candle, 8" 2-hdl. ftd.
        bowl, 8" pickle, low sugar and creamer, salt

LORIS DRUG STORE, LORIS, SC —Purchased:
    #115 Swan vase

JEANNETTE SHADE & NOVELTY CO., JEANNETTE,
PA—purchased:
    #1894 10" Wedding bowl w/lid
    #1700 Colonial candy jar w/lid, toothpick,
        mini lamp shade and base, bud vase
    #299 Bud vase
    #1820 Heart tray
    #51 Double Hands tray
    #1902 Small bell
    #999 Wildflower & Lace candle; pickle;
        ftd. compote; cream and sugar; han
        dled nappy; 4", 6", 8", 10" nappys,
        mayo or mini shade
    #240 Buzz Star punch bowl, pedestal, cup
    #1 Cat lid
    #1 Dove in hand
    #1870 Oblong bowl w/dancing sailors edge
    #64 8" Vase
    #1801 6" Blown vase
    #5 Lamp, vase

PAIRPOINT GLASS COMPANY, SANDWICH, MA—
    purchased:
    #3 Curtain tie back
    #58 Vase, blown
    #1 Small pig
    #61 Toothpick
    #1701 Trinket box
    #2 Strawberry ashtray
    Penguin figure
    #1776 Larkin salt
    Star coaster
    #1842 Baked apple
    #201 4½" Finger bowl (Princess Feather)
    #207 Tray
    #1 Lamp base
    #250 Bitters bottle
    Wiskbroom

PAIRPOINT GLASS COMPANY, SANDWICH, MA —
    (continued)
    Horn
    Blown revolver candy

PHIL ROSSO, PORT VUE, PA — Purchased:
    #752 Basket
    #32 Heart plate
    #62 Owl toothpick
    #299 Sugar, creamer, jelly with lid (File & Fan)
    #303 Punch bowl, cup
    #754 Bell
    #115 Swan toothpick
    #6 Standing rooster
    #5 Rabbit
    #4 Hen
    #3 Covered chick salt
    #10 Owl
    #750 Basket

Large Crimped bell
#75 Small bulldog
#7 5" Covered animals as follows: rabbit,
    duck, cat, lion, hen, rooster, swan
#1000 Creamer and shot glass
#1211 Cologne bottle
#1921 Cologne bottle with stopper
#1801 Cologne bottle with stopper
#73 Reamer
Elf stein; Lovers stein
#109 Cherry thumbprint cookie jar and
    lid, foot for cookie, 10" bowl, candlestick,
    cream and sugar
English Hobnail tall basket

PREMIER IMAGES INC., CLEVELAND, OH —
    purchased:
    Telephone receiver, mouth piece, stand

— EARLY AMERICAN PATTERN GLASS IN MILK GLASS —

My two main collections (there are many others!) are Early American pattern glass and milk glass. When I find a pattern glass pattern made in milk glass, it is a double bonus for me. The listing that follows shows Early American Pattern Glass patterns that have pieces made in milk glass. We don't know how many milk glass pieces were made in each pattern listed; usually just a few, although now and then we find a pattern with enough pieces to actually form a milk glass set.

ALMOND THUMBPRINT — rare
ART — rare
ASHBURTON — very rare
AURORA — chocolate
AUSTRIAN — Nile green, chocolate
AZTEC — reproduced by Kemple as Whirling Star
BASKET WEAVE — odd pieces — can make set
BEADED JEWEL (Jewel & Dewdrop) — reproduced by Kemple
BEADED SWIRL — rare
BELLFLOWER — very rare
BLACKBERRY — reproduced by Phoenix and Kemple
BLEEDING HEART — rare
BLOCK & FAN — can make set
BUCKLE — rare
BULL'S EYE — fiery milk in Flint

BULL'S EYE WITH DIAMOND POINT — rare
BUTTON ARCHES
CABLE — opaque green, white
CALIFORNIA — extensive reproductions
CAMEO — number of pieces
CANADIAN — reproductions in vase form resemble this pattern
CHERRY — reproduced by Westmoreland in many pieces
CLASSIC — extremely rare
COLORADO — rare in black
COSMOS
CROSSED FERN — can make set
DAISY & BUTTON — reproduced
DELAWARE — milk white with blue stain scarce; opaque ivory and white are rare

DEWEY — chocolate, Nile green, white, reproduced white by Imperial

DIAMOND POINT — green opal; colored opaque; white rare

DIAMOND THUMBPRINT — rare

FEATHER– pitcher only in chocolate

FINE RIB– opaque white, traslucent white rare

FLEUR-DE-LIS AND DRAPE

GOOSEBERRY — goblets and wine reproduced

HAIR PIN (Sandwich Loop)

HAMILTON WITH LEAF

HEART WITH THUMBPRINT

HOBB'S BLOCK– opaque blue and white

HOLLY — very rare

HONEYCOMB — white and green

HORN OF PLENTY

ICICLE — 21 pieces can make set

IVY IN SNOW — rare, reproduced

LIBERTY BELL — rare

LINCOLN DRAPE — rare

LOCKET ON CHAIN — very rare

LOOP & JEWEL — rare

MAIZE — can make set

MASCOTTE — very rare

MELROSE — chocolate

MICHIGAN — reproduced in many opaque and transparent colors

MONKEY — opalescent

MOON & STAR — reproduced by L.E. Smith & Kemple

ONE–O–ONE — blue, pink, white

OREGON — sugar reproduced by Imperial

PALMETTE — rare

PANELED GRAPE — WG reproductions in many pieces

PANELED DAISY — can make set

PLEAT & PANEL — very rare

PRIMROSE — rare

PRINCESS FEATHER — white, blue, very rare

PRICILLA — Fostoria

PRISM WITH DIAMOND POINTS — rare

PSYCHE & CUPID — 7" plate

RAINDROP — blue, white

RIBBED GRAPE — rare

ROMAN CROSS — can make set

ROSE IN SNOW — reproduced by Imperial

SANDWICH STAR — blue, lavender, very rare

SAWTOOTH — reproduced by Westmoreland, can make set

SCROLL — can make set

SHUTTLE — chocolate

SQUIRREL — chocolate, water pitcher only

STARS & STRIPES — odd pieces

STIPPLED CHAIN — rare

STIPPLED FORGET-ME-NOT — can make set, but rare

STRAWBERRY — can make set

SUNFLOWER — can make set

SWAN — reproductions creamer and sugar, set possible

SWAN & CATTAILS — can make set, reproduced

TEARDROP & TASSEL — can make set

TEXAS — reproductions of creamer and sugar

THUMBPRINT — rare

TORPEDO — black amethyst very rare

TREE OF LIFE — can make set

TULIP WITH SAWTOOTH — rare

VALENTINE — toothpick reproduced by Degenhart

VERMONT

VERSAILLES — can make set

VICTORIA, PIONEERS — chocolate

WAFFLE — odd pieces, rare

WAFFLE & THUMBPRINT — rare

WASHINGTON CENTENNIAL — rare

WHEAT — can make set

WILDFLOWER — reproduced

Plate 1 - LEFT: Beautiful 7" tall hand painted bottle burnished with gold. *$25.00 – 30.00.* RIGHT: Pansy pattern 10" dresser bottle. *$30.00 – 35.00.*

Plate 2 - TOP: **left and right**, 7" Barber bottles, one marked Witch Hazel, the other marked Toilet Water. *$70.00 – 90.00.* **Left center**, Roman Soldier cologne bottle with plastic cap. *$5.00 – 10.00.* **Right center**, 5½" all over embossed flower bottle is #2519 by Fostoria. Note the flower finial. A matching powder jar will be shown elsewhere in this book. *$40.00 – 55.00.*

BOTTOM **(l to r):** Leaf & Scroll 10" dresser bottle decorated with brown roses. Shown in the 1910 – 1912 Butler Brothers catalog. *$40.00 – 50.00.* Draped Leaf 10½" dresser bottle decorated with pink roses. Also found in the 1910–1912 Butler Brothers catalog. *$40.00 – 50.00.* Scroll footed dresser bottle, 11" tall. This rests on four scroll feet and has a crown-like stopper. *$35.00 – 40.00.*

Plate 3 - The Atterbury Duck bottle, probably one of the most elusive of the milk glass bottles. Patented by Thomas B. Atterbury on April 11, 1871. Without the stopper, it measures 11½" tall. *$300.00 – 375.00 w/o stopper. $550.00 – 600.00 w/stopper.*

Plate 4 - TOP (l to r): Hobnail 6½" cologne bottle. $8.00 – 10.00. 6½" Coquette cologne bottle by Campbell & Co., SDNY 2388, decorated with roses and silhouettes, bow-shaped foot. *$10.00 – 12.00.* Coaching scene 5" bottle. *$8.00 – 10.00.* "Mother" out of set of three bottles (Mother, Father, Child), 6½" tall with flat,

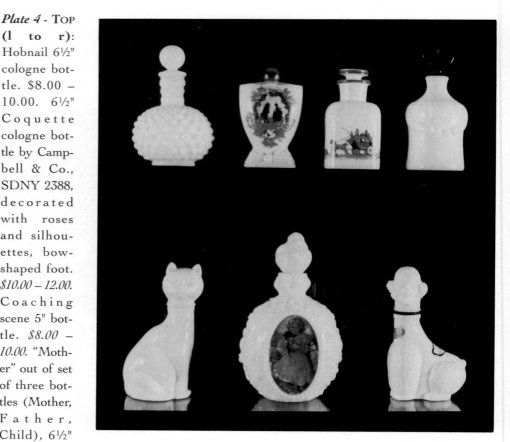

transparent glass head. Also have seen the heads in amber glass. *$35.00 – 40.00.*
BOTTOM: **left and right,** Cat and Poodle, 6½" wine bottles. Labeled Vintage 1971, Imported by Universal Wine & Liquor Co., Detroit, Michigan. Front label on Poodle reads "Rose Italian Wine - Gori Gori. Produced and bottled in Italy. Exported by Nello Gori Certaldo Firenze". *$20.00 – 25.00.* **Center,** Floral Window dresser bottle. The molding of this bottle is almost the same as the Jenny Lind bottle, but this has a convex clear panel with a picture inserted instead of the lady's head on the Jenny Lind. *$45.00 – 50.00.*

Plate 5 - This is a close-up of the unique and rare marble in a cage stopper for the Atterbury Duck bottle. Very difficult to find. *$550.00 – 600.00 bottle w/stopper.*

Plate 6 - l to r: Le Tsar bottle, smaller than bon-bon and separates at neck. Rare. *$300.00 – 325.00.* Clown, maker unknown. *$85.00 – 95.00.* Grandfather's Clock bottle. *$85.00 – 100.00.* Vase by Anchor Hocking, decorated with blue enameling. 1940's. *$15.00 – 20.00.*

Plate 7 - TOP (l to r): Columbus Column bottle, 13" tall plus 7" metal statue. Patented by Librowicz on January 17, 1893. The metal statue forms the stopper. Originally contained rye whiskey and manufactured by James Simms & Company of Philadelphia. Scarce with top. *$220.00 – 250.00 w/o lid, $500.00 – 575.00 w/lid.* Joan of Arc bottle, 16½" tall. Here is Joan in her armor on her way to liberate the city of Orleans from the English in 1429. Joan is now a Saint, canonized by the Catholic Church in 1919. Embossed around the base is JEANNE D'ARC and the word DE POSE (Patented) is on the bottom. *$275.00 – 300.00.* Statue of Liberty bottle. Base 8", statue 7⅜", overall height 15⅜". Another metal statue closure on a milk glass bottle. Scarce. *$220.00 – 250.00 w/o lid, $500.00 – 575.00 w/lid.*

BOTTOM: **left and right,** Le Tsar bottle 13" tall with La Tsarine on the right. Originally candy containers made to resemble Nicholas II and Alexandra of Russia. On the edge below the busts is the legend "LA TSARINE or LE TSAR NICHOLAS II" On both bases is embossed: "BONBONS" and "JOHN TAVERNIER". Blown molded and hard to find. *$275.00 – 325.00.* **Center,** Grant's Tomb bottle, 8½" high, 9" with stopper. Patented January 17, 1893. Very scarce. *$275.00 – 300.00.*

Plate 8 - l to r: 5⅝" tall dresser bottle with little feet and hand painted decor. *$25.00 – 30.00.* 8½" tall rose-pink perfume bottle with leaves and flowers in white. *$35.00 – 45.00.* 5" Czechoslovakian perfume bottle with floral decoration. *$30.00 – 35.00.*

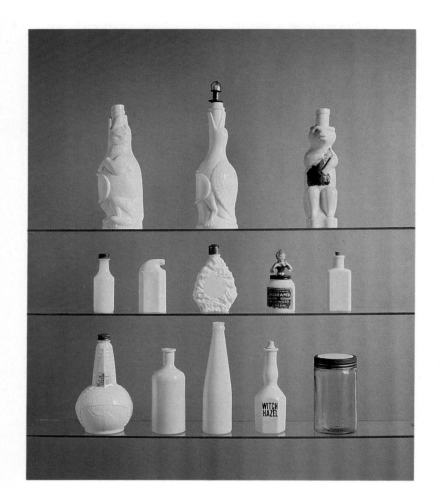

Plate 9 - TOP (l to r): Dawes Dog bottle, 11½" tall. Patented October 1, 1872, by John L. Dawes. Rare. *$450.00 – 475.00.* Atterbury Duck bottle, patented April 11, 1871. 11½" tall. *$300.00 – 375.00 w/o stopper, $550.00 – 600.00 with stopper.* Sitting Bear bottle, 10¾" tall. Also in dark green. Scarce. *$150.00 – 175.00.*

CENTER (l to r): Tooth Powder bottles (first two), *$15.00 – 20.00.* Hagen's Magnolia Balm. *$10.00 – 12.00.* Ingrams's Milkweed Cream, with Lady lid. *$15.00 – 20.00.* Witch Hazel Bottle, *$10.00 – 15.00.*

BOTTOM (l to r): New York World's Fair bottle, 9" tall with metal cap. Represents the globe with its continents and also the Perisphere. The neck resembles the Trylon. These were the two most famous buildings of the World's Fair. A band circles the globe bearing the legend: "1939 World's Fair, 1939." *$20.00 – 25.00.* Three barber bottles, various shapes, including Witch Hazel. *$55.00 – 65.00.* Canning jar with milk glass lid insert.

Plate 10 - Father's Bottle, 11⅝" tall. Contained ⅘ quart French Armagnac, Bahama Blenders ltd., Freeport. The attached lid is also glass but the screw-off nipple tip is wood. On the back are measurements suggesting what effect the brandy will have on you if you drink to each level! *$170.00 – 180.00.*

Plate 11 - 4½" tall, heavily sculpted cologne bottle. *$25.00 – 30.00.* 6½" Owl fruit jar with metal lid having a milk glass insert with embossed eagle. Sometimes found with blue glass eyes. *$100.00 – 125.00 w/lid insert.* Unusual 3¾" tall bottle resembling the old milk bottle carriers that the milkman used to transport your bottles of milk from the milk wagon to your doorstep. *$42.00 – 47.00.*

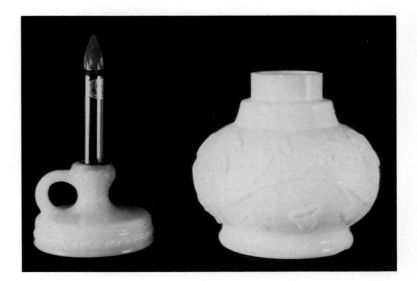

Plate 12 - LEFT: A mini candlestick made into a perfume bottle by some enterprising manufacturer. 4⅞" high overall, the candle bottle is inserted in a cardboard tube and then into the candlespace. Label underside reads: "Gardenia, Londer Distribution, 5th Avenue, NY." *$15.00 – 20.00*. RIGHT: Cologne bottle with embossed ivy leaves trailing around. Label on underside reads: "John Davis & Co., Manufacturers, Detroit, Michigan, and Windsor, Ontario." Has a potpourri recipe included so that one could fill the bottle with it when the cologne was used. *$20.00 – 25.00*.

Plate 13 - Grape pattern 11½" wine decanter by Imperial Glass, 1950 – 1968. Eight matching wine glasses completed the set. *$40.00 – 45.00*. 10⅜" modern refrigerator bottle. Seen in gift catalogs in the 1980's. Maker unknown. *$15.00 – 20.00*.

Plate 14 - LEFT: Draped Scroll 10" dresser bottle with rose-shaped finial. *$35.00 – 45.00*. RIGHT: Footed Scroll dresser bottle without stopper. This is in satin finished milk glass. *$35.00 – 45.00*.

Plate 15 - Some really lovely and interesting bottles were made to hold Avon products. **TOP (l to r):** Classic Decanter, 1969 – 1970. Ming Cat, 1971. Victorian Lady, 1972 – 1973.
BOTTOM (l to r): Dr. Hoot, 1977–1979. Leisure Hours, 1970–1972. Sitting Pretty, 1971 – 1973. *Range $8.00 – 12.00.*

Plate 16 - More bottles by Avon. **TOP:** Candle bowl, 1964 – 1966. Fragrance Touch, 1969 – 1970. **BOTTOM:** Grecian Pitcher, 1972 – 1976. Nesting Dove Candle, 1970. *Range $12.00 – 15.00.*

Plate 17 - Deco shape 8" bottle with finger ring hold handle. *$15.00 – 20.00.* Wreath dresser bottle, 10½" tall, satin finish with gold. *$30.00 – 35.00.*

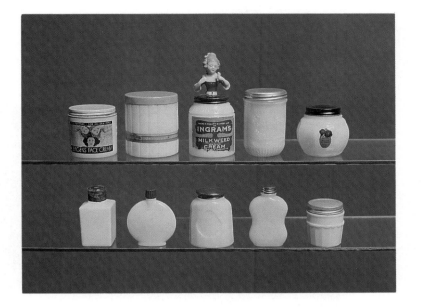

Plates 18, 19, 20 - Assortment of small, collectible milk glass jars. Range *$5.00 – 10.00.*

Plate 21 - Also for Avon. **TOP:** Capitol Decanter, 1976–1977. Uncle Sam Pipe, 1975 – 1976.
BOTTOM: Bon-Bon the Poodle cologne, 1972 – 1973. Base for Ultra Fluff, 1970. Cornucopia, 1971 – 1976. *Range $8.00 – 12.00.*

Plate 22 - An assortment of blue milk pieces by Vallerysthal. TOP: three-footed, handled nappy. *$25.00 – 30.00.* BOTTOM: Zipper & Bead three-footed, handled nappy, *$25.00 – 30.00.* Swirled Compote. *$30.00 – 35.00.*

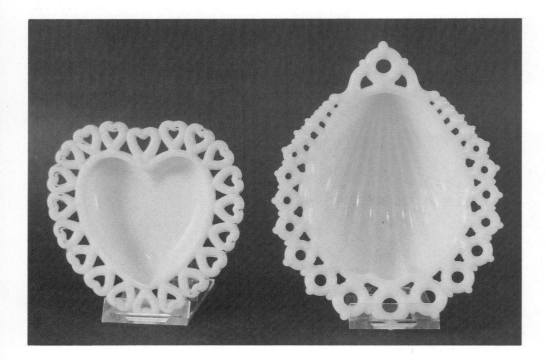

Plate 23 - LEFT: Small heart-shaped dish by Westmoreland. 3¾" to point of heart. *$10.00 – 12.00.* RIGHT: Shell dish with lacy edge by Fenton. 5⅜" including handle, 1⅝" high, sets on three little legs. *$12.00 – 15.00.*

Plate 24 - Monroe pattern, 10⅝"
diameter fruit bowl by Fostoria,
1960's. *$25.00 – 30.00.*

Plate 25 - Open lacy edge, 10¼"
diameter bowl by Atterbury. Later
Westmoreland used this same mold
for a lot of their lacy edge pieces.
$30.00 – 35.00.

Plate 26 - 8" x 4¾" handled bowl with a Daisy
Ray design. Also found in black. Maker
unknown. *$15.00 – 20.00.*

Plate 27 - TOP: Open Lattice 9" bowl with Trumpet Vine central painting. A Challinor, Taylor product. *$28.00 – 35.00.* BOTTOM: 9" diameter bowl with hand painted grapes, leaves, and flowers by Smith Brothers. Harry and Alfred Smith were Englishmen who decorated for Mount Washington Glass for two years. They opened their own shop in New Bedford, MA, in 1894 generally using Mount Washington blanks. Enamel decorations were applied, sometimes signed Smith Bros. in enameled script below the design. *$375.00 – 400.00.*

Plate 28 - Seashell, 3" tall, 4¾" diameter, three-footed bowl by Cambridge. *$45.00 – 50.00.*

Plate 29 - Grape compote by Anchor Hocking. Recently manufactured during the 1960's–1970's. Has that "skim milk" look of recent, lower quality glass. *$7.00 – 10.00.*

Plate 30 - Scroll pattern, 8½" diameter bowl by Imperial Glass, 1955 – 1960. Originally a Challinor, Taylor product called C-Scroll and made in a number of table pieces. Also found in blue, chartreuse, and olive green. Imperial pieces will often carry a label with the legend: "from the Belknap collection." *$15.00 – 20.00.*

Plate 31 - TOP: Bowl, 8½" x 12" long including handles. Daisy and Button panels, wing-like handles. No marks. *$18.00 – 25.00.*
BOTTOM: Randolph pattern 9¾" x 8¼" covered bowl by Fostoria. Also in pink, white, and turquoise opaque, 1950's and 1960's. *$30.00 – 35.00.* Footed leaf or shell, 6" x 5¾" by Westmoreland. *$15.00 – 20.00.*

Plate 32 - TOP: Scroll & Eye, 6¾" shallow bowl by Challinor, Taylor 1885–1893. Also found in white. *$12.00 – 15.00.* **BOTTOM:** Gothic border bowl, 7½" diameter. Attributed to Canton Glass Co., by Belknap. *$20.00 – 25.00.*

Plate 33 - l to r: Daisy & Button, 2¼" tall by 5" wide, triangle shaped nappy with handle by Fostoria. *$25.00 – 30.00.* Heavy Drape 4" tall, rose bowl by Fostoria. *$25.00 – 30.00.* Crimped bowl, 3¾" tall by 5⅝" wide, by Fostoria. *$25.00 – 30.00.* All made during the 1950 – 1960 period.

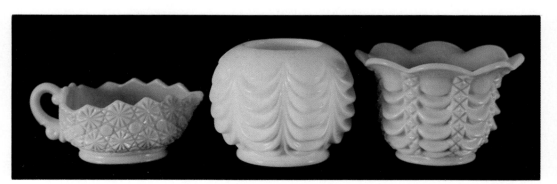

BOXES

Plate 35 - Two glove boxes. **TOP:** 10⅜" x 4" with scrolls and flower decals. *$55.00 – 65.00*. **BOTTOM:** 10½" x 3¾" with hand-painted roses and gold trim. Dithridge, about 1910. Bottom box is a grayish color rather than stark white. *$55.00 – 65.00*.

Plate 34 - An assortment of beautifully decorated dresser boxes, bottles, and trays. **TOP (l to r):** 5¼" x 3½" pin tray. 10" x 6½" comb and brush tray. 2½" x 4" hourglass shape box. **CENTER (l to r):** 6¼" square box with lid. 10½" bottle. **BOTTOM (l to r):** 3¾" star shaped box and lid. 3½" round box and lid. Pieces are probably by various makers, such as Dithridge, Eagle, Gillinder, etc. *Boxes range $10.00 – 15.00. Trays range $8.00 – 10.00.*

PLATE 36 - An assortment of small dresser boxes were produced in abundance from the 1880's into the early 1900's mainly by firms such as Dithridge, Eagle, Gillender, etc. **TOP:** 6" navette shaped box. *$15.00 – 20.00*. 4⅛" diameter flower top box by Boyd's Crystal Art Glass, 1980–1990. *$18.00 – 22.00*. **BOTTOM:** Assorted boxes. *Range $12.00 – 15.00.*

Plate 37 - LEFT: Dresser box with embossed little girl and doll on lid. 3⅞" diameter at widest. *$15.00 – 20.00*. RIGHT: Box in form of a shoe brush, 4¾" long. Originally produced by Challinor, Taylor Company about 1890, and also shown in a U.S. Glass Company catalog of 1891. (Challinor was listed as U.S. Glass's Factory C.) Originally called a match or toothpick holder. Made in milk glass and crystal. Scarce. *$85.00 – 100.00*.

Plate 38 - An assortment of Jenny Lind dresser pieces made by Fostoria in the 1960's. Roses & Poppies raised pattern with central lady head medallion. TOP: 10¼" x 4½" glove box. *$60.00 – 65.00*. 6" x 3⅜" pin tray. *$25.00 – 30.00*. BOTTOM: 10¾" cologne flask and stopper. *$85.00 – 90.00*. 11½" x 7½" comb and brush tray. *$45.00 – 50.00*. The set also included a 5" pin box and lid. *$20.00 – 25.00*. 3⅛" puff box and lid. *$25.00 – 30.00*. 2⅛" pomade and lid. *$20.00 – 25.00*. 5¼" x 2⅛" handkerchief box and lid. *$40.00 – 45.00*. 6" x 2" jewel box and lid. *$35.00 – 40.00*. Can be found in pink and aqua milk glass as well as white.

Plate 39 - TOP: Three Kittens handkerchief box, 5¾" x 5". *$65.00 – 70.00*. BOTTOM: 5½" diameter by 4½" tall cuff box with lid. Made by Westmoreland. Gold pattern has been enhanced to show more clearly. *$45.00 – 50.00*.

Plate 41 - TOP: 4¾" x 4" tall, all over floral embossed powder box by Fostoria. Matching cologne bottle will be found in the Bottle section of this book. *$40.00 – 45.00.* Oak & Acorns, 6" covered dresser box. *$30.00 – 35.00.*
BOTTOM: 3¾" diameter by 3¾" tall Beaded Shell hair receiver. About 1910. *$25.00 – 30.00.* 4" satin finished ring tree. About 1900–1910. *$25.00 – 30.00.*

Plate 40 - An assortment of dresser pieces in the Ray End pattern, **TOP:** 9" cologne bottle. *$35.00 – 40.00.* 11⅜" x 8½" comb and brush tray. *$30.00 – 35.00.*
CENTER: 3" x 3½" covered pin box. *$15.00 – 20.00.* 5½" footed rose bowl. *$20.00 – 25.00.*
BOTTOM: 7⅜" fern dish. *$25.00 – 30.00.* 5¼" diameter open dish. A product of Dithridge Company. *$15.00 – 20.00.*

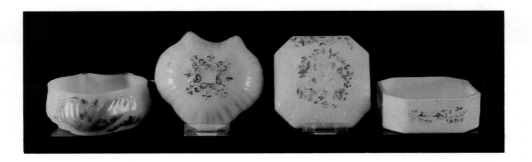

Plate 42 - Two dresser boxes about 4" in diameter. Shown in Butler Brothers catalog 1905–1910. Painting has been enhanced to show pattern. *Range $15.00 – 20.00.*

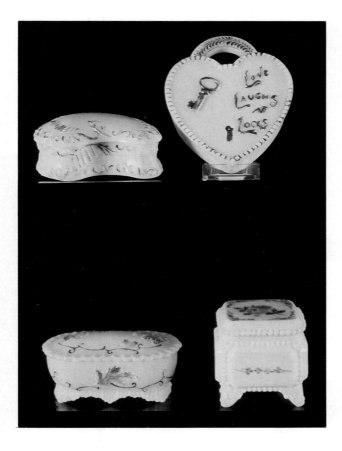

Plate 43 - Top: 2¼" x 3¾" comma-shaped dresser box by McKee. *$15.00 – 20.00*. Heart-shaped covered box, 4¾" hasp to point, 3¾" wide. "Love Laughs at Locks" embossed on lid. By McKee about 1889. *$75.00 – 80.00*. Bottom: 2¼" x 4" oval box with green leaf decoration and ruffled feet. *$15.00 – 20.00*. 2½" square trinket box by Westmoreland Glass. *$25.00 – 30.00*.

Plate 44 - Top: 4½" x 6½" Rib & Scroll covered bowl with feet. 7" high to top of finial. By Vallerysthal. *$30.00 – 35.00*. Bottom: 6" square, 2½" tall covered puff, pin, or desk box by Imperial Glass, 1950–1952. *$35.00 – 40.00*.

Plate 45 - Round, 6½" diameter, covered candy with divided, three-section base and lovely hand painted floral lid. Maker unknown. *$25.00 – 30.00*.

Plate 46 - Collar box, about 8" diameter. Notice lid with convex domed top. Bow tie at base. Used in those old days when linen or celluloid collars were attached to the man's shirt so it would not be necessary to wash it after each wearing. *$75.00 – 80.00*. Patented April 10, 1894.

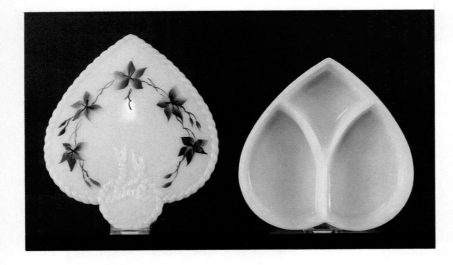

Plate 47 - Heart-shaped, 8½" x 7¼", divided candy box by Consolidated Con-Cora line in the 1950's. Note the rope around the lid that ties in a bow at the center. Beautifully hand painted. *$40.00 – 45.00.*

Plate 49 - TOP: 3½", Flower Square covered box. Measures 6¼" to top of finial. Marked Valerysthal inside base. *$25.00 – 30.00.* BOTTOM: Versailles dresser box, probably for powder or perhaps cuffs. 5¼" diameter by 6" tall. *$40.00 – 45.00.*

Plate 48 - TOP: 6" diameter, round covered box with scattered flowers. Maker uncertain. *$40.00 – 45.00.* 6½" x 10½", oval covered box by Consolidated. Highly embossed flowers cover lid and sides of box while under the lid is a beautifully done embossed design containing birds. The finial is a unique "S" shape. *$125.00 – 130.00.* BOTTOM: 7" x 4½" covered box by Consolidated in the Five Fruits pattern. Highly sculpted design covers lid and sides of box. Martele line, 1930's. *$75.00 – 80.00.* 8¼" x 4" covered dish, divided inside, in the Pond Lily pattern by Consolidated. This beautiful box has waterlilies on sides and bottom with dragonflies on lid top along with lovely hand painted roses. Inside the lid the water lily design is continued. *75.00 – 85.00.*

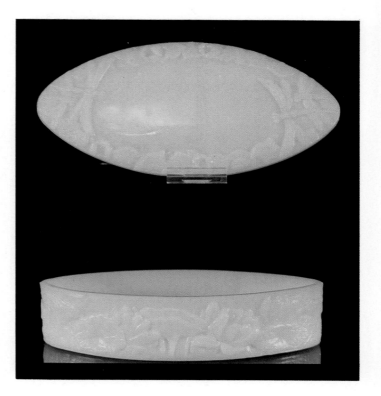

Plate 51 - Top is lid, bottom is base of this lovely Pond Lily, 11" navette shaped box by Consolidated. Notice the dragonflies on the lid—under that lid are more water lily or lotus flowers! A wonder of the mold-makers art. *$75.00 – 85.00.*

Plate 50 - Top row is lid, bottom is base, 3¾" x 5". Santa Maria covered cigarette box by Consolidated and shown in 1931 catalog. This is the flagship of Columbus's fleet. Note the dolphins sculpted around box sides. Ten pieces were made in this extremely rare set including dolphin console set, ship console set, covered cigarette jar with ship, upright ship ashtray, small tray with ship, covered cigar jar with ship, footed cigarette holder with ship holding the pack of cigarettes, vanity or smokers tray with ship, and the box shown. *$125.00 – 130.00.*

Plate 52 - Oriental Boy covered jar, 3¾" tall. Made by Westmoreland Specialty Company. This is one of a pair of jars—one with boy and one with girl—that probably were used for tea. The panel facing has the boy figure. Opposite him is a Chinese junk and on side panels are raised Oriental motifs. *$35.00 – 40.00.* Pink Beehive, 4⅛" covered honey jar by Jeannette Glass Company. Part of their line of pink milk glass from 1958–1959. *$30.00 – 35.00.*

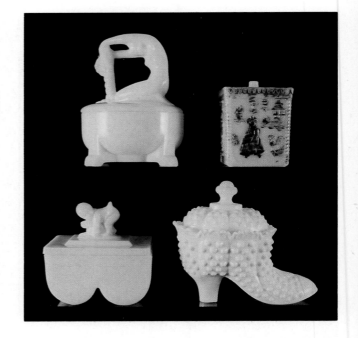

Plate 53 - Hummingbird, 7" diameter, covered box by Consolidated. Hard to find in this color wash over the milk glass. *$125.00 – 130.00.*

Plate 54 - TOP: 5¾" tall, Rapunzel covered puff box. Also found in frosted colors. *$100.00 – 120.00.* 3⅜" tall Oriental Girl condiment box by Westmoreland Specialty Co. See matching Boy in Plate 52. *$35.00 – 45.00.*
BOTTOM: Boy with Dog. Oddly shaped, 4¼" box, divided inside. Also called Puppy Love. Found in frosted colors besides the milk white. *$175.00 – 185.00.* 5¼" Hobnail covered shoe candy dish by Fenton Art Glass. *$35.00 – 40.00.*

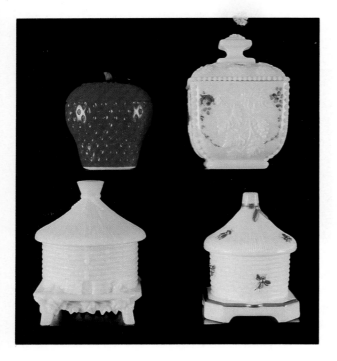

Plate 55 - TOP: 3¾" covered Strawberry, painted over milk white. *$10.00 – 15.00.* 5¼" Beaded Grape covered box with hand-painted roses. A product of Westmoreland. *$25.00 – 30.00.*
BOTTOM: 5½" Beehive with Vines honey dish by Vallerysthal. *$95.00 – 100.00.* 4⅞" Beehive covered honey by Imperial Glass. *$30.00 – 35.00.*

Plate 56 - Parakeet candy jar and lid by Imperial Glass, 1958–1960. Mold is now being used by Summit Art Glass and made in various transparent colors. *$50.00 – 65.00.*

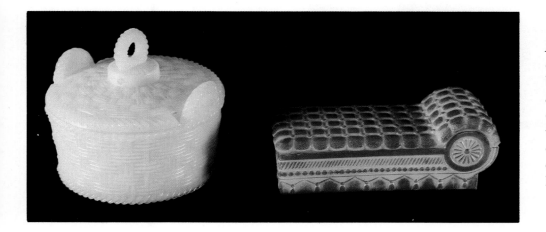

Plate 57 - Hinged Basket covered dish. 4" diameter, two handles and braided finial, by Vallerysthal. *$40.00 – 45.00.* Fainting Couch covered dish, 5⅛" long, 2" wide. One of those wonderful little Victorian novelty pieces from about 1890. May originally have been made to hold hairpins. Scarce. *$200.00 – 250.00.*

Plate 58 - TOP: 6¼", Roses & Ribbons ginger jar with lid. *$35.00 – 40.00.* 4½" squared corner rose bowl by Fostoria. Shown in 1900 catalog. *$30.00 – 35.00.*
BOTTOM: Base and lid for 5¼" diameter by 3⅞" tall cuff box. Decorated as souvenir piece, but place name is unreadable. Probably Dithridge manufacture. *$40.00 – 45.00.*

Plate 59 - TOP: Quilted pattern cookie or perhaps dresser jar. 4⅛" diameter, 8" tall to cube-shaped finial. Could be Old Morgantown. *$25.00 – 30.00.*
BOTTOM: Salt box with wooden lid. 6¼" diameter, 5¾" to top of hanger. *$95.00 – 100.00.*

Plate 60 - l to r: 5" decorated jar with metal screw-on lid. *$25.00 – 30.00.* Beautifully painted jar by David-Lynch Glass Company, Star City, WV. Made for L.G. Wright in the early 1970's. Wright did the decorating. *$60.00 – 65.00.* 4¾" jar with screw-on glass lid. *$25.00 – 30.00.*

Plate 61 - TOP (l to r): 2½" x 3" shaving mug by Akro Agate Company. Contained Orloff Attar of Petals flower potpourri. Made for the Jean Vivadou Company of New York. *$20.00 – 25.00.* Flower embossing very similar to that of the Actress or Jenny Lind items. Roses & Poppies with a clear glass covering over center medallion. Sometimes found with a picture under the glass. 8½" x 5½". *$40.00 – 45.00.* 3½" x 3" Basketweave covered jar with large embossed and painted rose. *$40.00 – 45.00.* BOTTOM (l to r): 8" x 4" Rose covered jar. This large attractive piece is footed and has large blown-out roses on the sides and a rose finial. *$45.00 – 50.00.* 7" x 3½" covered jar for Jean Vivaudou Co., Inc. of New York. Made by Akro Agate Company and listed as an apothecary jar. *$50.00 – 55.00.* Consolidated Glass, 6" x 6½" Tufted Pillow jar with hand painted gold and violet spray. *$65.00 – 70.00.*

Plate 62 - TOP: Lady powder jar by Akro Agate. Found in white, blue, and other colors. *$40.00 – 55.00.* CENTER: Covered candy on pedestal base, Consolidated Con-Cora line #45-5, done in the 1950's. Decorated with pink flower sprays and gold. *$45.00 – 50.00.*

BOTTOM (l to r): Lillian VII puff jar. The Lillian torso has shown up on several different bases and dates from the 1920's. *$150.00 – 160.00.* Another Consolidated candy box on pedestal base. This time with pink roses. *$45.00 – 50.00.* Spring Nymph powder jar. The elaborate finial consists of a kneeling nude under what appears to be a horseshoe shaped flower wreath. The lady has a drape of cloth across her lap. May also be found as a lamp in various frosted pastel colors. *$150.00 – 155.00.*

Plate 63 - l to r: 4½" Scroll & Lace footed candlestick with beaded rim on candle bowl. Early 1900's. *$30.00 – 35.00.* 7" candles decorated with scrollwork and hand painted flowers and bands. Two different color schemes are shown. Late 1800's. *$35.00 – 40.00.* 4" Pineapple candlestick by Indiana Glass Co. 1980's. *$7.00 – 10.00.*

Plate 64 - Rope handled candlesticks with tassels embossed on sides. Shown in 1905 Butler Brothers catalog. Probably Dithridge. *$30.00 – 35.00.*

Plate 65 - 13½" shaded candle attributed to Old Morgantown. 1960 – 1970's. *$25.00 – 30.00.* 9¼" Dolphin candlesticks by Westmoreland. *$65.00 – 75.00 pr.*

Plate 66 - TOP: Satin finish glass with embossed roses. 4" tall. *$25.00 – 30.00.* Newbound pattern double candleholders by Imperial Glass. Depression era. *$30.00 – 40.00 pr.*
BOTTOM: Open leaf edge in Betsy Ross pattern by Fostoria. *$25.00 – 30.00 pr.* Jewel & Dewdrop candles by Kemple. *$25.00 – 30.00 pr.*

Plate 67 - TOP: Ray End candlestick by Dithridge. *$18.00 – 22.00.* Cinderella candlestick by McKee. Around 1899 on both of these. *$20.00 – 25.00.*
BOTTOM: We thought this was a shallow candlestick until we discovered it was designed as an inkwell and pen tray. Much gold, late 1800's. *$40.00 – 50.00.* Ball Edge candle by Anchor Hocking. 1960's. *$7.00 – 9.00 pr.*

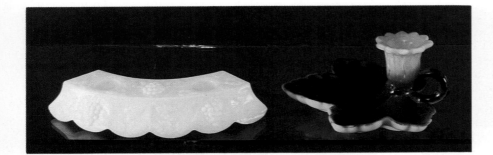

Plate 68 - Here is one part of a sectional candleholder that, along with three more sections forms a round centerpiece. Each section is 8½" long. By Westmoreland. *$35.00 – 40.00 ea.* Maple Leaf shape candle with finger hole. Heavily enameled and lovely, graceful shape. *$40.00 – 45.00 ea..*

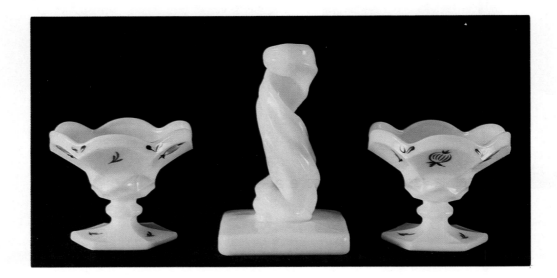

Plate 69 - LEFT AND RIGHT: Octagon shaped candlestick in the Georgian style. Decorated with Delft-style painting. Maker unknown. *$25.00 – 30.00 pr.* CENTER: Spiral candle 6" tall by Westmoreland. *$25.00 – 30.00 pr.*

Plate 70 - Three of the popular Crucifix candlesticks. LEFT: 11" candle with base resembling rocks above a section of vertical ribbing. The candle cup has a floral pattern below a finely ribbed top band. Made in milk and crystal in three sizes and shown in a 1893 U.S. Glass catalog. INRI above figure is a Latin abbreviation for "King of the Jews." *$75.00 – 80.00 ea.* CENTER AND RIGHT: 9⅝" tall and 8¾" tall candles by Cambridge. 1903. *$65.00 – 70.00. ea.*

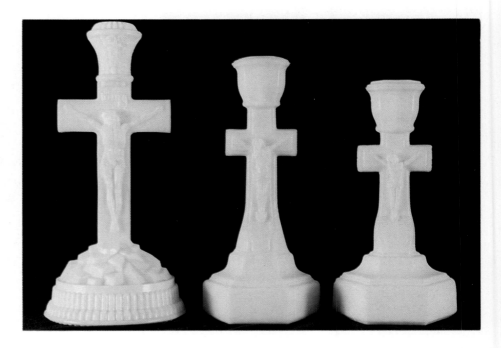

Plate 71 - 6¼" tall, double English Hobnail candlestick by Westmoreland. *$65.00 – 70.00 pr.* 10⅝" Crucifix candle by Cambridge. *$65.00 – 70.00.*

Plate 72 - Compote and candlesticks in the Vinelf pattern by Imperial Glass 1950–1965. Candlesticks, 7½" tall. *$45.00 – 50.00 pr.* Fruit compote, 8½" tall by 8¼" diameter. Mold later purchased by L. E. Smith. *$55.00 – 60.00.*

Plate 73 - Lamb, child's table set. **l to r:** 4¼" covered sugar. *$135.00 – 145.00.* 2⅝" spooner. *$175.00 – 200.00.* 2⅞" creamer. *$175.00 – 200.00.* 3¼" diameter butter. *$145.00 – 155.00.* Shown here in pink milk glass, a product of Boyd's Crystal Art Glass 1985–1989. Also made by Imperial Glass in various colors. From old molds of whose origin we are uncertain. *$45.00 – 50.00 set of Imperial.*

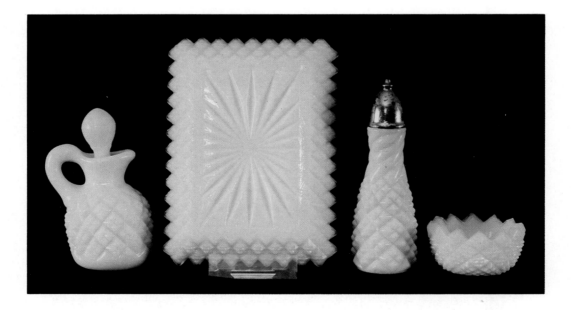

Plate 74 - Line 300 individual condiment or child's condiment set by Westmoreland. Tray is shown inverted. **l to r:** Cruet, 3" tall. Tray, 4½" x 3¼". Shaker, 3½" tall. Salt dip, 1¾" diameter. Originally made in crystal and milk glass, some pieces have been reproduced in colors. *Range $35.00 – 45.00 per set.*

Plate 75 - Miniature Swirl patterned candlesticks in white and blue. LEFT AND RIGHT: Taller sticks are 3¼" tall. CENTER: Chamberstick is 1¾" tall. You have to look at these very carefully because we have seen them with the word "Taiwan" embossed around the top rim of the candle cup. Mainly these are French production. *Range $25.00 – 30.00 pr.*

Plate 76 - LEFT AND RIGHT: Dutch Boudior candles, 3" tall. Attributed to U.S. Glass—1910. *$120.00 – 125.00 pr.* Boy with dog is embossed. Early set recently reproduced by Mosser Glass of Cambridge, Ohio. *$20.00 – 25.00.* CENTER: Candlestick is 3" tall and made by Indiana Glass for their Tiara line. *$10.00 – 15.00 pr.*

Plate 77 - Tiny milk glass child's set made in Japan. Also found will be plates and a small compote. The teapot measures 1½" tall. The sugar and creamer are ¾" high. The saucer is 1½" in diameter. The cup is 1" diameter. *Pieces range from $2.00 if you're lucky to $7.00 if your not!*

Plate 78 - Flattened Diamond & Sunburst table set. Also known as File and Fan and Thumbelina. **l to r:** Creamer is 2³⁄₈" to spout top. *$10.00 – 12.00.* Covered butter is 3½" diameter. *$12.00 – 15.00.* Sugar, 2¼"

tall. *$10.00 – 12.00..* Designed by Westmoreland Glass about 1890, appearing in crystal. In milk glass only the three pieces shown were produced and appear in 1950 – 1958 catalogs. Also were made by Westmoreland in several colors during the later years. New pieces being made for Phil Rosso and we have even seen them in the gift shop at Pairpoint Glass.

Plate 79 - Monk Stein set. Large is 4" tall. *$75.00 – 80.00.* Small, 2⅛". *$25.00 – 30.00.* Advertised in the 1910 Butler Brothers catalog with various color trims. Small mugs will be found with a horizontal ribbing at the top, as shown here, or plain. Also found in crystal.

Plate 80 - Nursery Rhyme punch bowl, 4⁵⁄₈" dia., 3³⁄₈" high. *$95.00 – 110.00.* Cups 1⁵⁄₈" dia, 1³⁄₈" tall. *$18.00 – 22.00.* Made by U.S. Glass Company at Gas City, Indiana, and advertised in Butler Brothers 1910 catalog. Also in blue milk glass, clear, and cobalt. Depicted are scenes from *Little*

Red Riding Hood—Grandma's House (shown), Wolf in Grandma's clothing, Little Red Riding Hood, and a tree. A table set, water set, and berry set were also made in this pattern in crystal. *$250.00 – 300.00 a set.*

Plate 81 - Wild Rose child's table set. **l to r:** 1⅞" tall spooner. *$55.00 – 60.00.* 2" tall creamer. *$55.00 – 60.00.* 1⅞" tall sugar. *$55.00 – 60.00.* Roses may vary on different pieces. Candlesticks were also made in this pattern.

Plate 82 - Wild Rose butter with lid. There is an inverted rose on the bottom of this piece. *$70.00 – 75.00.*

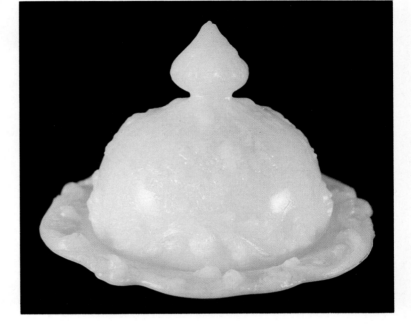

Plate 83 - Wild Rose punch set (6 cups in set). Bowl, 4¼" tall, 4" dia. *$85.00 – 90.00.* Cups, 1½" diameter. *$20.00 – 25.00.* Shown in Butler Brothers 1910 catalog in milk glass and crystal. Milk glass sets had red, green, blue, or silver trim. A dozen sets wholesaled for $2.10! *$200.00 – 225.00 set.*

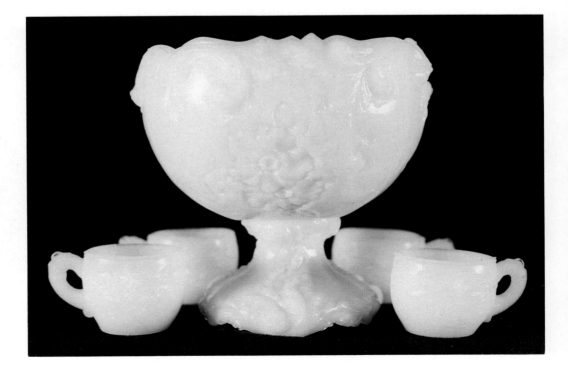

Plate 84 - Tappan child's table set. **l to r:** 2¾" tall creamer. *$25.00 – 30.00*. 3⅛" tall butter. *$30.00 – 35.00*. 4" covered sugar. *$30.00 – 35.00*. Originally made as Waffle and Button by McKee, 1894–1925 in crystal. Made in milk glass by Kemple at East Palestine, OH, until 1956, when plant burned. Continued at Kample's Kenova, WV, plant in 1957, in a number of transparent colors plus milk glass—cobalt, black, light amethyst, green, light and honey amber, aqua, Old Virginia blue, and West Virginia Centennial red (1963).

COMPOTES, EPERGNES & CAKE STANDS

Plate 85 - Two lovely blue compotes by Porteiux - Vallerysthal. Swirled Split Rib. *$30.00 – 35.00*. Zipper & Rib. *$20.00 – 25.00*.

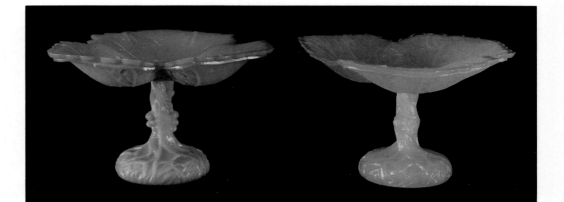

Plate 86 - Large Grape Leaf bowl compotes, one in blue, one in yellow. These have an interesting grape stem and root-like foot. Vallerysthal. *Blue $35.00 – 40.00. Yellow $45.00 – 50.00.*

Plate 87 - Bird Pedestal compote, 4⅛" tall, 7" diameter. Guernsey Glass in Cambridge, Ohio, made a similar piece shaped as a spooner in transparent and opaque colors sometime in the 1970's. Maker of the original mold is unknown. *$40.00 – 45.00.*

Plate 88 - Light blue open work edge combined with basket weave. This was advertised as a fruit bowl by Challinor, Taylor, 1885–1893. *$120.00 – 130.00.*

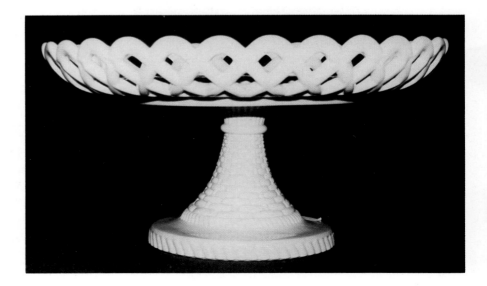

Plate 89 - Squared Arlington pattern, 9⅞", tall compote by Fostoria. 1960's. *$30.00 – 35.00.*

Plate 90 - TOP: 10" x 6½" Arlington pattern compote by Fostoria in the 1960's. This is a two-piece mold with the stem being applied to the bowl. *$30.00 – 35.00.* 5½" x 5" compote or footed candy jar without its usual lid. Imperial Glass, 1950–64. #425 line. *$35.00 – 40.00.*

BOTTOM: 6½" x 10" Con-Cora line covered compote by Consolidated, design inside. This is the smaller of two similar pieces. *$40.00 – 45.00.* Deep Ribbed Stem is 9" tall and 8" in diameter with a 3" deep bowl. This one has a 2" deep bowl. There is also a cake stand in this pattern, made by flattening the bowl section. A similar compote was made by Imperial Glass 1955–1964, having a rounded side bowl rather than a straight-sided bowl. Listed as #203F it was also made in the cake stand form. *Old, $70.00 – 75.00. IG, $35.00 – 40.00.*

Plate 91 - TOP: Daisy and Button with petticoat edge compote, 6" x 6" tall. *$25.00 – 30.00.* Dolphin Stem compote with shell bowl, 8½" x 5½" tall. Westmoreland Glass. *$40.00 – 45.00.*
BOTTOM: Bull's Eye covered candy, 6⅛" x 11" to top of finial. *$25.00 – 30.00.* 6" x 4½" Vintage Grape compote by L. E. Smith. *$25.00 – 30.00.*

Plate 92 - TOP: 8¼" x 7¾" Jenny Lind compote by Challinor, Taylor 1889 – 1893. There is a difference of opinion whether the figure on the stem is Jenny Lind or Columbia, Goddess of Liberty. Since the piece was designed and produced close to the date of the World Columbian Exposition in Chicago in 1892, it is very probable that it was indeed meant to be Columbia. *$90.00 – 95.00.* 5⅛" x 5½" Old Quilt small compote or mint dish by Westmoreland Glass. *$20.00 – 25.00.* BOTTOM: 6½" x 5¼" lacy edged compote produced by Imperial Glass 1954–1960 as #749F. Sometimes found with a metal handle which was added during 1962. *$15.00 – 20.00.* 9¾" x 8¼" tall Grape pattern compote by L. E. Smith. Shown in their 1975–1976 catalog. *$30.00 – 35.00.*

Plate 93 - Doric Border compote, 11" diameter, with three-column stem. *$35.00 – 40.00.* Matching candleholders, 4½" tall. *$25.00 – 30.00.* By Westmoreland Glass.

Plate 94 - Jewel and Dewdrop 6⅛" tall compote. *$125.00 – 130.00 for Phoenix.* 3⅝" tumbler. *$45.00 – 50.00 for Phoenix.* These were produced during the Phoenix ownership of the mold. Originally made by Duncan Glass and later made by Kemple. See more pieces of this pattern in various treatments throughout this book.

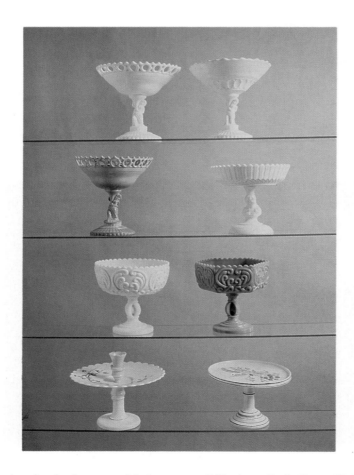

Plate 95 - 1ST ROW: Atlas compote, 8¼" tall, shown in lace edge and scalloped edge styles. Made in white, blue, and green opaque colors by Atterbury. The lace edge is harder to find; base is the same on both styles. *$100.00 – 150.00, lace edge. $75.00 – 90.00, scallop edge.*

2ND ROW: Green Atlas is shown along with Jenny Lind. Jenny was designed by David Barker and patented in 1877. The Crystal Glass Company of Pittsburgh, first made them with a Beaded Panel bowl. After they, and Challinor, Taylor joined the U.S. Glass Company it was made with the flute panel bowl. It was also made with two different stems; the base on one is smooth with a floral impression underneath. On the other version, the base under the bust is ribbed. *$90.00 – 95.00.*

3RD ROW: 8" Scroll compotes in both round and hexagonal style bowls, the hexagonal being more difficult to find. You will find a variety of table items in the Scroll pattern having been made by Imperial 1953–1962 and sometimes marked with a paper label stating "The Belknap Collection." *$45.00 – 50.00, hex. $40.00 – 45.00, round.* 4TH ROW: Cake plate with and without center handle, both by Challinor, Taylor, 1885–1890. *$50.00 – 55.00.*

Plate 96 - Two covered dishes by Westmoreland Glass. 5½" tall by 6¼" diameter, English Hobnail footed candy bowl. *$45.00 – 50.00.* 9" tall and 6¼" diameter, Sawtooth covered compote. *$45.00 – 50.00.*

Plate 97 - 9½" x 7" ribbed compote originally by Atterbury and later produced by Westmoreland. The Atterbury stem, however, has a vertical center support column while Westmoreland's version has a stem with curved columns. Also, the Westmoreland version has a much thicker "tablet" at the stem top, attaching to the bowl of the compote. *$35.00 – 40.00.* 8" tall, 6" diameter, Fleur de Lis footed candy with lid and Fleur de Lis finial made by Imperial Glass, 1957–1960. *$35.00 – 40.00.*

Plate 98 - Lace & Dew Drop pattern made by Kemple Glass. 8½" tall covered compote. *$20.00 – 25.00.* 4½" candleholders. *$20.00 – 25.00 pr.* The molds were later sold to Wheaton Glass in New Jersey. See more of this pattern elsewhere in this book.

Plate 99 - Fostoria's #2679 line puff box with lid. 4½" tall, 5¾" diameter. *$35.00 – 40.00.* 6½" tall, 6" diameter covered compote in the Colony pattern also by Fostoria. *$45.00 – 50.00.*

Plate 100 - Open Hand, 8¾" tall, 9⅛" diameter. Shown in the 1881 Atterbury catalog. *$75.00 – 85.00.* Basketweave, 10¼" tall, 8" diameter compote. Patented in 1874 and shown in the 1881 Atterbury catalog. *$80.00 – 85.00.*

Plate 101 - Strawberry pattern, 7½" covered compote, patented in 1870, by John Bryce and produced by Bryce Brothers of Pittsburgh, PA. This is a fine flint glass made in many pieces and fairly difficult to find. *$150.00 – 155.00.* 8¼" tall Blackberry compote. Patented in 1870, by W. Leighton, Jr., and produced by Hobbs Brockunier and Co. of Wheeling, WV. This is another pattern with a long history of mold sales. From Hobbs, the molds went to Cooperative Glass of Beaver Falls, PA, then to the Phoenix Glass Co. of Monaca, PA. They stayed there until about 1942, when they were purchased by John Kemple Glass of East Palestine, OH. *$150.00 – 155.00.*

Plate 102 - 11" tall, 5" square, wedding bowl by Westmoreland. Originally, wedding bowls were used at long-ago weddings to serve individual pieces of wedding cake. They were traditionally used in pairs. In Westmoreland wedding bowls, one can set the lid down, upright, on a flat surface and place the stemmed piece over it, forming a large pedestal. Or, the lid could be turned upside down on top of the bowl. This made a special place for serving the bride and groom with the first piece of cake. Several glasshouses made very similar wedding bowls, among them L. E. Smith (4" x 8" #5000, 1963–64 catalog), Duncan Miller (6" dia, 12" tall; 5" dia. 10" tall; 4" diameter, 5½" tall), and Jeannette Glass who made 6½" and 8" sizes as early as 1940, the 6" low footed bowl being most elusive. *$45.00 – 55.00.* 6½" x 5" beaded edge covered candy. Recent, by Indiana Glass. *$8.00 – 10.00.*

Plate 103 - 9¼" tall Grape stack set by Imperial Glass, or as they called it "Three Section Ivy Tower." Made 1958–1968, also made in a four section version. *$45.00 – 50.00, 3 high. $60.00 – 65.00, 4 high.* 8½" covered compote or candy, also found in white by Vallerysthal/Porteiux. *$45.00 – 50.00.*

Plate 104 - Imperial Glass Candlewick line single horn epergne. Bowl is 9" x 6" tall; 11½" tall with horn inserted. This will be found with the ball-edged horn also. Made 1950–1960. Note the leaf pattern around base and also on bottom of bowl. *$75.00 – 85.00.*

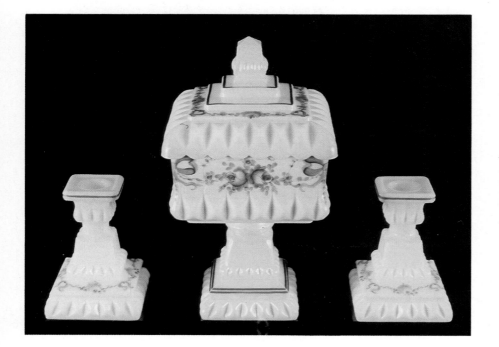

Plate 105 - Wedding bowl and candlesticks set by Westmoreland Glass. Pearlized box has hand painted Roses and Bows decoration. Box is 9¾" tall. *$85.00 – 90.00.* Candles, 4½". *$40.00 – 45.00 pr.*

Plate 106 - Ribs & Scallops, single-horn epergne by Vallerysthal/Porteiux. PV sticker. *$75.00 – 85.00.*

Plate 107 - 6" tall by 9⅛" diameter, cake stand by Challinor, Taylor, 1885 – 1893. Also came in 10" size. Note the lovely hand-painted floral trim which is, alas, so often found today almost completely worn off, as well as the multicolored rings and edge of plate. *$40.00 – 45.00.*

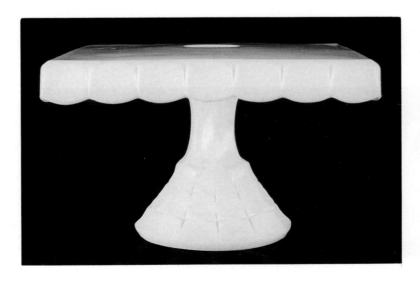

Plate 108 - Cake stand by Indiana Glass. 6¾" tall, 10⅜" square. Has a 1¾" hole in the center of the plate. 1960's–1970's. *$10.00 – 12.00.*

Plate 110 - The American Hen Covered dish. 6⅛" long. Inspired by the Spanish-American War, this eagle shelters three eggs marked "PORTO RICO, CUBA & PHILIPPINES". A banner along both sides of the base says "THE AMERICAN HEN" and on the base is "PAT APPLIED FOR." Has been reproduced in several colors. *$85.00 – 95.00.*

Plate 109 - The Boar's Head covered dish. 9½" long. By Atterbury, patented May 29, 1888. The date will be found on the base and lid. Also in blue. A large piece, much desired by the advanced collector. *$1500.00+*

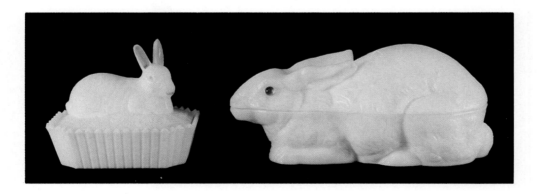

Plate 111 - Mule-eared Rabbit on Picket Base. 5½" long, 4½" tall. Corners of the base are cut on a diagonal and form an octagon. Hard to find in blue, blue with white head, or white with blue head. Even more elusive in blue with custard head. Made by Westmoreland Glass. Also made in Caramel Slag iridized and white carnival along with other colors. Being reproduced today; offered in milk glass, milk hand painted by Rosso in 1990 – 1991. *$45.00 – 65.00.* 9½" Large Rabbit with pink glass eyes by Imperial Glass, 1953 – 1958. Originally patented by Atterbury, the patent date of March 9, 1886, will still be found on the base of the Imperial piece along with the IG logo. Originally manufactured by Atterbury in opaque blue as well as white. The Imperial rabbit has become almost as scarce as the original. Also found in a 6¼" size. *$150.00 – 175.00 for IG version. $200.00 – 250.00 for Atterbury.*

Plate 112 - The British Lion covered dish. In England, the Lion is comparable to our Eagle as a symbol of patriotic pride. This was a centennial piece but, we have found nothing to tell us the maker. *$225.00 – 250.00.*

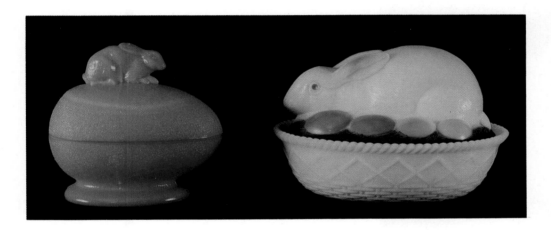

Plate 113 - Rabbit on Egg, 5" tall, 5¼" long. Made by Vallerysthal in white as well as blue. This piece was shown in their 1914 catalog, but had disappeared by the 1933 catalog. *$195.00 – 225.00.* Rabbit on Diamond Basket with Eggs. 4¾" tall, 7⅜" long. By Westmoreland. Will be found hand painted in pastels with green grass and also with a brown basket and brightly colored eggs. Recently produced (1990's) by Fenton in a pearlized finish with pastels. *$95.00 – 125.00.*

Plate 114 - Jack Rabbit on fine ribbed base. 4¼" tall to top of rear end, 6¼" long. Generally thought to be Flaccus. *$180.00 – 190.00.* Beehive, plain base sugar and lid by Vallerysthal. 5¼" tall, 4" square base. This is the version without the vinery at the base. *$65.00 – 75.00.*

Plate 115 - Ribbed Base Lion, 5½" tall, 7" long. patented August 6, 1889, by Atterbury. The Fox will also be found on this ribbed base. The same lion lid will be found on a lacy base as well. *$200.00 – 225.00.* Westmoreland Lion on Diamond Basket base. 6" tall, 7⅜" long. Reproduced from the Atterbury Lion lid, but usually marked WG. The same lion has been made by Kemple and Imperial. Imperial put their logo IG in the upper inside of the lion's head. Westmoreland's lion will be found on a lacy base in a number of colors. *$85.00 – 95.00.*

Plate 116 - The Westmoreland Lion on Lace Edge box. The lion was originally an Atterbury design of 1889, but will not be found on this base. Westmoreland's lion can also be found in blue milk glass as well as white and several other colors. The same lion was made by Imperial in 1957–1960 and Kemple Glass. *$125.00 – 135.00.*

Plate 117 - Lion on Scroll Base. 4¼" to top of head, 5⅜" base length. Not much seems to be known about the origin of this lion. *$70.00 – 90.00.*

Plate 118 - TOP: Kemple, 5½", Dome Top Rabbit on split rib base. The top of the rabbit dish is taken from the old Greentown rabbit, but the underside of the lid rim is stippled, which is a characteristic of Kemple. Made in blue milk by Rosso in 1986. *$65.00 – 75.00.* Lamb on Split Rib Base, this one by Boyd Crystal Art Glass, was made as a convention piece for the National Milk Glass Collectors in 1991. The lid is a Westmoreland mold. *$80.00 – 85.00 for Westmoreland.*

BOTTOM: McKee Horse on Split Rib Base. *$250.00 – 265.00.* McKee Turkey lid on split rib base. *$25.00 – 30.00.* Another convention piece made for National Milk Glass Collectors Association in 1993, by Boyd's Crystal Art Glass. As you can see the split rib bases have been used by many glasshouses for many years and the fact that the tops are virtually interchangeable, leads to many a marriage so hard to sort out after a few years. McKee & Brothers Glass Factory (1853–1899) produced a variety of animal covers on their split rib bases. Some are signed McKee in script on the lid or base or both. Some, but by no means all! From 1899–1903, McKee was, along with many other glasshouses, part of the National Glass Company, which meant molds could be loaned out among a number of factories. Kemple bought many McKee molds in 1951. St. Clair Glass Co. and Degenhart also produced animals on split rib bases. According to some informed collectors, only McKee split rib bases had the straight sides, however, a few signed McKee bases have been found with flared sides! Edges on flared bases seem thicker than those on straight-sided bases. Some collectors feel there is a slight difference in the rays on the bottom of the base, but this is difficult to detect. For the most part, I would advise don't pay McKee prices for a piece unless it is *signed* McKee.

Plate 119 - TOP: 6" tall Robin on Nest. This piece by Westmoreland began production about 1952. It was produced in as many as 24 different colors! This was originally a Portieux-Vallerysthal piece which is shown in their 1908 catalog. Most Westmoreland robins will be signed, but if you're not certain, the older French version has a solid glass head, whereas Westmoreland's robin has a hollow head. The French version came in blue and white milk glass and in a transparent amber. The Westmoreland mold was at one point acquired by Blenko Glass Company of Milton, WV. *$75.00 – 95.00 for Westmoreland. $125.00 – 150.00 for Portieux.* Westmoreland's 8½" tall, Standing Rooster, introduced by Westmoreland around 1948, this proud rooster was also a French original, shown in a 1933 Portieux catalog. Some collectors maintain that the very top of the Portieux base has feathering right up to the top edge, whereas the Westmoreland version has a fine, smooth, very narrow band all around. Originally made in white and blue opaque and amber transparent, Westmoreland's rooster has been produced in many colors. L. E. Smith produced a very similar rooster shown in their 1963–1964 catalog. The mold is currently owned by Phil Rosso and being produced by Summit Art Glass in several colors, for instance, blue milk glass in 1990. *$40.00 – 45.00 for Westmoreland. $90.00 – 100.00 for Portieux.*

BOTTOM: Westmoreland Specialty Company Dog and Cat, both on wide rib bases. Both made in various plain colors and combinations of blue and white milk glass. Notice that they face in opposite directions! Blue and blue/white combinations are harder to find. Cat has been made in amethyst, cobalt, and green slags and also blue milk and pearlized white for Rosso in 1990. *$40.00 – 45.00 white. $50.00 – 55.00 blue/white.*

Plate 120 - Top: 5½" tall, 5¾" long, Resting Camel by Westmoreland. Introduced in the 1930's and designed by Westmoreland. Can be found in blue milk as well as other satin or frosted colors. *$110.00 – 120.00, white. $175.00 – 190.00, blue.* 5¼" tall, 7" long, Stagecoach by Fostoria. Produced in the 1950's, this is a great piece! *$200.00 – 250.00.*

Bottom: 7½" long Fish on Skiff. Although this piece is relatively easy to find and has been around for a long, long time, the maker is still unknown. *$50.00 – 60.00.* Robin with Berry on split rib base. This particular one is by Boyd's Crystal Art Glass. Originated by Greentown on a diamond top basket base. Also made by Degenhart, Kemple and St. Clair. *$45.00 – 55.00.*

Plate 121 - Top: Love Birds, 6" x 4¾" x 5" tall, covered dish by Westmoreland. Came in blue and green milk in 1974 and 1977 for Levay Company. Mold now owned by Summit Art Glass. *$65.00 – 75.00.* 4" diameter, 3¾" tall, Love Bird dish made in Taiwan and found in dime stores about ten years ago. Note hand-painted holly and berries on lid. *$12.00 – 15.00.*

Bottom: L. E. Smith Coach, 5" long and 4¼" tall. A larger size was made also. *$75.00 – 90.00, small. $125.00 – 150.00, large.* 4⅝" tall Hen on two-handled basket by Westmoreland. Mold now being used for reproductions by Summit Art Glass and Phil Rosso. *$35.00 – 45.00.*

Plate 122 - TOP: Uncle Sam on Battleship. 5½" tall, 6⅝" long. Probably a product of the Spanish-American War era. Many collectors attribute the piece to Flaccus. Be careful, however, as this was shown in milk glass in the 1974–76 AA Importing catalog. $65.00 – 75.00. Snail on Strawberry, 5⅛" tall. A product of Vallerysthal shown in their 1870, 1900, 1914, and 1933 catalogs. Also made in a somewhat larger size. $100.00 – 125.00. 4¾" tall, 5⅜" long, Santa on Sleigh, an original creation by Westmoreland Glass. Mold now being reproduced by Summit Art Glass in many colors & treatments. $75.00 – 95.00.

BOTTOM: Two 6" tall, 7½" long, Westmoreland Roosters on diamond basket bases. The beautiful slag fellow on the right was made in the 1980's for a jobber. Both have glass eyes. $55.00 – 65.00, white. $75.00 – 85.00, slag.

Plate 123 - Raised-wing Swan by Atterbury, 5¼" tall, 10" long. Note the red glass eyes. Westmoreland's raised wing swan has shallow eye sockets, with the eyes sometimes painted black and sometimes unpainted. Both swans have the basket weave pattern inside the base. The Atterbury base has a ³⁄₁₆" ledge to support the cover while the Westmoreland edge is ¼" wide. There is an Atterbury variant

top which is scarce. In this lid, the swan floats on a 1" slab rather than Westmoreland's ¼" thick slab. Most Westmoreland are marked. $175.00 – 200.00, Atterbury. $95.00 – 125.00, Westmoreland. Atterbury Hen on lacy base. 7¾" tall to tail tip, 7" long. Atterbury white hens can be found with blue heads in several opaque shades as well as cased, which are more elusive. Also produced in blue, red, yellow, brown, and green marble. As with all Atterbury hens, the distinguishing features are the flat, round eye sockets made for red glass eyes. Westmoreland's similar hen has oval, molded eyes. $200.00 – 250.00.

Plate 124 - Dolphin covered pitcher-shaped piece. 7" long and sometimes found in pairs. The base has an oval medallion in the center which leads one to believe it was first made for something having a label affixed to it, but so far we have not uncovered the maker. *$55.00 – 65.00.* 6½" tall, 7¼" diameter, Chick on Egg Pile with lacy base. Made by Atterbury, 1889. Also found on a tall, three section pedestal base. Both have been produced by Westmoreland, but in the tall, pedestal version, the Atterbury vertical center support is missing. Will be found with eggs painted in either pastel or bright colors. This piece was made in several colors by Westmoreland and is now being reproduced by Summit Art Glass. *$95.00 – 125.00.* 6¼" tall, 6" diameter, Shell & Dolphin covered bowl by Westmoreland with dolphin feet and snail shell finial. Originally a Vallerysthal piece made in two sizes. This Westmoreland version has a space separating the loops of shells that circle the lid; also, the Westmoreland dolphins are sad in comparison to the French smiling version. See Vallerysthal pieces pictured elsewhere in this book. Mold now owned by Dalzell-Viking. Westmoreland made the piece in 1976, in mother-of-pearl finish with pastel painted shells. Also other transparent and satin colors. *$35.00 – 40.00 for Westmoreland.*

Plate 125 - Civil War Cannon on Snare Drum, 3⅜" x 4" diameter, by Westmoreland Specialty Company. The cannon with its pile of shot can be found on the base shown or on the Kettle Drum base which is identi-

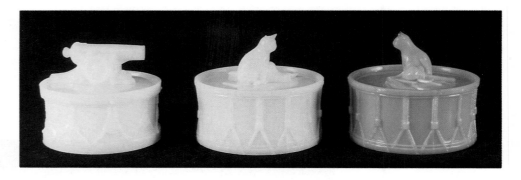

fied with Westmoreland's #200 line. The snare drum is hardest to find. *$80.00 – 90.00.* Cats on Drums. 3¾" x 4¾" dia., by Portieux, which is usually marked on the base. The blue version is thought to be made later than the white. *$100.00 – 125.00.*

Plate 126 - 5" long, 5" tall, Squirrel atop Fancy Dish by Vallerysthal in the early 1900's. *$90.00 – 120.00.* 4¾" tall, 5" long, Dogs on Steamer Rugs with floral bases. Blue piece is signed Vallerysthal while the yellow bears a paper label. *$195.00 – 200.00, yellow. $175.00 – 185.00, blue.*

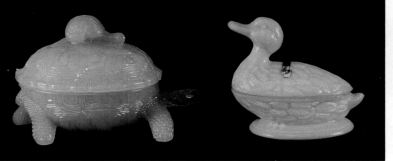

Plate 127 - Turtle with Snail Finial. 4¾" tall, 7½" long overall. This pink opal piece is marked P.V. France. *$175.00 – 200.00.* Swimming Duck, 4½" tall, 5" long. Marked P.V. France on sticker with "Opale Verrtable" on cartouche. Vallerysthal catalog mentions two sizes. The 5" size is called a sugar and the 5¾" a butter. Pictured in the 1914 catalog but not in the 1933 issue. *$75.00 – 95.00.*

Plate 128 - 6⅛" Robin on Pedestal Nest. Originally a Vallerysthal piece, pre World War I (1908). Shown again in Portieux 1933 catalog. Also copiously made by Westmoreland in more than 25 colors. The head of the French robin is solid glass whereas you can fit a little finger into the hollow head of the Westmorland version. French will also be found in blue and white milk glass and transparent amber. Mold now owned by Blenko Glass. *$75.00 – 95.00 for Westmoreland. $100.00 – 125.00 for Vallerysthal.*

Wavy Base Duck, 4¾" tall, 8½" long. Originally a Challinor, Taylor product, part of their Farm Yard Assortment advertised in 1891. Made in white, light blue, and olive green. Challinor's base has a ¾" rim with wavy pattern on both sides. Reproduced by Westmoreland and by Fenton in light blue with satin finish (1977). Also in production by U.S. Glass. Westmoreland's duck is marked with their logo and is thicker and heavier than the original, although it is only 8" long. This is a difficult piece to accurately judge the maker. The realistic glass eyes are missing on the duck pictured. *$125.00 – 135.00 for Challinor. $85.00 – 100.00 for Westmoreland.*

Plate 129 - Dove Box made by Imperial as their "Atterbury Dove Box" in 1957 – 1960. It is 7½" tall, 8½" long. Base is milk glass and lid is satin crystal. *$95.00 – 100.00.*

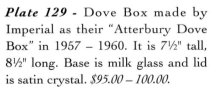

Plate 130 - Setter Dog covered dish, 6½" tall, 6" long. Produced by Vallerysthal between 1914 and 1933. This mold is a dream, with the dog resting on various pieces of hunting equipment, including the horn. What moldmakers they had! *$200.00 – 250.00.*

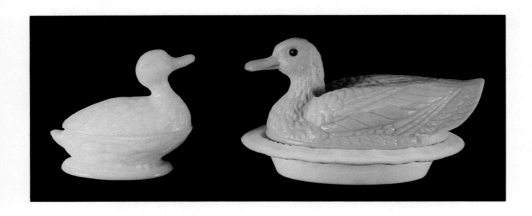

Plate 131 - White version of Vallerysthal's Swimming Duck box. 4½" tall, 5⅛" long. 1914–1932. *$75.00 – 80.00.* Another version of the Wavy Base Duck, this time by Tiffin Glass. *$90.00 – 100.00 for Tiffin version.* Notice the glass eyes and the lovely pale green wash of color on the body. Along with this dish, Tiffin included the following story: "In the archives of the Tiffin Glass Factory at Tiffin, Ohio, the 106 year old moulds were found which produced the Tiffin Duck. This duck was originally produced at the Challinor, Taylor and Co. factory in Tarentum, PA. The Challinor facility began producing glass items in 1870 and remained in business as Challinor, Taylor and Co, until July 1, 1891, when it became part of the U.S. Glass Co., a combine of 18 then-existing glass factories throughout Ohio, Pennsylvania, and West Virginia. The duck mould was sent to the Glassport, PA, plant shortly after 1894. Glassport was then part of the U.S. Glass combine.

"In 1932, the then 62 year old mould was sent to the Tiffin Glass plant, the more prestigious of all the U.S. Glass companies. Upon close examination, the duck mould was found to be damaged. Tiffin's ingenious chief moldmaker, however, was able to replace the damaged section with a metal plug which still remains in the mould. If you look closely at the underneath section of the tail on today's duck, you will see a neatly repaired rectangular patch. If you own one of the original ducks without such a patch mark, you can be sure that it was made prior to 1932, and is truly a bit of early American. Although the duck mould equipment is 106 years old, the detail today is still so realistic that you can almost see the feathers rippling as the duck settles over its nest. The intricate detail of the mould creates a fine example of American pressed glass for today's collector and of the workmanship done by the skilled craftsmen of the Tiffin Glass Factory...the oldest existing glass factory in America...built and in operation on its present site since 1887."

Of course, Tiffin is not in operation as of this writing, having closed its doors in 1980, after being purchased by several different companies.

Plate 132 - Hen on Chick Base. 4½" tall, 6¼" long. Attributed to Flaccus by most collectors. The piece is unusual in that the chicks are on the base, with Flaccus' usual great mold. *$250.00 – 260.00.* Robin on Nest covered dish, 6" tall, 6" long. This difficult to find bird on its intricate nest is commonly attributed to the Indiana Tumbler & Goblet Company (Greentown). *$150.00 – 165.00.*

Plate 133 - Here we have the Block Swan in two versions. 6¼" tall, 7⅛" long on Challinor, Taylor's basket base. *$295.00 – 300.00.* Strangely, it is the swan on the right that is pictured as part of their Farm Yard Collection in the 1891 catalog. The swan on the right is 6¼" tall and 8" long. Perhaps it was offered on either base? Scarce in blue. *$295.00 – 300.00.*

Plate 134 - Closed Neck Swan on diamond basket base. 4¾" tall, 5½" long. Made by Westmoreland Specialty Company. *$75.00 – 80.00.* Open Neck Swan covered dish, 5½" tall, 5⅜" long. By Vallerysthal. Also found in green and perhaps other colors. Shown in their 1914–1933 catalog. This is one of the reproductions you will find in the catalogs of places like AA Importing, usually in a slag, so be careful. *$100.00 – 120.00.*

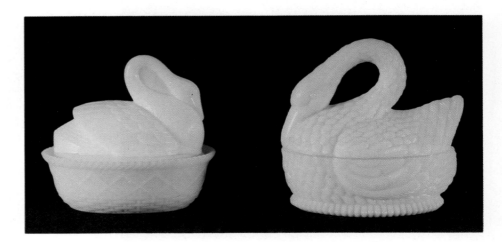

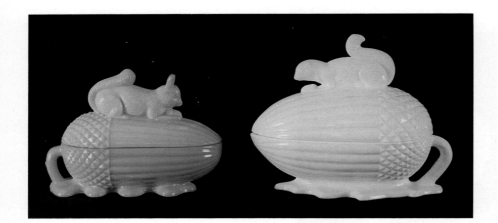

Plate 135 - Squirrels on Acorn bases. AA Importing product of about the early 1980's. 5" high, 6¾" long overall. *$12.00 – 15.00.* Vallerysthal piece, measuring 6½" tall, 7¾" long. The squirrel has shorter, squared ears and sits on a large acorn while holding a small acorn in its paws. Base is an Oak Leaf. Shown in the 1914 Vallerysthal catalog, but disappeared by the 1933 issue. *$95.00 – 100.00 for Vallerysthal.*

Plate 136 - Fox on Diamond Basket base. 5¾" tall, 7⅜" long. By Kemple Glass and marked with the "K" logo. *$100.00 – 120.00.* Cow on Diamond Basket, 4¼" tall, 7⅜" long. Also a product of Kemple Glass. *$80.00 – 95.00.*

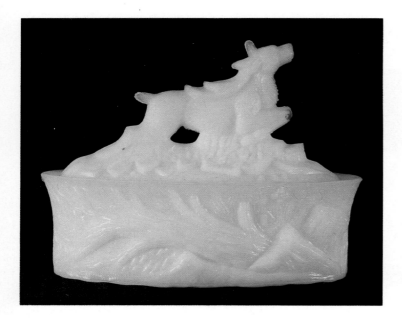

Plate 137 - Deer on Fallen Tree base. 5" tall, 6⅝" long. Another intricate piece by Flaccus. Horns and tail are very opalescent. Also found in crystal, but both are scarce. *$180.00 – 240.00.*

Plate 138 - Wooly Lamb on Bo Peep base. 3¾" tall, 6⅛" long. Notice the base with Bo Peep reclining with her sheepherder's crook. Again a great mold by Flaccus. Scarce. *$275.00 – 295.00.*

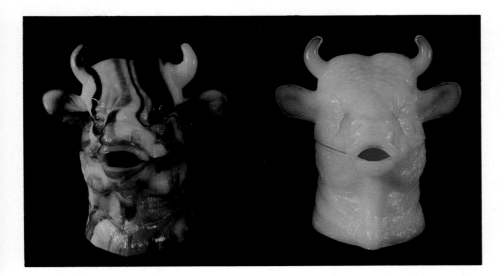

Plate 139 - Here we have two Bull's Head mustards. 4¼" to top of horn, 3¾" across ears, base is 3⅝" long. The jar on the left is purple slag from L. G. Wright. The white bull on the right is Atterbury, patented July 17, 1888. This particular one bears an embossed "PATT-APPLD-FOR," but not all pieces will have this. Originally made with a ladle that extends from the mouth to resemble a tongue. Eyes are molded in the L. G. Wright model. *$40.00 – 60.00 for slag. $165.00 – 175.00 for old white.*

Plate 140 - Flat Fish covered dish. 8¼" long. An unusual dish wherein the tail is part of the base while the main body of the fish is the lid. The base has wide vertical ribs topped by a ½" flange which has a net pattern on the underside. Atterbury – hard to find. *$190.00 – 200.00.*

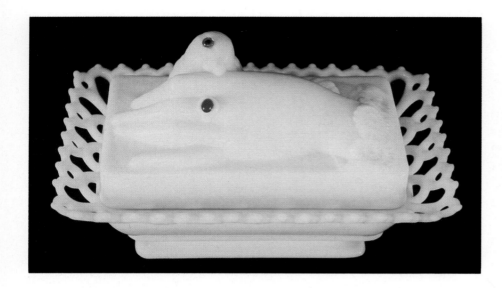

Plate 141 - Hand and Dove covered dish, 6⅜" long. Patented August 27, 1889, for Atterbury. Later produced by Westmoreland in blue and white with their WG logo. The dove has a blue glass eye, while a ring on the hand sports a red glass stone. A lace cuff is at the wrist. *$125.00 – 130.00 for Atterbury. $100.00 – 125.00 for Westmoreland.*

Plate 142 - Fox on Lacy Base, 8" long. Originally an Atterbury mold, the fox shown is by Westmoreland. He will be found on the ribbed base, the Basketweave base, and the Lacy Edge base. Imperial Glass and Kemple both made the same piece and it would be difficult to tell them apart without the company logos. Getting hard to find by any maker. *$85.00 – 110.00 for Westmoreland. $150.00 – 160.00 for Atturbury.*

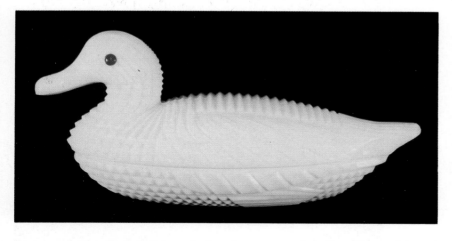

Plate 143 - The Atterbury Duck covered dish, 11" long. Note the distinctive Atterbury red glass eye. Patented March 15, 1887. Original Atterbury ducks will have the patent date or Patent Applied For on the bottom of the base. They were made in white, white with blue head, and white with amethyst head. These have been copiously reproduced. Fenton made a blue and white slag for L. G. Wright in 1955, along with purple and white slag for Phil Rosso and L. G. Wright. Has recently (1990–1991) been made in purple and in blue slag with glass eyes for Phil Rosso. In reproductions the thumb indentation area under the tail is rounded and narrow rather than flat and broad as in Atterbury molds. Atturbury head opening is squared and tail is thinner than in reproduction. *$265.00 – 275.00.*

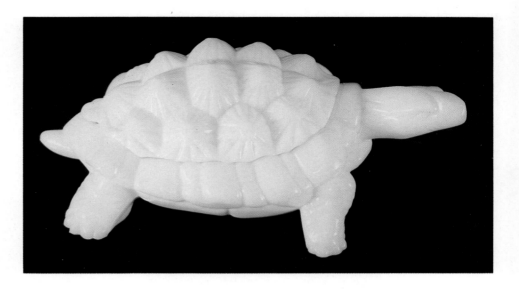

Plate 144 - Snapping Turtle, 9¾" long. Carapace or outer shell is very highly sculptured on this handsome fellow. The lid section is rather small compared to the overall size of the figure. Made at one point for L. G. Wright in several transparent colors. Original mold source remains unknown. *$250.00 – 300.00.*

Plate 145 - Cat on Lacy Base, 8⅛" long. Originally an Atterbury design patented August 27, 1889. Westmoreland purchased the mold from Atterbury and produced it in several colors besides milk glass. The lacy base has the familiar Dancing Sailors design. *$95.00 – 100.00 for Westmoreland. $150.00 –175.00 for Atturbury.*

Plate 146 - Entwined Fish covered dish. Cover is 6" in diameter. Patented August 6, 1889, by Atterbury. Both fish have ruby eyes. Also found (rarely) on tall-stemmed lacy base. *$200.00 – 250.00.*

Plate 147 - TOP Pintail Duck, 5½" long, on diamond basket base. By Westmoreland Specialty Co. Also found in blue with white head, white with dark blue head, all white, and in assorted applied colors. *$50.00 – 60.00.* Lion on Picket Base. Also by Westmoreland Specialty Co., and found in blue/white combinations. *$50.00 – 60.00, white. $80.00 – 85.00, blue/white.* BOTTOM: Little Red Schoolhouse. *$95.00 –*

125.00. Log Cabin. Each are 3¾" tall, 3⅝" long. Both these cute little houses were made by Westmoreland Specialty Co. as mustard containers. They were designed with very thin glass at the chimney opening which was to be removed and then used as a bank. The lids are interchangeable, however the school has shingles with rounded ends while the cabin has straight wood shingles. *95.00 – 125.00.* Chick emerging from Egg on Sleigh. Also Westmoreland Specialty Co., 5⅜" long. Usually with much gold. *$60.00 – 75.00.*

Plate 147-A - This is a close-up of the labels found on the bottom of the Little Schoolhouse piece, giving instructions on using the piece for a bank, and also tells about the mustard inside.

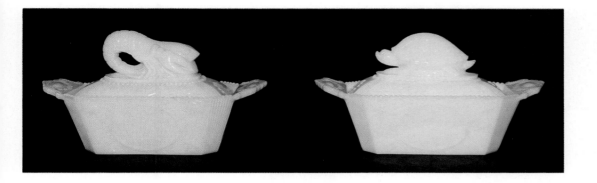

Plate 148 - Crawfish Cover handled dish. *$200.00 – 250.00.* Turtle cover handled dish. *$175.00 – 190.00.* Bases are identical with an open, oval medallion shape on the side, possibly for a label. 4¼" tall, 7¼" handle to handle. These are old pieces recently attributed to Westmoreland Specialty Company.

Plate 149 - Robed Santa on Sleigh, 8" long. Patented 1901 by Harry Thomas. Patent is assigned to John A. Dobson & Co. of Baltimore, MD. *$175.00 – 190.00.*

Plate 150 - Chicks Emerging from Eggs on 4⅛" diameter, handled basket. Westmoreland Specialty originated this mold, which held mustard. The oval medallion on the front of the basket is often found with elaborate, hand-painted decor. Sometimes the

chicks are painted as shown, sometimes entirely gilded. *$100.00 – 150.00 depending on amount of decoration.* Turkey covered dish by Imperial Glass, 1952 – 60. Also made in carnival and various colors. *$45.00 – 50.00.*

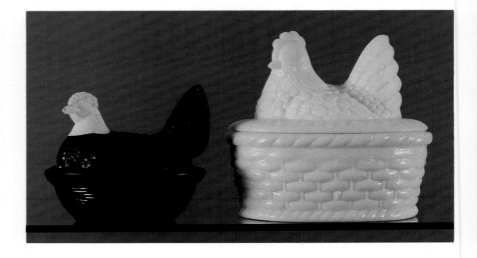

Plate 151 - Rabbit on Eggs, 7⅛" long. This version is by Fenton Art Glass and was first made from old Westmoreland molds in 1992. It has a pearlized or lightly iridized finish. The eggs have colored and white tiny glass beads fused to make the design. *$35.00, current retail.* Rooster on 8" lacy base by Westmoreland. Painted comb and wattles and glass eyes. Also found on diamond basket base as illustrated elsewhere in this book. *$90.00 – 95.00.*

Plate 152 - Black, 5⅛" long Hen on Basket (white head), 4½" tall to tail tip. Base is Challinor, Taylor. This particular hen belonged to Bill's grandmother. *$95.00 – 110.00.* Hen on Deep Basket base, 6⅛" overall height. Basket measures 5" x 6⅞" x 3" deep. The base on this piece is blown into a mold. Maker unknown. *$85.00 – 95.00.*

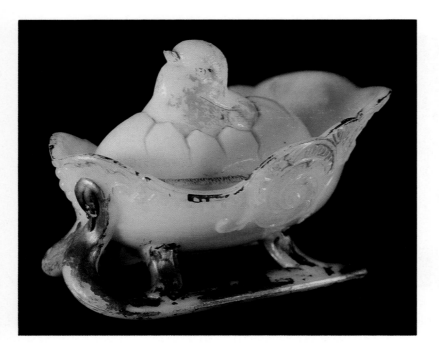

Plate 153 - Chick Emerging from Egg on Sleigh base. 4¾" long. By Dithridge in the 1800's. Upon close examination, the sleigh is different from the Westmoreland Specialty Company sleigh. *$125.00 – 150.00.*

Plate 154 - Here we have an assortment of new covered dishes, purchased during the 1990's. TOP: *left:* 5½" Rooster on wide rib base, decorated with hand-painted roses. Made for Phil Rosso. *$12.50, retail.* **Center and right:** Hens by Fenton Art Glass. 5½" long. Center lid is in pink carnival, at right is milk glass with transparent cobalt head. *$30.00 – 40.00.*

BOTTOM: Two Standing Roosters from the old Westmoreland molds. Black with white head, red comb and wattles, yellow beak, and much gold in feathers and legs. *$17.50, current retail.* Milk glass with painted comb, wattles, and feet; gold feathers, and hand-painted roses. Both made for Phil Rosso. *$17.50, current retail.*

Plate 155 - Breakfast Set by Vallerysthal and marked as such on the tray where the covered hen rests. Tray measures 10⅛" x 11". The set consists of covered hen on basket base, six chick-based egg cups, and round covered basket for salt. *$350.00 – 360.00.*

Plate 156 - Hen on Scalloped Basket base, 5" tall, 5¾" long. This is the Vallerysthal piece that fits on the Breakfast Set tray. *$45.00 – 55.00.* Hen on Braided Weave basket, eyes missing. 6" tall, 7¼" long. By Challinor, Taylor. *$90.00 – 95.00.*

Plate 157 - 9¾", Standing Rooster on Log by Kanawa Glass. Shown in their 1970's catalogs. *$40.00 – 45.00.* Blue Standing Rooster, 8½" tall, by Vallerysthal. Similar roosters were produced by Westmoreland and L. E. Smith, as illustrated elsewhere in this book. *$95.00 – 100.00.*

Plate 158 - 6⅞" long, Vallerysthal Hen on Basket. The molded eye is rounder than the Westmoreland look-alike. Found in white and opaque green with or without painted accents. Generally marked on inside of base. *$85.00 – 90.00.* 5½" – 6" Westmoreland Specialty Co. Hen on Diamond Basket base. The hen continued to be made by Westmoreland in many colors and combinations right up to their closing in 1985. *$30.00 – 35.00.*

Plate 159 - TOP: We have three sizes of Westmoreland covered Hens from 2½" up to 6". Note that the smaller two have heavy weave basket bases while the larger has the familiar diamond basket base. Generally marked with the WG logo. *7", $50.00 – 55.00; 5½", $30.00 – 35.00; 3½", $20.00 – 24.00; 2½", $12.00 – 15.00.*

BOTTOM: Westmoreland Specialty Company Rooster on Wide Rib Base. This piece has been made for Phil Rosso in 1990–1991 in milk glass, milk glass hand painted, blue milk, green, and cobalt marble. *$30.00 – 35.00 for Westmoreland.* West-

moreland experimental Hen on Diamond basket. Only a few of these lavishly decorated pieces were produced. They feature hand-painted roses and much gold. Westmoreland first produced their Hens on Nests in 1889, and continued up until closing in 1985. *$85.00 – 95.00.*

Plate 160 - Large, 7½" x 6" x 3¾" Atterbury Hen on lacy base. *$225.00 – 235.00.* 7⅞" x 6½" x 3½" Westmoreland Hen on lacy base. *$110.00 – 125.00.* Confusing? You bet! First of all, notice the differences in measurements. The Westmoreland hen is heavier, weighing 3 lb. to the Atterbury's 2½ lb. One very important difference is that the Atterbury hen has the round, flat eye socket originally found with a glass eye, while the eye on the Westmore-

land hen is oval with a raised pupil generally accented with a dot of red paint. Except for measurements and weight, the bases are so much alike that if not marked, it is very difficult to tell the difference, especially when you find one at a flea market or mall.

Plate 161 - Old Abe Eagle Jar, 6½" tall. Attributed to Crystal Glass Company. On the banner across the front is "E Pluribus Unum." The jar itself was originally one of those mustard jars so popular in the 1870's, and a Centennial Exposition piece in frosted glass. Old Abe was a real eagle, and his story is a fascinating one. The baby eagle was captured in 1861 by a Chippewa Indian. He brought the eagle into Chippewa, Wisconsin, and sold him for a bushel of corn. After passing through several hands, the eagle was presented to the Eau Claire Badgers, Company C., 8th regiment. He was sworn into the U.S. Service as Old Abe, the mascot. A standard was made on which he could be carried and thereafter the eagle always rode on the left of the color bearer. From then on, the Wisconsin Eagle Regiment became known all through both the Union and Confederate armies During battles, Old Abe would spread his wings and utter his fierce scream, heard all over the battlefield. Many are the stories of Old Abe and his valor and loyalty. With only a few slight wounds, he returned home to Wisconsin hale and hearty with his regiment. He attended the Milwaukee Soldiers Reunion in 1880, along with General Grant, but it was to be his last appearance. In 1881 a fire started in the State Capitol building where Old Abe lived and he died a day or so later. Old Abe and his regiment fought in 39 battles and skirmishes during the Civil War and his story was known to almost every person in the country. Old Abe was still alive at the time of the Centennial Exposition and Wisconsin sent him to Philadelphia for display in the Agricultural Hall. Civil War veterans came to look at the bird they'd heard so much about on the battle-grounds. *$100.00 – 125.00.*

Plate 162 - Moses in the Bulrushes, 5" long covered dish. The flowered resting place is raised ½" or so above the base edge. A similar top on a split-rib base has been found marked McKee. Maker unknown. *$200.00 – 250.00.*

Plate 163 - Owl Covered Jar, 7" tall. This popular jar has a long history, with the original patent for the design having been registered on October 19, 1888, to Matthew Turnbull who was a glass manufacturer at the Cornhill Glass Works, Southwich, Sunderland Co., Durham, England. Our owl next turns up in the U.S.A. being made by Atterbury Co. of Pittsburgh, PA. The Atterbury owl has red glass eyes instead of the yellow glass used later when made by Imperial Glass. The main distinguishing feature between the old jar and the relatively recent Imperial jar is that on the old there are "lugs" on the cover that fit into indentations on the rim of the base which keep the cover from sliding around. The Atterbury owl can be found in white, blue, and yellow opaque, black, butterscotch marble, clear turquoise, amber, and cobalt. The Imperial owl was made around 1955–1960. You will find the jar in milk glass, both glossy and satin and in several slag colors such as purple and green, or caramel which is very attractive and realistic looking. Often found with a paper sticker reading "From the Belknap Collection" and generally marked with the IG logo. *$125.00 – 135.00 for Atturbury. $40.00 – 45.00 for Imperial.*

Plate 164 - A close-up of the "lugs" under the lid of the Owl Jar by Atterbury.

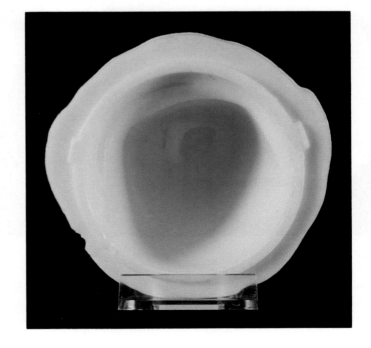

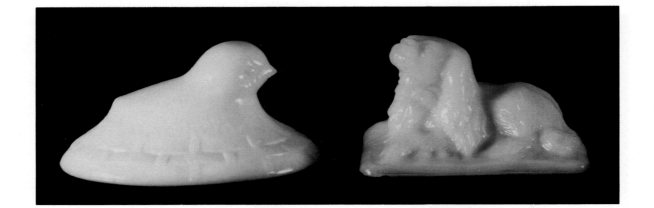

Plate 165 - Here are two of my "bottomless pets" that are worth showing even without their bases. Chick cover by Fenton Art Glass made in many colors from the early 1950's onward. He should be on the scalloped basket base, sometimes with a milk base and transparent lid. *$75.00 – 90.00 complete.* Little spaniel type dog who should be on a diamond stippled base or rarely on a ribbed base. This wonderful little fellow is often attributed to Sandwich but at the Sandwich Museum they told us that he was made by the Alton Manufacturing Company who operated out of the old Boston and Sandwich Glass Company building for less than one year. They were, according to the Museum, the last manufacturer of glass in Sandwich, making Trevaise Art Glass, pressed novelty items, and covered dishes. *$90.00 – 100.00, lid only. $500.00 – 700.00, complete.*

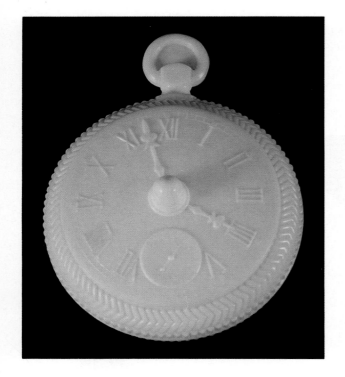

Plate 166 - Pocket Watch covered candy box, 5¾" diameter. Made by Imperial Glass 1958–1960. The mold work is very nice and sharp on this piece, which even sports a separate little dial for the second hand and a herringbone type edge. *$40.00 – 50.00.*

Plate 167 - Picnic Basket, 5" tall to top of handle. Made by Westmoreland with original having been a Portieux product. When we were taking the photos, this basket dropped into a number of pieces, but Bill managed to glue it together to have its picture taken. *$45.00 – 55.00.*

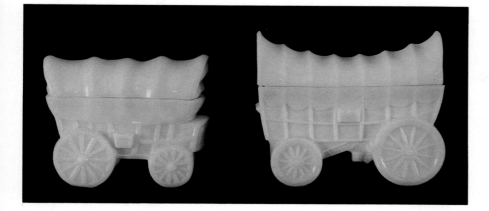

Plate 168 - Prairie Schooner, 5⅞" long. Designed by K. R. Haley and shown in Haley Glassware Company, Greensburg, PA, catalog in 1948. This has a five-rib frame while the Smith Conestoga Wagon has eight ribs. Kemple bought the mold from American Glass Co. in 1958. *$175.00 – 195.00.* Congestoga Wagon, 6½" long, made by L. E. Smith in the 1950's. *$160.00 – 180.00.*

Plate 169 - Pie Wagon, 5" tall, 6¼" long by Imperial Glass. Made in caramel slag in 1982. *$165.00 – 175.00.* Cinderella's Coach, 5¾" tall, 6½" long. Made in the 1950's by L. E. Smith. The same coach in a smaller version was also made by Smith. *$125.00 – 150.00.*

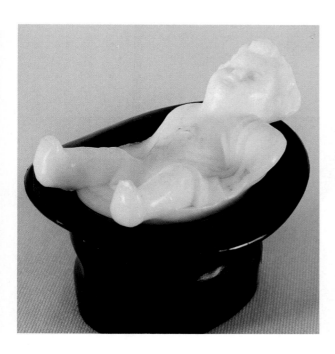

Plate 170 - Baby on Top Hat. Original called a match holder, but with a cover! 4½" tall. This is a great Victorian-Edwardian whimsical piece. The baby is very detailed, wearing a nightdress. Her underside is ribbed for striking matches (Ouch!). Baby will be found in either satin or glossy finish. Scarce. *$300.00 – 325.00.*

Plate 171 - Dewey on Tile base, 6¾" long. The word "DEWEY" is embossed just beneath the bust. Attributed to Flaccus. A Spanish-American War commemorative. *$70.00 – 85.00.*

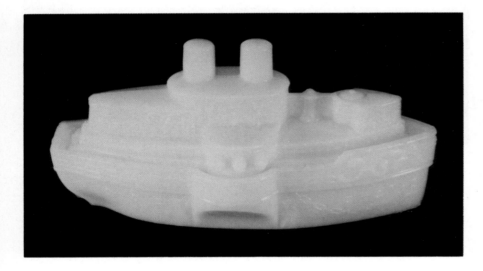

Plate 172 - Battleship Maine, 7⅞" long. "Maine" is embossed on the foredeck. A momento of the Spanish-American war of 1898. *$65.00 – 75.00.*

Plate 173 - Melon with Leaf and Net covered dish or sugar. 5½" tall, 5½" long, by Atterbury in 1878. The melon surface has a cantaloupe netting plus leaves at the larger end. Hard to find. *$45.00 – 50.00.* Flatiron Box, 7" long. Very simple, with a deep base and a shallow lid. Maker has eluded us. *$50.00 – 60.00.*

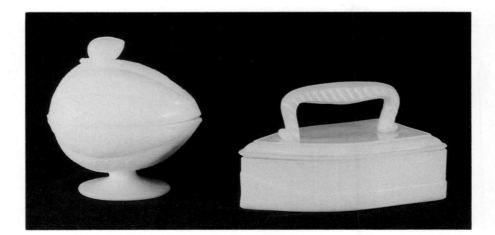

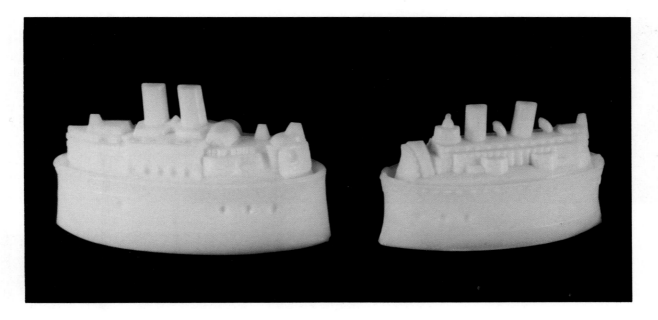

Plate 174 - Another of the popular battleship pieces, this one 7½" long. Other similar ships are the Wheeling, Olympia, and Oregon. Battleship Newark, 6¼" long. Originally by E. C. Flaccus Company, Wheeling, WV, as a prepared mustard container. *$65.00 – 75.00, for each.*

Plate 176 - Here we have England and America side by side with two glass jars. Bust of Queen Victoria makes the lid of this 8¼" tall jar, with fancy embossing on the sides. *$135.00 – 140.00.* Eagle jar, 8½" tall, with raised stars on the lid. This was part of L. E. Smith's Bicentennial line. *$45.00 – 55.00.*

Plate 175 - Santa Claus, 9½" tall covered jar. Made by Fostoria Glass in 1955, presumably to go along with their sleighs, which were made about the same time. Very hard to find. *$350.00 – 400.00.*

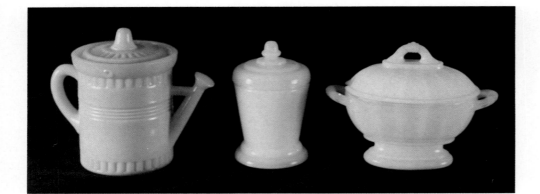

Plate 177 - l to r: Covered 4½" x 3⅛" watering can. A product of Westmoreland Specialty Co. *$45.00 – 50.00.* Covered 3¾" tall jar. Marked H.A. for Hazel Atlas. *$12.00 – 15.00.* Tureen-shaped 3⅞" tall, 5" long including handles, covered dish. Maker unknown. *$15.00 – 20.00.*

Plate 178 - Dolphin candy box, 8¾" tall. Made by Fenton Art Glass in 1989–1990 for Gracious Touch, a home party plan by Clevenger & Associates. *$50.00 – 55.00.* Candy jar, 9" tall by L. E. Smith in the mid 1960's. Has alternating cane and fruit panels including pear (shown) and apple. *$25.00 – 35.00.*

Plate 179 - Pink opaque candy and lid, 5¾" tall. Diamond pattern by Fostoria. 1950's. *$35.00 – 40.00.* Ginger jar, 7½" tall. Regent line by Consolidated. Hand painted and signed RAC. *$30.00 – 40.00.*

Plate 180 - Beautiful hand-printed biscuit jar, 5½" tall to shoulder. Silverplate handle and lid marked "Canada, Silverplate." Golden Poppy pattern shown in L. G. Wright catalog from 1970's. *$75.00 – 80.00.*

Plate 181 - Bulldog Humidor, 6¼" tall, 5⅜" diameter. Alledged to be unmarked Wavecrest. There are three bulldogs on one side with "Three Guardsmen" written under the heads. On the reverse side is an elaborate old pipe. The brass lid originally had a sponge insert to keep the contents from drying. *$300.00 – 350.00.*

Plate 182 - Tufted Pillow Cookie Jar, 7½" diameter, 8½" tall. In the Con-Cora line by Consolidated. Artist initialed by Matilda Davidson. 1950's – 1960's. *$65.00 – 75.00.*

Plate 183 - Cherry Thumbprint, 7¾" tall cracker jar by Westmoreland. *$100.00 – 120.00.* Biscuit jar with hand-painted scene. 6"tall to rim, 7½" to finial. Rim and lid are pewter, over-handle is brass. Inside the lid is ingraved "Mrs. John Fennel to Mrs. and Mr. Carl E. Kaiser, Berlin, June 28, 1883, Canada." On the rim it is marked with a shield inside a circle, "MERHEN - B. Co." with scales inside the shield also. Piece is mold-blown with ground pontil and applied foot. *$125.00 – 150.00.*

Plate 184 - 7½" tall Pineapple covered dishes by Vallerysthal. One in opaque yellow and one in opaque blue. *$70.00 – 75.00, yellow. $65.00 – 70.00, blue.* 6½" diameter Cabbage also by Vallerysthal. *$75.00 – 80.00.*

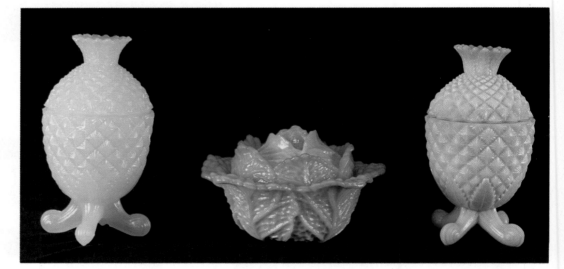

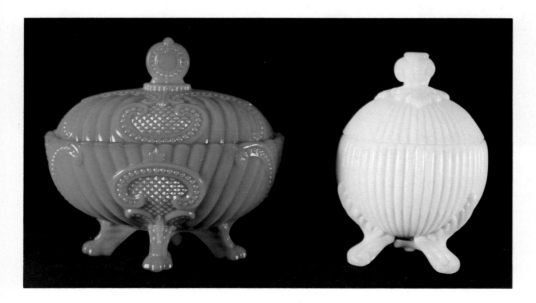

Plate 185 - Rib & Scroll covered compote or butterdish, 6¾" tall by Vallerysthal. Also in white milk, shown elsewhere in this book. *$70.00 – 85.00, blue.* Rib sugar bowl or covered dish. The three feet extend into leaves and the lid finial rests on leaves. By Vallerysthal in their 1908 catalog. Also produced by Westmoreland and extremely difficult to tell from the original. *$55.00 – 60.00, Westmoreland. $65.00 – 70.00, Vallerysthal.*

Plate 186 - Another Tufted Pillow cookie in Consolidated's Con-Cora line. This time in roses painted by Helen Fitzgerald. *$65.00 – 75.00.*

Plate 187 - Grape & Leaf footed, 5½" tall, covered jars by Vallerysthal. Later made in pink milk glass by Jeannette Glass and recent, pretty ugly reproductions by Indiana Glass in transparent colors. *$40.00 – 45.00 for Vallerysthal. $15.00 – 17.00 for pink milkglass by Jeannette.*

Plate 188 - LEFT: 3⅞" tall covered Apple with glossy paint. A product of the 1940–1950 era. Maker unknown. *$10.00 – 15.00.* CENTER: Two, 3" Pigs on Drum by Vallerysthal. Marked PV. *$75.00 – 95.00.* RIGHT: Baseball 3⅛" covered dish. 1940's–1950's Maker unknown. *$35.00 – 40.00.*

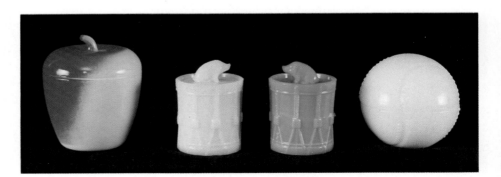

Plate 189 - **l to r:** Dolphin & Shell sugar bowl, 5" diameter, in caramel. *$65.00 – 75.00.* Dolphin & Shell butter dish, 5½" diameter, in light blue. *$45.00 – 55.00.* Sugar bowl, 5" diameter, medium blue. *$45.00 – 55.00.* All Vallerysthal, 1908–1914. Porteiux 1933. Later produced by Westmoreland as a covered dish called Seashell & Dolphin. Made in a number of colors. Original has continuous, unbroken chain of shells and the dolphins smile rather than sneer as on the Westmoreland version.

Plate 190 - Tyrolean Bears mustard jar or sugar, 4⅛" tall. By Westmoreland Specialty Co. Besides the Resting Bear shown, the piece contains a bear with a walking stick over his shoulder and another one holding a rifle and walking cane while climbing a rocky slope. Turn of the century. *$125.00 – 130.00.* Watering can, 4" tall, blue, also Westmoreland Specialty Co., 1904. *$35.00 – 40.00.* Covered Pineapple marmalade jar with ladle, 5¾" tall, by Imperial Glass, 1959–1965. *$30.00 – 35.00.*

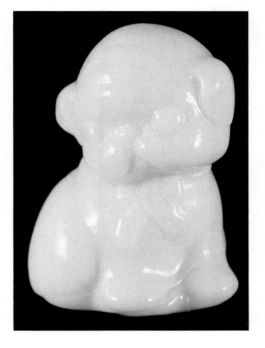

Plate 191 - Chubby Dog Figure, 5" tall, solid, heavy glass. Everybody thinks they recognize this little fellow from some old cartoon or other but nobody can put their finger on which one! Possible Gillinder? *$35.00 – 40.00.*

Plate 192 - Bear bookend, 8¾" tall. Weighs a hefty 4½ pounds. This appears to be a clambroth shade of glass with a white coating. Probably an import. *$35.00 – 40.00 each.*

Plate 193 - Sleigh candlesticks, 3½" tall, 6" long, by Boyd's 1985. Santa Head fairy light, 5½" tall, Fenton, 1988. *These items currently available at retail.*

Plate 194 - TOP (l to r): Boyd Deer, 2¼", 1985. Mosser Angel, 3½". Mosser Easter Bunny, 5¼". Boyd Chuckles Clown, 3¾", 1988. Boyd Colonial Man, 4¼", 1991, in Patriot White, 1989 in Pearl, 1987 in milk.
BOTTOM (l to r): Fenton duck, 2¼" long. Boyd Debbie Duck (2¾") and Ducklings. Fenton chick, 2¾" long. Fenton Hen, 2⅝" long. Fenton pieces introduced about 1989. *Items currently available at retail.*

Plate 195 - TOP (l to r): Mosser Glass Snowman, 4⅝" tall. *$15.00.* Fostoria Standing Deer, 4⅜" tall. *$50.00 – 55.00.* Fostoria Reclining Deer, 2⅜" tall. *$50.00 – 55.00.* Both Fostoria pieces made in 1950. Gibson Glass Snowman, 5¼" tall. *$20.00 – 25.00.*
BOTTOM (l to r): Merry Mouse bottle by Avon, 3½" tall, 1970–1980. *$4.00 – 7.00.* Mosser Sleigh, 3½" long, current production. *$16.00, retail.* Mosser flat-backed Santa Face, 3¾" long, current production. *$10.00, retail.* Precious Chickadee bottle by Avon, 3" tall, 1970–1980. *$4.00 – 7.00.*

Plate 196 - TOP: Fenton Nymph figure with separate flower frog, 7" tall, late 1920's. *$100.00 – 125.00.* Fenton 6¾" Bridesmaid figure, iridized. 1980's on. *$45.00 – 55.00.*

BOTTOM: - Fenton, 2⅝" Iridized Bird with applied porcelain roses & leaves and narrow pink ribbon bow. 1988. Spaniels by Fenton, 2⅝". Part of their "natural painted" line in 1985. *Bird and Spaniels currently available at retail.* Owl ring tree, 4¼" tall, by Fenton in the 1950's. *$25.00 – 30.00.*

Plate 197 - TOP: Fenton Southern Girl, 8" tall. She is holding her big hat and has hand-painted accents. Designed by Kathy See and limited to several months production in 1993. 6¾" Fenton Bear still on sprue. This is taken off and the bottom of the figure finished.

BOTTOM: 4" and 4½" Clown figures by Fenton. They have Hearts and Flowers decor and were Designed by Debbie Barlow in 1988. There are two more clowns in the set. Fenton 3½" tall Panda. *All items currently available at retail.*

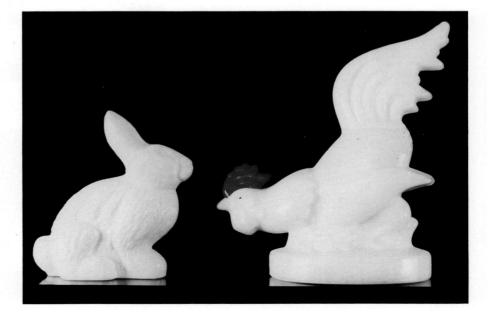

Plate 198 - Solid, heavy 6" tall Rabbit by Mosser Glass, Inc. *$20.00 – 25.00.* 8¼" Fighting Cock. Originally bookends designed by K. R. Haley, later produced by Kemple Glass. The designs were first introduced in 1945, and continued to the early 1960's. *$45.00 – 55.00 ea.*

Plate 199 - TOP: 2⅛" Duck on Basket, 1991. Tugboat, 3" long, 1983. Tractor, 2⅞", 1991. BOTTOM: Eagle, 2½" tall, 1990's. Panda, 3⅛" tall, 1987. Little Luck, 2⅛" tall, 1990. This little fellow was decorated especially for the Friends of Gladys Taber convention. He has a silver horn and a violet wreath around his neck. Gladys often spoke of her unicorn who had the silver horn and hoofs and who would crop the fresh spring violets in the evenings. 3" bird figure. All these are products of Boyd's Crystal Art Glass. *All items currently available at retail in many colors.*

Plate 200 - TOP: Standing Rooster, 3" tall, by Summit Art Glass. Note the very opalescent comb. *$12.00 – 15.00.* Westmoreland 3⅛" long Pig created in the early 1970's. The underside is hollowed out. No mark – generally just a paper label. *$15.00 – 20.00.* 2½" Horse by Summit Art Glass. *$12.00 – 15.00.* BOTTOM: Reclining Lion limited edition figure. 4⅝" long. Done in 1981 in "Snow Sparkle," iridized milk glass. *$20.00 – 25.00.* Wren on Perch, 3½" tall, 3" square base. Westmoreland, revised from an old mold in the 1970's. Found in all white, all black, and with colored bird on either white or black base. *$30.00 – 35.00.*

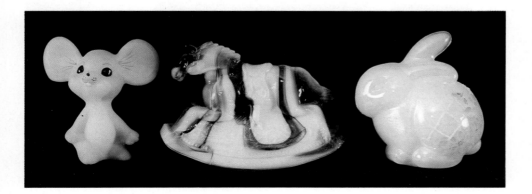

Plate 201 - Fenton 2⅜" Mouse, 1980's onward. *Currently available at retail.* "Rocky," 2⅞" rocking horse in Carousel Slag for Guernsey Glass of Cambridge, OH. November 1981. Rocky was taken from a mid-1920's Cambridge candy container mold. Marked with a "B" inside a triangle for Harold Bennet, owner of Guernsey Glass, and dated. *$25.00 – 30.00.* Bunny, 3⅛" tall by Fenton. From 1980's onward. *Currently available at retail.*

Plate 202 - **TOP:** Parlor Pups. 3½" and 3¼" tall. These were made in 1987 by Boyd's in milk white opal. Originally an Imperial mold, a set of three dogs was made in various colors and discontinued in 1971. *$45.00 – 65.00 ea.* Guernsey Glass Bridge Hound, 1⅝" tall. Originally a Cambridge Glass mold and used to hold one's pencil during a card game. *$30.00 – 35.00, Cambridge.* **BOTTOM:** 2⅞" and 5" Scottie Dog figures by L. E. Smith. *$35.00 – 40.00, large. $25.00 – 30.00, small.* 2½" Bulldog in satin milk glass with painted collar & rhinestone eyes. By Westmoreland. *$25.00 – 30.00.*

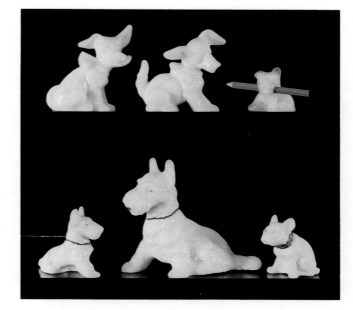

Plate 203 - All figures by Boyd's Crystal Art Glass. **TOP:** 4" Rooster holder in Patriot white, 1991, originally an Imperial Glass mold. 3¼" Lucky Unicorn, 1987. 4⅛" Louise Doll, 1991. **BOTTOM:** Boyd Plane, 4" long, 1980's. Miss Cotton the Kitten, 3⅛" tall, 1985 and 1989 milk white. Owl, 3⅜" tall. Olympic white, 1984; Snow, 1982; milk white, 1987; 1989, Patriot white, 1991. *All items currently available at retail in various colors.*

Plate 204 - Open Swan, 9" long, by L. E. Smith about 1930. Also found in black. *$35.00 – 40.00.* Jumping Horse, 9½" long, 7" tall. Designed by Haley and produced in crystal in 1947. Mold later acquired by Kemple Glass and made in milk glass. *$60.00 – 70.00.*

Plate 205 - Imperial Glass, 4½" Hen. *$35.00 – 40.00.* 5¾" Rooster. *$35.00 – 45.00.* Chicks, 1½". *$10.00 – 15.00, head up. $5.00 – 10.00, head down.* Originally produced in crystal by Heisey in 1948–1949. Later made by Imperial in milk glass (1978). Chicks are as they come from the press — still on the "sprue." Later they are cut off and the bottom finished.

Plate 206 - Girl and Boy angels by Fenton. 5½" tall, about 1988 and still in production in various color treatments. *Currently available at retail.* 7" Madonna by Mosser Glass, 1980's. *$15.00.*

Plate 207 - 208 - Here are a group of mugs plus a sugar bowl in the very confusing Swan and Block Swan patterns. **TOP (l to r):** 3⅝" mug. Covered 6" tall sugar. Pay attention to the ring and bead handles on all these pieces. Notice that the sugar is the only one that has three tiny beads on the outer edge of the ring handle. Some researchers feel these are Atterbury—some disagree. Some feel the blocks under the swans on the compote make it a different pattern—again, some disagree. So far these lovely pieces are destined to remain a mystery.

BOTTOM (l to r): Pink, 3⅝" mug. 2⅝" mug. Handled nappy or small compote, 2⅞" tall. Handles are the same on all three pieces, but swans on the compote are different and have a block pattern under them. *Prices on these unidentified beauties not available.*

Plate 209 - Dwarf Mug, 4⅞" tall, by Westmoreland Specialty. This was another condiment container and should have a rather pointy lid. Panels show dwarfs or gnomes bowling in woods with the legend "Ein Lustig Spiel Frewt Jung und Alt," which translates "A happy game enjoyed by young and old." Another panel shows them at the table, drinking, "wohl Bekomms" or "To your health"; then walking in the woods with keg and mugs, "Ein Kuhler Trunk, Ein Gruner Wald" or "A cool drink, a green forest." *$65.00 – 75.00.* 3¾ footed mug with hand-painted decor. *$25.00 – 35.00.*

BOTTOM: Scenic, hand-painted, 4" tall mug. *$30.00 – 35.00.* Ribbed Base, 3⅜" mug marked as Souvenir of Webster Springs, WV. *$25.00 – 30.00.* Cathedral Arches and Roses, 3¼" mug with gold paint. *$25.00 – 30.00.*

Plate 210 - On the top we have three steins from the Westmoreland Specialty Company's "Rookwood" Tankard and Stein Set, made from 1910 to 1915. They were painted with purple or "Rookwood Brown" backgrounds. Steins are 4¼" tall. There is an accompanying 9¼" tall tankard, not shown here. The poem on the top left stein is as follows: *$45.00 – 55.00.*

"Here's to the prettiest, Here's to the wittiest,
Here's to the truest of all who are true.
Here's to the neatest one, Here's to the sweetest one,
Here's to them all in one — Here's to you."

The four steins on the bottom row were made by Fostoria as part of their Art Decorated line from the 1900–1910 era. All these steins were made of white milk glass, then sprayed with brown, green, or lavender shaded backgrounds. A lighter, shaded area was left on which a transfer decoration was applied. Many different transfers were used such as Indians, Monks, and Elks. More Fostoria Art Decorated pieces will be found in the Vase section of this book. *$40.00 - 45.00.*

Plate 211 - 4¼" green background mug with Three Gentlemen transfer. *$40.00 – 45.00.* 6½" Lovers Stein with lid by Westmoreland Specialty Co. Also called "Troubador" or "Wedding Stein." Shows a man playing lute on one panel, lady with hand across breast, and a couple standing together. Each has a German phrase, but they do not seem complete and we were unable to translate them. This was made in various colors through 1983. *$60.00 – 65.00.* Lavender shaded Art Decorated mug, 4⅜" tall by Fostoria. This one has an Elk transfer and is marked "Henry's (?) Detroit, 1910." *$40.00 – 45.00.*

Plate 212 - Drape or Puffed, 3¾" tall tumbler by Fostoria. Made during the period when they were in Fostoria, OH, before moving to Moundsville, WV, in 1891. *$25.00 – 35.00.* Bleeding Heart, 3¼" tall. Made by King, Son & Co. in 1870's and later by U.S. Glass Co. 1898. *$30.00 – 35.00.* Eastlake or Bird and Wheat, 3¼" tall by Atterbury around 1881. Made in several sizes with 4⅛" tall being rarest. Also found in many colors. Flat foot rings are probably later than the one shown. Enhanced with gold to bring out the pattern. *$30.00 – 35.00.*

Plates 213, 214, 215, 216 - An assortment of decorated mugs made by Anchor Hocking and Hazel Atlas during the 1940's. Made for advertising, for children, as commemoratives, and for most any other reason you could think of! *$4.00 – 6.00.*

Plate 217 - TOP: Westmoreland Della Robbia iced tea, 6" tall with matching 4⅞" goblet. *$18.00 – 20.00.* Note the gold line trim on the goblet. Evidently they were made with and without gold. BOTTOM: 3⅞" Souvenir of Chicago tumbler very opalescent. *$20.00 – 25.00.* 4⅞" Souvenir of the St. Louis Exposition in 1904. Shows Palace of Agriculture, Palace of Machinery, St. Louis Union Station, Louisiana Purchase Monument, and Cascade Gardens. Very intricate moldwork. *$25.00 – 30.00.* 4⅜" Scroll tumbler by Imperial Glass. Label is marked "From the Belknap Collection," 1955–1958. *$12.00 – 15.00.* There were 22 items in the Belknap Collection including: bridesmaid bowl & lid, wedding bowl & lid, Rabbit on Nest, 7½" Grape vase, 6¼" Rose vase, 8½" Tricorn vase, 9¼" Celery vase, 10" cake stand, 8½" fruit bowl, 4-toes sugar & creamer with lids, oval sugar & creamer with lids, 8" Scroll berry bowl, 5" Scroll nappy, Salz & Pfeffer set, one quart Grape pitcher, 6 oz. footed Grape tumbler, 60 oz. Scroll pitcher, 12 oz. Scroll tumbler, 3¼" candle, 7" candle, Owl sugar & creamer, Owl jar & lid. Discontinued by 1968.

Plate 218 - TOP: Dewberry, 6" tall goblet by Kemple Glass. Taken from an 1890 pattern. *$12.00 – 15.00.* Jewel & Dewdrop also by Kemple from old molds. *$15.00 – 20.00.* BOTTOM: Diamond & Dart, 6", maker unknown. *$12.00 – 15.00.* Hobnail by Fenton Glass, made for many years. *Item currently available at retail.*

Plate 219 - Beautiful 3¼" tall cup and 5" diameter, saucer. Thick glass with lots of fire. Maker unknown. *$25.00 – 30.00.*

Plate 220 - Various cereal bowls and sherbets made by Hazel Atlas from the 1940's onward. *$5.00 – 8.00*.

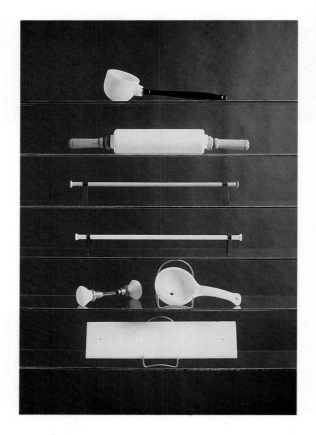

Plate 221 - 1ST ROW: 14" long wooden handled ladle. Cambridge Glass, 1903–1924. *$50.00 – 55.00.* **2ND ROW:** Rolling pin with wooden handles, also Cambridge. *$55.00 – 60.00.* **3RD & 4TH ROW:** Towel bars, green and milk glass about 16" long. *$15.00 – 18.00.* **5TH ROW:** Set of door knobs. *$8.00 – 10.00.* Pickle dipper, you dipped into the crock of dills and the juice ran out the little hole. *$25.00 – 30.00.* **6TH ROW:** Plain tray or plaque. *$10.00 – 12.00.*

Plate 222 - Here we have a selection of kitchenware by Fire King from the 1950's. **TOP:** 6", 7½", and 8¾" mixing bowls with hand-painted fruit design. *6", $6.00 – 8.00; 7½", $8.00 – 10.00; 8¾", $12.00 – 15.00.* **MIDDLE (l to r):** Plain gravy boat. *$5.00 – 7.00.* Patriotic design shakers and butterdish: Shakers say "God Bless America, it's Great to be an American." *$25.00 – 30.00.* Butter has Lincoln head and railsplitter fence. Rare and unusual set. *$40.00 – 45.00.* Another commemorative mug, this one advertising Christmas at Crowley's. *$6.00 – 8.00.* **BOTTOM:** Covered casseroles and loaf pan by Fire King, 1950's. *$7.00 – 12.00.*

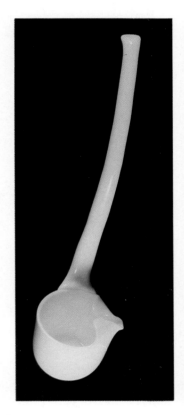

Plate 223 - Ladle with curved handle and ice lip. 13¾" long. *$40.00 – 45.00.*

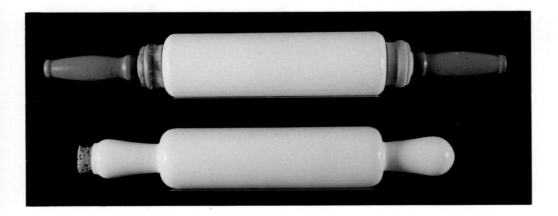

Plate 224 - **TOP:** Rolling pin with wooden handles; marked Cambridge. Milk glass section 9" long, 20½" long overall. One wood handle has been replaced. *$50.00 – 55.00.* **BOTTOM:** 15" blown glass rolling pin with cork. Maker unknown. *$120.00 – 130.00.*

Plate 225 - Acanthus lamp, 8¼" tall. Embossed decoration found plain or with pink, green, or yellow painted trim. *$245.00 – 250.00.* **RIGHT:** Embossed Leaf lamp base, 4½" tall to shoulder of milk glass. Found with round globe shade or umbrella shade in white and blue milk, vaseline, blue and green transparent glass and blue opalescent. Cold painted in various ways. *$55.00 – 60.00.*

Plate 226 - Electric lamp featuring reclining nude with harp. Milk glass part is 5¾" tall, overall 11½". Depression era, reproduced for Levay by L. E. Smith in 1980. *$30.00 – 35.00.*

Plate 227 - Cosmos Variant oil lamp. 6¼" to shoulder of milk glass. Found in a number of colors and with various fixtures and shades. 1940's. *$70.00 – 75.00.*

Plate 228 - Electric, vaseline opalescent "font" on milk glass base. 12" to shoulder of hobnail section; 25½" overall. *$40.00 – 45.00.*

Plate 229 - Dancing Couple electric lamp, 7⅝" high to top of figural section. From the 1940's. Made in a number of colors in transparent, satin, and opaque with various shades. *$35.00 – 45.00.*

Plate 230 - Violets in the Snow, 8¾" lamp and 4⅛" candlesticks by Fenton Art Glass. *$125.00 – 150.00.* Lamp base and candlesticks are the same mold, but a clear glass candleholder fits onto the stick, and the lamp shade sets on that. Shown in 1982 catalog.

Plate 231 - Two little cartoon character-type lamps. 6½" Chubby Dog, shown by Heacock in *The Glass Collector #4* pg. 28–30. Attributed to Consolidated. He called it the Puppo lamp after a cartoon dog by Grace Wiederseim, creator of the Campbell Soup Kids. Also see figurine section. *$150.00 – 175.00.* 8½" little girl. Whoever made Puppo probably made this cutie also. *$150.00 – 175.00.*

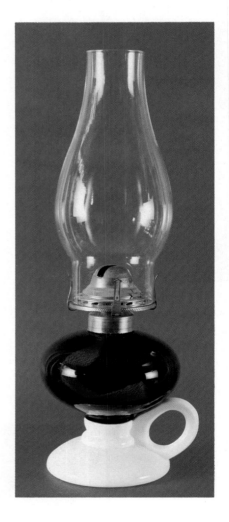

Plate 232 - Milk glass and cobalt lamp by Mosser Glass. Height to cobalt shoulder 4½". Still in production. *Item currently available at retail.*

Plate 233 - Wide and narrow beaded panels with raised flowers inside the wide ones. 15½" tall. *$75.00 – 100.00.*

Plate 234 - Alternating wide and narrow panels with embossed flowers on wide sections and oak leaves and acorns embossed on narrow. Much gold paint. Lacy metal base. About 16" tall. *$90.00 – 125.00 w/shade.*

Plate 235 - Elaborate footed shape with scrollwork, cross-hatching, and embossed flower trim. *$90.00 – 125.00 w/shade.*

Plate 236 - Nellie Bly, 9" tall. Chimney and shade in one piece on this lamp. *$130.00 – 140.00.* Embossed cross-hatching and flowers. 7½" tall. Also found in blue or green milk glass. *$125.00 – 130.00.*

Plate 237 - Banquet Lamp, 17" to shoulder of top glass section. Hand-painted flower trim, lacy metal base. *$100.00 – 120.00.*

Plate 238 - A fat little lamp, 4½" tall to shoulder, with decorative embossed panels at base, narrowing into body and gold painted. *$50.00 – 60.00 w/shade.*

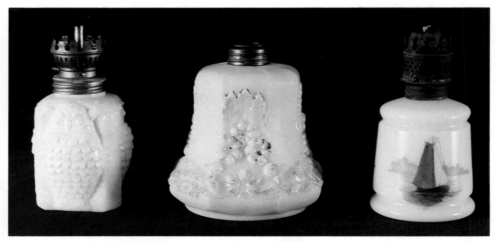

Plate 239 - Three Owls embossed around base. 2¾" tall to shoulder of milk glass section. *$35.00 – 40.00.* Star Night Lamp, 3½" to shoulder. By Consolidated 1896 – 1902. Has embossed floral design. Came with round globe shade. Also found in pale aqua green. *$35.00 – 45.00.* Bristol Type, ring top and base, straight sides. Hand painted with gaff-rigged sloop on one side, barn and trees on other. 2¾" tall to shoulder. Found with scenes painted in green, gray, and brown. *$35.00 – 45.00.*

Plate 240 - Art Deco styling in a 21" tall lamp. By Pittsburgh Lamp, Brass and Glass Company, and shown in their undated catalog #13. Strings of tiny glass beads hang from the shade. Green stenciled or transferred in Art Deco pattern. Also came in ruby stain on straw glass or carmine on opal. *$350.00 – 370.00.*

Plate 241 - Plain Jane lamp, 8" to shoulder. Graceful in shape with no decoration whatsoever. *$50.00 – 75.00.*

Plate 242 - Bundling Lamp by Imperial Glass. 8" tall. *$50.00 – 60.00.* Fleur de Lis, 7" tall by Eagle Glass, Oct. 10, 1901. Also found in clear with painting. Reproduced in pale green and cobalt by Imperial Glass. *$200.00 – 220.00, old.*

Plate 243 - l to r: Half-Barbell Glo Lite, 5" tall. Globe screws on with the wick in it. By the Glo Night Lamp Company of Boston. Found in clear, milk glass, green, blue, purple, amber, and ruby. Also in clear base with milk glass shade or milk glass base with ruby shade. Patented 1895, still in catalog in 1906. *$140.00 – 150.00*. Basket Weave, 6¾" tall with acorn burner. *$240.00 – 250.00*. Grecian Key, 5⅝" tall, acorn burner. *$165.00 – 170.00*.

Plate 244 - l to r: Mission Octagon pattern, 6½" tall. By U.S. Glass and shown in Butler Brothers 1912 catalog. Found also decorated in pink, green, and yellow with black panel outlines. *$100.00 – 125.00*. Christmas Tree or Shag, 6½" tall, same base as shakers. *$145.00 – 150.00*. Four-sided Grape, 2⅝" to shoulder. Butler Brothers 1912 catalog. Also found in pairs as shakers and sometimes with an undertray. See Shaker section of this book. *$45.00 – 50.00*.

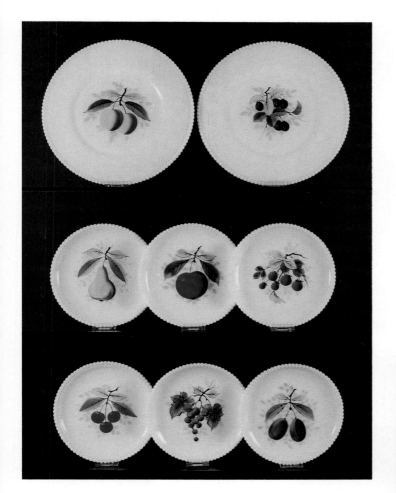

Plate 245 - An assortment of Westmoreland Beaded Edge fruit patterned plates, ranging in size from 7½" to 10½".
TOP (l to r): Peach. Blackberry.
CENTER (l to r): Pear. Apple. Strawberry.
BOTTOM (l to r): Cherry. Grapes. Plum. *All fruits $10.00 – 15.00.*

Plate 246 - A set of eight Westmoreland Beaded Edge Bird plates, 7½" diameter.
TOP (l to r): Bluebird. Goldfinch.
CENTER (l to r): Yellow Warbler. Cardinal. Titmouse.
BOTTOM (l to r): Chickadee. Mockingbird. Scarlet Tanager. All were also made in the 15" torte plate. *All birds $18.00 – 20.00.*

Plate 247 - An assortment of Floral and Bird plates on the 7½" Beaded Edge by Westmoreland. **TOP (l to r):** Iris. Bluebell. **CENTER (l to r):** Poppy. Violet. Pansy. *All florals $12.00 – 15.00.* **BOTTOM (l to r):** Parakeet. *$18.00 – 20.00.* Chicks. *$18.00 – 20.00.* Apple Blossom. *$18.00 – 20.00.*

Plate 248 - More Westmoreland Beaded Edge plates. 7½" diameter. **TOP:** Iris. **BOTTOM:** Columbine. Daisies. Hand painted. *All $12.00 – 15.00.*

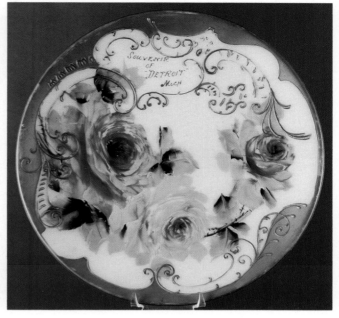

Plate 249 - Coupe plaque, 16" diameter. This gorgeous plate features a central medallion with hand-painted man and woman in garden scene. All is surrounded by hand-painted roses, leaves, and gold. These rounded-bottom plates were called "Plaques" in the old catalogs, and were meant to hang on the wall. *$50.00 – 60.00.*

Plate 250 - Souvenir of Detroit, Michigan, coupe plaque, 12" diameter. This is a beauty with much gold and beautiful painted roses. Some folks call these "flue covers" but in order to be a chimney flue cover, they would have had a metal edging to hold them into the opening. *$20.00 – 25.00.*

Plate 251 - Eagle and Shield coupe plaque, 15" diameter. Marked MarCor. *$45.00 – 50.00.*

Plate 252 - Moss Rose, 12" diameter coupe plaque, beautifully hand painted with a satin finish. $20.00 – 25.00. Kewpie doll, 10⅛" diameter coupe plaque with darling Kewpie baby figure and much gold work on the raised scrolls $25.00 – 30.00.

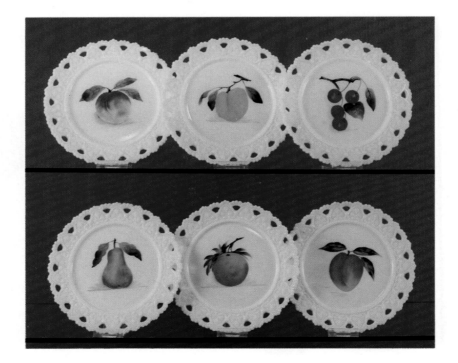

Plate 253 - A set of six Lacey Edge, hand-painted plates by Kemple. 7¼" diameter. There seem to be two peaches; we call them "one ripe" and one "not ripe." $10.00 – 12.00 ea.

Plate 254 - Partial set of Petalware plates with the ribbon edge. 8" diameter by MacBeth Evans Glass Co. 1930–1940. *$12.00 – 15.00 ea.*

Plate 255 - Shown here is an assortment of Petalware plates ranging from 8" in diameter to 11". Made by the MacBeth Evans Glass Company during the 1930's and 1940's. These plates are gorgeous and fun to collect since there are so many different patterns available. Some, like the 8" fruits, can be found in sets of eight. Other patterns came in complete dinnerware sets. *$15.00 – 20.00.*

Plate 256 - TOP: Yacht and Anchor, 7½" plate. *$20.00 – 25.00.* Three Bears, 7½" plate by Westmoreland. Legend says "From Uncle Tom, Crystal Lake." Also found in blue milk. *$30.00 – 35.00.* BOTTOM: Three Kittens plate by Westmoreland. Found in 7", 8", and 9" sizes, the 7" being the most common. *$30.00 – 35.00.* Rabbit & Horseshoe plate, 7½" dia., patented August 16, 1902, by George R. West for Westmoreland Specialty Co. Also found in blue. These were included in Westmoreland's "Bakers Dozen" plates that were produced at various times throughout their history. *$45.00 – 50.00.*

Plate 257 - TOP: Heart border, 8" plate by Westmoreland. Baltimore Oriole decal. *$20.00 – 25.00.* Club & Shell Border, 7" plate with hand-painted pears by Kemple Glass. *$18.00 – 22.00.*

BOTTOM: Lacey Edge, 7¼" scenic plate with hand-painted winter view by Kemple Glass. *$12.00 – 15.00.* Bar & Scroll Edge, 7¼" plate. Colonial Hearth black decal by Kemple Glass. *$10.00 – 12.00.*

Plate 258 - TOP: H-border plate, 7½", by Atterbury in 1890. *$20.00 – 25.00.* Souvenir of Tashmoo Park, 8" coupe plaque. Tashmoo Park was located on Harson's Island at the north end of Lake St. Clair in Michigan. *$20.00 – 25.00.*

BOTTOM: Scroll & Waffle, 7¼" plate by McKee in 1800's. Script signed. *$15.00 – 18.00.* Daisy & Branch Border, 7½" plate. *$15.00 – 20.00.*

Plate 259 - TOP: Coupe plaque, 10" diameter. Roses & gold, hand painted. *$25.00 – 30.00.* Coupe plaque, 10" diameter with hand-painted carnations. *$25.00 – 30.00.*

BOTTOM: Block border, fancy, 8¼" plate with hand-painted pansy decor in center. A very deep plate. *$45.00 – 50.00.* Angel Head 9" plate, pink rose center. *$30.00 – 35.00.* Comes in 7½" and 8½" sizes also by Westmoreland Glass and Kemple. Reproductions now sold by Phil Rosso, in many colors.

Plate 260 - **Top:** Club & Shell border, 9½" plate by Kemple. Baltimore Oriole, Audubon, decal. *$30.00 – 35.00.* Passenger Pigeon, Audubon decal. *$30.00 – 35.00.*
Bottom: Club & Shell border, Columbus plate. Individually decorated with bits of stamps, as was the fad for awhile. *$30.00 – 35.00.* Cherries, hand painted, Kemple Glass. *$15.00 – 18.00.*

Plate 261 - **Top:** Closed Lattice Edge, 10½" plates. *$35.00 – 40.00.* **Bottom:** Open Lattice Edge, 10½" plates. *$45.00 – 55.00.* Originally by Challinor, Taylor in floral designs. Two styles will be found, one with very heavy latticework and large openings. Also produced by Westmoreland Glass in 11" sizes decorated with hand-painted game birds (turkey, pheasant, bobwhite grouse, snipe, wood cock, mallard, blue jay, and red bird) and also with flowers.

Plate 262 - **Top:** Here we have two 6½" Lacey Heart border plates by Kemple Glass that are perfect for the fisherman. A "Gray Ghost Streamer" lure. *$10.00 – 12.00.* A small-mouth black bass. *$10.00 – 12.00.*

Bottom: A third fisherman's plate featuring the lake sturgeon. These are decal-trimmed by Kemple. *$10.00 – 12.00.* A 9" Forget-Me-Not border plate with old silk flag ribbon threaded into the border. In the center is a hand-tinted photo of a great trotting horse, Major Delmar (1:59¼). *$45.00 – 55.00.* This was a bay gelding born in 1897, whose last race was in 1903. His record time of 1:59¼ was very fast for the era and he was described as "a large, powerful gelding" and one of the first two-minute performers. He ran the record on Oct. 27, 1892, driven by Alta McDonald. We learned a lot about Standard Bred Trotting horses while researching this plate and thank the U.S. Trotting Association for their help.

Plate 263 - **TOP:** Lotus Flower edge, 7⅝" diameter plate. *$20.00 – 25.00.* H-Circle border, 8¼" diameter. Colonial folk in garden decal by Kemple Glass. *$18.00 – 22.00.*
BOTTOM: Fan & Circle Square, 10½" plate. *$20.00 – 25.00.* Grape, 8¾" plate by Imperial Glass 1954–66. *$12.00 – 15.00.*

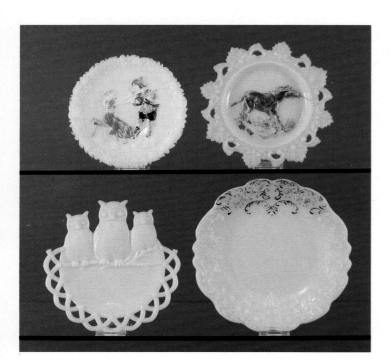

Plate 264 - **TOP:** 11" Open Lattice border plate by Westmoreland with a beautiful pheasant, which is one of the series of eight game bird designs. *$55.00 – 60.00.*
CENTER: 8½" Lace Edge plates with an Irish Setter decal and Floral painting. Anchor Hocking. *$6.00 – 8.00.*
BOTTOM: 5½" very opalescent Ring and Dot border plate issued as a souvenir of Gaines, Michigan, which is in Southeast Michigan. *$15.00 – 20.00.* 8½" Club & Shell border plate with Carlton-decorated pine tree by Westmoreland. *$15.00 – 20.00.* 5¼" Leaf plate almost completely covered in green paint. *$10.00 – 12.00.*

Plate 265 - **TOP:** The Serenade, 6½" plate. *$40.00 – 45.00.* Contrary Mule, 7" plate by Westmoreland. Sometimes this one has "I'm from Missouri, Show me," above view of mule. *$30.00 – 35.00.*
BOTTOM: Three Owls, 7½" plate by Westmoreland. *$30.00 – 35.00.* Flower & Scroll, 8⅜" plate, maker unknown. Painting enhanced to show detail. *$12.00 – 15.00.*

Plate 266 - **Top:** Deep Block border, 8¼" plate. This deep plate comes in blue as well as white and in 7½", 8½", and 9" sizes. *$15.00 – 25.00.* Diamond & Shell border, 8¼" diameter. Original also came in blue. This plate has a lovely hand-painted rose bouquet and was made by Kemple Glass. *$18.00 – 20.00.*

Bottom: Plain, 9" plate with a wide border featuring a hand-painted "South Sea Island" scenic view. *$12.00 – 15.00.* Gothic Edge, 9⅛" plate. Will be found in black as well as blue and white and in sizes ranging from 6" to 9¼". Originally a product of Canton Glass Company. This particular plate features a child's sepia tone photo under glass plus a little judicious gold line trimming. *$25.00 – 30.00 w/ photo.*

Plate 267 - **Top:** Sheaf of Wheat (or Diamond & Shell) border, 6" plate with hand-painted Dutch girl scene. *$20.00 – 25.00.* Also comes in 7½" and 8½" sizes. Kemple Glass. Spring Meets Winter, 7¼"plate. The character on the left is Spring. Winter on the right, is evidently trying to blow Spring back. Unusual border found almost exclusively on this plate. *$45.00 – 50.00.*

Bottom: Cupid & Psyche, 7½" plate by Westmoreland Glass. *$30.00 – 35.00.* Flag, Eagle, and Fleur de Lis, 7¼" plate by Westmoreland. Patented Sept 8, 1903, for Westmoreland Specialty Co. Two commemorative plates made on this blank are rare. One is "Wyoming Monument near Wilkes-Barre, PA. Pat. Sept. 8, 1903. This commemorates the 125th anniversary of the 1778 Revolutionary War Wyoming Valley Massacre. The other commemorates the Roger William Statue in Providence, RI, and shows the Memorial in the center. *$20.00 – 25.00 as shown.*

Plate 268 - **TOP:** Star plate, 5⅝", Maker unknown. *$8.00 – 12.00.* Chick & Egg tray, 5⅛" long. By Westmoreland Glass. *$15.00 – 20.00.* **BOTTOM:** "No Easter Without Us," 6¼" plate by Dithridge about 1900. *$40.00 – 45.00.* Chick in Egg Cart, 6½" plate. Maker unknown but probably the turn of the century era. *$35.00 – 40.00.*

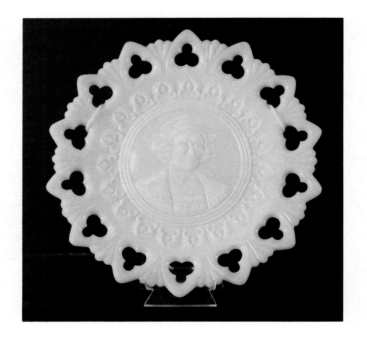

Plate 269 - **TOP:** Heavy, scroll-edged, 12" plate with a rose decal center and gold accents. *$25.00 – 30.00.* **CENTER:** Three Dogs, 6" plates. This features three puppies in full figure, contemplating a couple of hand-painted butterflies. The loop border is identical to Westmoreland's Three Kittens plate, so we assume this is also a Westmoreland product. *$60.00 – 65.00.* Garfield Monument, 7" plate with Leaf & Loop border. Millard calls it "Ancient Castle" but this plate is marked Garfield Monument and so it is. *$30.00 – 35.00.* Located in Lake View Cemetery in Cleveland, Ohio, the 165 foot tower was built of Ohio sandstone and completed in 1890. **BOTTOM:** Diamond & Shell border, 7" scenic plate, hand painted. *$35.00 – 40.00.* Lacey Edge, painted windmill scene. *$20.00 – 25.00.* Both by Kemple Glass.

Plate 270 - Columbus plate, 9¾" diameter. A big, heavy plate with a bust of Columbus in the center, having 1492 – 1892 across his chest. Shell & Club Border. *$40.00 – 45.00.*

Plate 271 - Top: Single forget-me-not border, 7¼" plate painted as a "Souvenir of Adrian, Michigan." Adrian is in southeastern Michigan close to the Ohio border. *$20.00 – 25.00.* Crown border plate, 8¼", gold trimmed. *$20.00 – 25.00.*
Bottom: Panelled Edge, 7¼" fruit decal plate, marked "John E. Kemple Glassworks, East Palestine, Ohio." *$20.00 – 25.00.* Lacey Edge, 7¼" plate with a farm scene, marked "Hand Painted Lenore (?)," by Kemple. *$15.00 – 20.00.*

Plate 272 - Top: Owl Lovers, 7½" plate. Why what is obviously a parrot is watching the owls, I don't have a clue... *$40.00– 45.00.* Easter Opening, 7½" plate. The words appear at the bottom. Two chicks, one just emerging from the egg, rest in a patch of lily of the valley. *$55.00 – 60.00.*

Bottom: Lincoln on Backward C border, 9¼" diameter. "Lincoln" is marked under the bust. This is one of the Civil War Centennial anniversary plates by L. E. Smith in 1960. *$50.00 – 55.00.* Same borders will be found with Jefferson Davis and John Kennedy. Iron Cross border, 10½" plate. Photo shows the back of this deep plate; the topside is plain. The border is slightly crimped and quite unusual.

Plate 273 - TOP: Taft campaign plate, 7½" diameter. Features William Howard Taft, president in 1908, surrounded by a border of eagles, flags, and stars. The same blank will be found with the face of Bryan, another with a Monk, and one with only the border. *$50.00 – 55.00.* Lincoln, 8½", Rail Splitter plaque. The rails are really split on this particular piece, due to the mold not being completely filled when it was made. Very scarce in the original and even difficult to come by in the Kemple product (1945–1970). *$100.00 – 150.00.* BOTTOM: Angel Head border, 9½" plate. This is one of the appealing photo gift plates occasionally found. Here we have a baby photo under glass. Painted in gold around the photo is "Jessie to Fred" and "Merry Christmas." Unfortunately no date. Made by Dithridge and later by Westmoreland. *$40.00 – 45.00 w/ photo.* 101 Border, 8¾" plate. Hand-painted central decoration has a horseshoe and flowers with banner saying "luck." *$25.00 – 30.00.*

Plate 274 - TOP: 6¾" Easter Rabbits plate. The word "Easter" is above two bunnies cavorting in a cabbage patch. Dithridge, late 1800's. *$35.00 – 40.00.* 6" Woof Woof plate by Westmoreland. *$45.00 – 50.00.*
BOTTOM: Chicks on Wooden Shoe, 6½", Lacey Heart border plate. *$50.00 – 60.00.* 7⅛" dia. Alphabet plate. A Westmoreland product. *$45.00 – 50.00.*

Plate 275 - A 12" wall plate or torte plate in the Roses pattern by Imperial Glass 1950–64. Top of this beautifully sculpted plate is shown here. *$25.00 – 30.00.*

Plate 276 - Bottom of the Previous Imperial Roses plate, showing panels of roses and daisies. Beautiful mold work.

Plate 277 - TOP: Wicket border, 8⅝" plate with hand painted flowers. *$15.00 – 20.00.* Diamond & Shell border plate with waterlilies. Marked "Hand Painted" on the back. Probably by Lornita Glass for Kemple. *$15.00 – 20.00.*
BOTTOM: Club & Shell with Loop, 8⅜" plate with Colonial scene decal. *$15.00 – 20.00.* "S" border, 8½" square plate with hand-painted scene on the surface and not fired. Somebody's hobby, no doubt, but interesting all the same. *$20.00 – 25.00.*

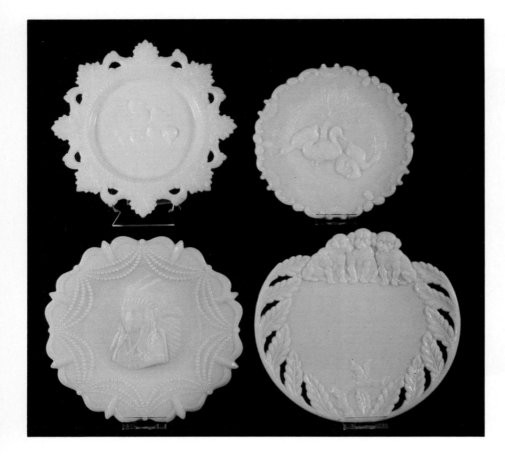

Plate 278 - TOP: Easter Chicks, 7¼"
plate by Westmoreland on Leaf & Loop
border. *$30.00 – 35.00.* Easter Ducks
plate in rather a grayish glass by
Dithridge about 1900. *$35.00 – 40.00.*
BOTTOM: Beaded Loop, 8" Indian Head
plate by Westmoreland. *$35.00 – 40.00.*
Three Puppies, 8½" plate with the Open
Leaf border that is rarely found. At the
bottom of the plate is a squirrel which
the puppies are no doubt thinking of
chasing. *$60.00 – 65.00.*

Plate 279 - TOP: 7½", Plate, forget-me-not
border with gold painted flowers and
threaded through with old silk flag ribbon.
In the center is a decal of the USS Potsdam. Since Potsdam is one of the major
German cities, perhaps the ship shown
here was one that carried immigrants to
our shores. *$45.00 – 50.00.* Anchor and
Belaying Pin plate, patented August 20,
1901, by M. Tonnemann. This is heavily
and gaudily painted as a "Souvenir of Niagra Falls." *$25.00 – 30.00.*
BOTTOM: Sheaf Border (or Diamond &
Shell), 7½" plate by Kemple. Hand
painted with a lovely red bird. Marked
"HAND PAINTED." Probably by Lornita Company, a decorating firm located
near Point Marionk PA. *$30.00 – 35.00.*
Angel with Harp on Single Forget-Me-
Not border. Certainly the instrument is
not a harp, but more likely a mandolin.
Westmoreland Glass. *$20.00 – 30.00.*

Plate 280 - Pair of Tomato shakers, 2¾" tall with pewter lids. *$10.00 – 15.00 pr.* See more tomato items in the Sugars & Creamers section.

Plate 281 - **TOP (l to r):** Vertical Beaded, 3⅛" shaker shown in Butler Brothers 1905 catalog. *$20.00 – 25.00 pr.* Palmer Cox Brownie, 2¼" shaker. Early 1900's. Palmer Cox was born in Canada and wrote story poems about the adventures of the little creatures he called Brownies. There are several shapes of shakers decorated with Brownies, a number of them with hand-painted figures rather than the embossed one shown here. *$90.00 – 95.00 pr.* 2½" shaker with embossed dogwood-type flower. *$20.00 – 25.00 pr.*

BOTTOM (l to r): Flower Sprig, 3" shaker. *$20.00 – 25.00 pr.* 3½" Beaded Bottom shaker. *$20.00 – 25.00.* 4¼" Feathered Scroll. *$20.00 – 25.00.*

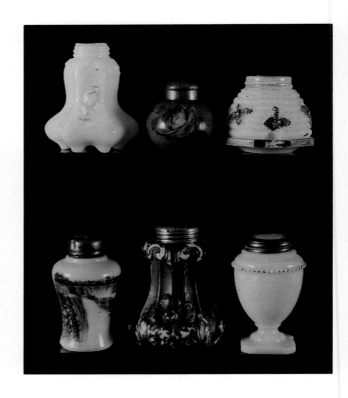

Plate 282 - TOP (l to r): Tassel, 3¼" tall. *$25.00 – 30.00 pr.* Tomato, 2¾" tall. *$10.00 – 15.00 pr.* Clover, 3¼" tall. *$18.00 – 22.00 pr.*
BOTTOM (l to r): Paneled Cross, 4" tall. *$20.00 – 25.00 pr.* Cylindrical, 4¼" tall with lovely hand-painted roses. *$20.00 – 25.00 pr.* Paneled Daisy, 3⅛" tall. *$20.00 – 25.00 pr.*

Plate 283 - TOP (l to r): Embossed Rose, 3" tall, footed shaker. *$30.00 – 35.00 pr.* Green, 2" ball-shaped shaker with hand-painted rose. Shown in Butler Brothers 1905 catalog. *$20.00 – 25.00.* Beehive, 2¼" shaker with gold-encrusted bees all around. *$35.00 – 40.00 pr.*
BOTTOM (l to r): Souvenir shaker, 3⅜" tall painted with Niagra Falls scene. *$30.00 – 35.00 pr.* Paneled Scroll with Wild Rose, 3¾" tall. *$25.00 – 30.00 pr.* Beaded Urn shaker, 3½" tall with row of beads on shoulder as only decoration. *$20.00 – 25.00 pr.*

Plate 284 - TOP: Grape Cluster, 3" tall shakers with 5½" x 2⅜" tray. *$22.00 – 28.00 set.*
BOTTOM (l to r): Hen & Rabbit egg-shaped, 3" shaker with head of hen on one side and rabbit head on the other. Design patent to M.T. Thomas early 1900. *$50.00 – 60.00 pr.* Tulip, 4" sugar shaker. *$60.00 – 65.00.* Gaudy Rose, 3" shaker. *$20.00 – 25.00 pr.*

Plate 285 - John and Mary Bull, 6" shakers by Imperial Glass. Called "Salz and Pfeffer," 1955–1960. Also made by IG in carnival colors. **RIGHT:** John originated with Atterbury as a "Saloon Pepper." *$25.00 – 30.00.* **CENTER:** Imperial made Mary to form a set. *$25.00 – 30.00.* **LEFT:** Notice side view of John showing off his tail coat.

Plate 286 - Arlington pattern, 5" tall salt shaker and pepper mill by Fostoria in the 1960's. *$30.00 – 35.00 set.*

Plate 287 - **TOP:** Quilted shakers in basket, 3" tall, 4" long. Imperial Glass 1952–1966. *$25.00 – 30.00 set.* Chubby Floral shakers with two different lids. Bases look like they might fit into a condiment set. *$10.00 – 12.00 each.*

BOTTOM (l to r): Hobnail and English Hobnail, 4¼" shakers. When I bought these at the store years ago, they told me the English Hobnail one was for the pepper. Through the years, however, I begin to wonder if they just put these together either inadvertently or on purpose. *$25.00 – 30.00.* 3" shakers by Kemple after McKee patterns. *$10.00 – 12.00 pr.* Paneled Scroll, 3¾" tall. *$20.00 – 22.00 pr.*

Plate 288 - **TOP:** Blue, 2½" Fleur-de-Lis shakers. *$20.00 – 25.00 pr.* 2¾" tall Ribbed shakers with hand-painted floral accents. *$15.00 – 20.00 pr.*

BOTTOM: Grape pattern, 4¼" shakers, recent. *$5.00 – 10.00.* Blooming Flower, 4¼" by Westmoreland. *$20.00 – 25.00.*

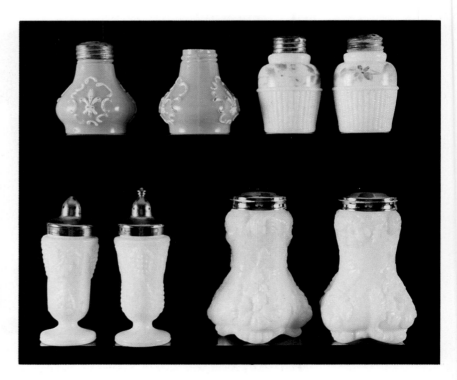

Plate 289 - Three-bottle Cattail-decorated condiment set with wire handle. Shakers, 3½" tall; base, 5¼" diameter. *$30.00 – 35.00.* Two-bottle Caster Set with glass handle. 2¾" tall shakers, 5" long base. By Imperial Glass, 1951–1955. *$25.00 – 30.00.*

Plate 290 - Creased Bale three-bottle condiment set by Dithridge about 1894. Wire handle. Shakers, 2⅞" tall; base, 6¼" diameter. *$125.00 – 130.00.* Three-bottle condiment set on Fan shaped base with wire handle. 3⅝" tall shakers, 6" flat side measurement of fan base. Hand-painted decorations. *$115.00 – 125.00.*

Plate 291 - TOP: 3⅞" long Swan salt. Purchased from Carl Forslund Company of Grand Rapids, Michigan, in 1960. Maker unknown. *$15.00 – 20.00.* 1½" Basket Weave individual salt by Atterbury. Marked "Patented June 30th., '74," (1874). *$20.00 – 25.00.* 3" long Fostoria Bird salt. *$15.00 – 20.00.*
BOTTOM: 2⅛" tall Daisy footed salt. *$10.00 – 12.00.* 2⅝" tall Blackberry salt. *$18.00 – 20.00.* 5¼" long Westmoreland Duck salt. *$18.00 – 20.00.*

—— SUGARS, CREAMERS, BUTTERS & PITCHERS ——

Plate 292 - English Hobnail, 4¼" tall footed sugar. *$8.00 – 10.00.* 4¾" tall footed creamer. By Westmoreland for many years. *$8.00 – 10.00.*

Plate 293 - Close-up view of the English Hobnail pattern.

Plate 294 - Betsy Ross pattern by Fostoria, 1960's. 4" creamer. *$10.00 – 12.00.* 3⅝" sugar. *$10.00 – 12.00.*

Plate 295 - Cow & Wheat, 3⅛" x 4⅞" sugar. *$75.00 – 90.00.* 4⅝" creamer. *$75.00 – 90.00.* Very unusual and hard to find set. Consensus of opinion is English manufacture.

Plate 296 - 1ST ROW (l to r): Horizontal Rib sugar with lid. *N.P.A.* Bow-finial sugar with lid. *N.P. A.* Blue Scroll sugar with lid. *N.P.A.* Two pieces of The Family, very opaque and heavy. *Mother, $300.00 – 325.00; Father, $325.00 – 350.00; Boy, $150.00 – 175.00; Girl, $200.00 – 225.00.* There are flat eye sockets from which the eyes are missing in the pieces shown. The set consists of Mother covered sugar, Father covered butter, Little Boy creamer, and Little Girl spooner.

2ND ROW (l to r): Lacey Edge by Atterbury, later produced as Randolph by Fostoria. *$30.00 – 35.00.* By Atterbury, produced in green/white marble also. *$45.00 – 50.00.* G.E. Refrigerator sugar (also see further photos with matching shakers). *$45.00 – 50.00.*

3RD ROW (l to r): Crossed Fern with Ball and Claw covered sugar *$45.00 – 50.00* and spooner. *$35.00 – 40.00.* Fern was patented by Atterbury in 1876. Oval Medallion by Challinor, Taylor, also in clear, white and purple mosaic. *$50.00 – 65.00.*

4TH ROW (l to r): Vertical Rib creamer and covered sugar. *N.P.A.* Roman Cross covered butter and covered sugar. Unusual square shape, maker unknown. *$55.00 – 60.00, butter. $50.00 – 55.00, sugar.*

Plate 297 - TOP: Maltese Cross sugar with lid. *$25.00 – 30.00.* The Pittsburgh Commercial Gazette, July 29, 1886, stated: "The newest pattern this year is a Maltese Cross, the old 5th. Army Corps badge." Grape pattern, three-toes sugar & creamer by Imperial Glass 1952–1971. *$12.00 – 15.00, sugar. $12.00 – 15.00, creamer.*

BOTTOM: Westmoreland Grape & Cherry covered creamer and sugar. Has cluster of cherries on one side, grapes on other. Both pieces have lids. Also found with fruits painted. First produced around 1889 as mustard containers. Re-introduced in the

1930's until 1970's. Has been reproduced recently. *$20.00 – 25.00 ea. Painted $30.00 –35.00.* Strutting Peacock covered sugar and creamer by Westmoreland. Found in all white or with blue lids as shown. *$30.00 – 35.00.* Created at the turn of the century as mustard jars. These are the only pieces made by Westmoreland in this pattern. Westmoreland Specialty Co. also made in amehtyst carnival during the early teens. Blue milk was made in the 30's, 40's, and 50's and is most difficult to find.

Plate 298 - A selection of Tomato pieces, makers generally unknown. **TOP:** 5¼" plate. *$12.00 – 18.00.* 3¼" green sugar. *$12.00 – 15.00.* **BOTTOM:** 3" creamer. *$12.00 – 15.00.* 3¼" red sugar. *$15.00 – 18.00.* 3⅞" creamer. *$15.00 – 18.00.* Set shown in center and at right are included in the 1910 Butler Brothers catalog.

Plate 299 - **TOP:** 6⅛" covered sugar. *$20.00 – 25.00.* 4⅜" creamer in the Cactus pattern. *$18.00 – 20.00.* Originally by Greentown, and later produced by Fenton.
BOTTOM: Sunflower pattern, 4½" creamer. *$30.00 – 35.00.* 4½" spooner. *$30.00 – 35.00.* Originally Lily pattern in Atterbury 1881 catalog. Panels have both sunflowers and lily of the valley.

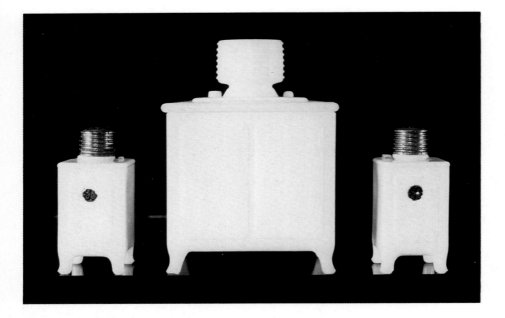

Plate 300 - Shakers and covered sugar made to resemble the old two-door, Monitor top General Electric refrigerator. The 5" sugar depicts the refrigerator with the Monitor top unit. This was one of the first refrigerators on the market. *$45.00 – 50.00.* The 3" shakers have corks underneath as well as screw-on tops. Note the round paper labels on the shaker fronts, using the GE logo. *$25.00 – 30.00.* Maker unknown.

Plate 301 - TOP: Paneled Wheat 5¾" creamer. *$35.00 – 40.00.* 7¾" covered sugar. *$40.00 – 45.00.* **BOTTOM:** 5¼" tall spooners. *$35.00 – 40.00 ea.* Ptd. by J.H. Hobbs for Hobbs, Brockunier & Co. in 1871. Variations in the pattern are illustrated by the spooners. The scalloped rim spooner and creamer and the sugar have ringed waists while the straight rim spooner does not. It has a much deeper base, almost a pyramid shape. Originally made in crystal, it is one of the rarest patterns in milk glass.

Plate 302 - A grouping of Westmoreland Specialty Company sugars and creamers used before the turn of the century as condiment containers. **TOP:** 4¾" covered sugar. 5" Paneled Forget Me Not covered sugar.
BOTTOM: 3¼" creamer with rim for lid. 5½" Flute and Crown sugar. *All range from $10.00 – 25.00.*

Plate 303 - TOP: Swan with Beaded Ring handles and finial. See more about this pattern in the Mugs section of this book. *$40.00 – 45.00.* Imperial's 3½" Owl creamer and sugar with yellow glass eyes. *$20.00 – 25.00 ea.* Originally a Challinor, Taylor product and shown in their 1891 catalog. The little sugar has the owl face both front and back. An almost identical owl face was produced by Bryce, Higbee of Pittsburgh, PA, during the same time frame (1885–93).

BOTTOM: Primula or Primrose sugar and creamer by Westmoreland Specialty Co. Both are six sided and have eight scalloped feet. These were sold as mustard containers and made in white, blue, and green milk glass as well as clear and transparant colors. *$30.00 – 35.00, set.* 4¼" tall creamer marked "Hand made, Baker, Finland." *N.P.A.*

Plate 304 - A group of spooners. 4½" Blackberry pattern. Another mold with a long history. Blackberry was patented in 1870, by Wm. Leighton, Jr. and manufactured at Hobbs, Brockunier & Co. of Wheeling, WV. After this, the molds went to Co-Operative Glass Co. of Beaver Falls, PA, and finally to the Phoenix Glass Co. of Monaca, PA, where it was made until about 1942. Some of the old creamers in this pattern were made with the 1870 date. John Kemple bought the Blackberry mold in

1946. Original Hobbs pieces included various sizes of covered compotes, egg cup, 4-piece table set, pitchers, honey dish, salt, pickle, celery, and syrup plus bases for oil lamps. *$50.00 – 55.00.* Challinor, Taylor's, #313 ware called Tree of Life. (Also called Daisy pattern by Belknap pg. 122.) Made from 1885 – 1893 in white as well as shades of blue, green, and perhaps pink, either plain or hand-painted. Original production included an openwork-edged bowl, 8" comport, cracker jar, syrup or "molasses can," condiment tray, nappy, cruet, nut bowl, creamer, butterdish and lid, spooner, 7" oval dish, and sugar bowl. *Spooner, white, $35.00 – 40.00. Spooner, pointed, $45.00 – 50.00.* Strawberry spooner patented by John Bryce in 1870, and made by Bryce Brothers in fine quality flint glass. Hard to find. *$50.00 – 55.00.*

Plate 305 - Two Lace & Dewdrop covered sugars (6" tall). *$25.00 – 30.00.* 4¼" creamer. *$20.00 – 25.00. Blue painted, $40.00 – 45.00.* The all milk white pieces are by Kemple Glass. The blue-painted version is by Phoenix. This pattern was first named Beaded Jewel and created in the 1880's by George Duncan Glass Co., Pittsburgh, PA. At that time, the line was made in crystal only. In 1902 when Duncan went out of business, the molds were sold to Co-Operative Glass Co. of Beaver Falls, PA, who made this pattern, called their "1902 line" in milk glass until 1929. The molds were then purchased by the Phoenix Glass Co. of Monaca, PA; they made the pattern in milk glass and painted the pieces in various colors for several years. In 1946, after a very short stint with Westmoreland, a glass jobber, H. M. Tuska, sold the molds to John Kemple. He made the line in milk glass at the East Palestine, OH, plant and at the Kenova plant in blue and honey amber transparant colors. Molds now are owned by Wheaton Glass of New Jersey.

Plate 306 - Betsy Ross pattern by Tiffin Glass. Sugar, 7" to top of finial. *$25.00 – 30.00.* Urn, 7½" to top of handle. *$25.00 – 30.00.* Creamer, 5" to top of spout. *$25.00 – 30.00.* Shown in undated catalog; made after 1956.

Plate 307 - Viking pattern covered sugar, 8" tall. A Centennial Exposition item made by Hobbs, Brockunier and originally named Centennial. Design patented Nov. 18, 1876. Oddly, some pieces have four feet and some only three, leading one to believe that the mold was altered at some time. It is uncertain how many pieces of the pattern were made in milk glass, as the main bulk of production was in crystal. The following pieces have been seen in milk: shaving mug, creamer, sugar with lid, butter with lid, bread tray. The covered sugar shown has five heads (4 as feet and one as finial). All pieces are extremely rare in milk glass. *$500.00+.*

Plate 308 - Four-piece table set in the Banded Shells Varient by U.S. Glass. **TOP:** Sugar, 6" tall. Creamer, 4⅝". **BOTTOM:** Butter, 7" diameter. Spooner 4¼" tall. Hand-painted decoration. *$125.00 – 150.00 set.*

Plate 309 - TOP: Victorian Urn, 4⅞" sugar without lid (5¾" with lid), by Westmoreland Specialty Co. The lid is seldom found on this sugar probably due to the fact that, upside down, it resembles a salt dip and probably has been sold as such by unknowing dealers. *$50.00 – 65.00 w/lid.* Chubby, 4⅞" coverd sugar. *$10.00 – 12.00.* Tall, slender 6" tall covered sugar, Slender Panel shape. *$12.00 – 15.00.*
BOTTOM: Cherry Thumbprint, 3½" creamer by Westmoreland. *$15.00 – 18.00.* 3⅞" tall creamer in Aztec pattern originally by McKee Glass but probably produced in milk glass by Kemple. *$10.00 – 12.00.* Della Robbia, 3" creamer by Westmoreland. *$6.00 – 8.00.*

Plate 310 - TOP: Individual covered sugar and creamer. Pattern is the same Ribs and Scallops as shown in the epergne section and made by Vallerysthal. *$35.00 – 40.00 set.* BOTTOM: Maple Leaf, 3⅝" creamer. *$10.00 – 12.00.* 3¼" sugar. *$10.00 – 12.00.* By Westmoreland.

Plate 311 - Pear sugar, 5" tall by Westmoreland Specialty Co. The pear part is only the lid; the rest of the piece being leaves resting on a base. Originally a mustard container. *$65.00 – 70.00.* Cornucopia sugar bowl, 5½" tall, also by Westmoreland Specialty Co. Sugar has two cornucopias with points turned in and crossing at base. The matching creamer has one cornucopia. Also in blue milk. Hard to find. *$70.00 – 75.00.*

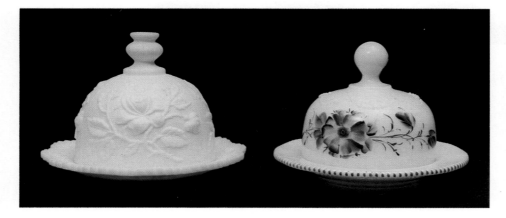

Plate 312 - Imperial Roses butterdish with lid, in doeskin finish. 5½" tall, 7¾" diameter. *$35.00 – 40.00.* Heisey Beaded Drape butter with hand-painted decor. 5½ x 7½" diameter. *$50.00 – 55.00.*

Plate 313 - Large, 7½" tall Owl pitcher by Challinor, Taylor and shown in their 1891 catalog. Has the realistic glass eyes. Terriffic mold work front, back, and sides! Hard to find. *$185.00 – 200.00.*

Plate 314 - TOP: 6" sugar. *$25.00 – 30.00.* 3¾" creamer in pink milk glass by Fostoria. *$20.00 – 25.00.* Randolph pattern, 1960's. Also produced in opaque white and aqua.

BOTTOM: 4¾" Westmoreland Swan and Cattail. Originally Westmoreland Specialty Co. condiment containers. This is one of the relatively few sets with covered creamer as well as sugar. Also produced in blue milk glass. *$25.00 – 30.00.*

Plate 315 - Lovely embossed roses and ruffles on this 6¾" diameter by 4" tall butterdish. Scroll Varient pattern? *$40.00 – 45.00.*

Plate 317 - Lace & Dewdrop covered butter by Kemple Glass. 6½" diameter, 6" tall. Very deep bowl. *$35.00 – 40.00.*

Plate 316 - TOP: Strawberry, 7" syrup pitcher missing the lid. *$65.00 – 70.00 w/lid.* Flower Swirl, 7" syrup pitcher, also no lid. *$85.00 – 90.00 w/lid.*
BOTTOM: Dot & Thumbprint, 6½" syrup with applied handle. *$50.00 – 55.00.* Imperial's Grape, 6¾" syrup with a keyed lid. 1955 – 1964. *$25.00 – 30.00.*

Plate 318 - Iris pattern, 8¾" tall pitcher. Manufactured by Westmoreland about 1910. *$95.00 – 100.00.* Fish pitcher, 4¾" tall, by Atterbury and shown in 1881 catalog. The fish is head up on one side and head down on the other. *$150.00 – 160.00.*

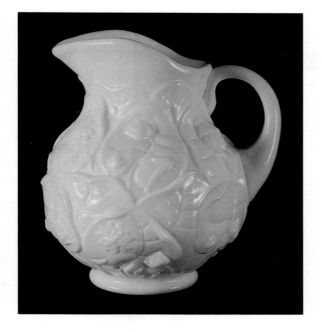

Plate 319 - Waterlily, 6⅞" tall pitcher by Fenton Art Glass. *$75.00 – 80.00.*

Plate 320 - Birds on Branch, 7" tall pitcher. Three little birds perch on branches on each side with leaves at the top. Hard to find. *$75.00 – 80.00.*

Plate 321 - Jenny Lind water set by Fostoria. 8¼" pitcher. *$90.00 – 100.00.* 4½" tumblers. *$20.00 – 25.00.* Produced in many pieces in the 1960's. See Fostoria catalog reprints and boudoir items pictured elsewhere in this book.

Plate 322 - Ball pattern, 7" tall, ice lip pitcher by Cambridge Glass. *$50.00 – 65.00.*

Plate 323 - **TOP:** Fenton Hobnail, 7" cruet, very opalescent, old label. *$35.00 – 40.00.* Imperial, 5½", Swirl mustard with lid and spoon. *$25.00 – 30.00.*
BOTTOM: Pair of Fenton Hobnail, 4¾" tall cruets on 7¾" long stand. *$40.00 – 45.00.* 3¾" Fenton Hobnail mustard pot with lid. *$20.00 – 25.00.* These Fenton items have been made for many years, and often in production today.

Plate 324 - Alligator Toothpick. 2¾" tall. Very delicate and fragile Victorian novelty piece. Hard to find. Also in light blue, amber, vaseline, and clear. In advertisements of the time, it was called both a match safe and a candlestick. *$75.00 – 85.00.*

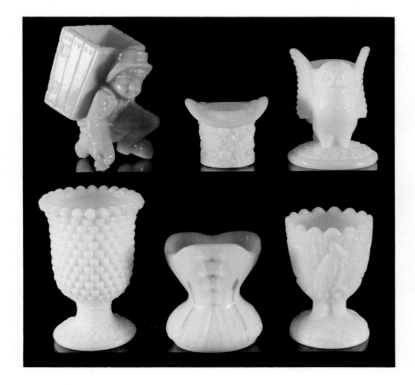

Plate 325 - Top: Boy with Basket toothpick holder by Vallerysthal. *$60.00 – 70.00.* Daisy and Button Top Hat, 1½" tall. Several makers. *$8.00 – 12.00.* Owl with Spread Wings toothpick, 3" tall by Westmoreland. *$15.00 – 20.00.* **Bottom:** Thousand Eye match holder. *$20.00 – 25.00.* Corset toothpick by Bellaire Goblet Co. *$65.00 – 70.00.* Heron in Marsh match or toothpick, 3½" tall. Swimming fish at foot. Also made in clear colors and has been reproduced. *$30.00 – 35.00.*

Plate 326 - Two book-shaped match safes. 3" tall. 4⅜" tall. Made by a number of glasshouses from the 1890's until the early 1900's. *Range $45.00 – 65.00.*

Plate 327 - Double hanging match box, 3¼" long by Eagle Glass & Manufacturing Co. 1898. Comes with plain, smooth back, and with raised diamond "scratcher" back. *$30.00 – 35.00.* 3⅛" Satchel wall match box. *$60.00 – 65.00.* Gamma Butterfly, 3¾" long, 2-compartment wall match box. *$50.00 – 55.00.*

Plate 328 - Top: 3¼" tall, Kemple Indian Head toothpick or match. Older version is divided down the center inside. *$50.00 – 60.00, Kemple. $75.00 – 85.00, old.* 4¾" tall, Indian Head match holder by Challinor, Taylor and shown in their 1891 catalog. This is a beautiful piece, very detailed and wonderfully sculpted. *$80.00 – 95.00.* Beggar's Hand holding ribbed match or tooth pick. Found in opaque colors of white, blue, and green. Also clear and frosted. By Vallerysthal-Porteiux, 1900. *$40.00 – 45.00.*
Bottom (l to r): Three Swan toothpick, 2⅜" tall by Westmoreland. *$25.00 – 30.00.* 2⅜" Eagle Drum toothpick, unknown. *$20.00 – 25.00.* Daisy and Button top hat, 2¼", many manufacturers. *$15.00 – 20.00.* Keg match holder, 2¾" tall. Has metal hoops, with the bottom hoop missing on this particular piece. Bryce-Higbee Co. Late 1800's. *$20.00 – 25.00.*

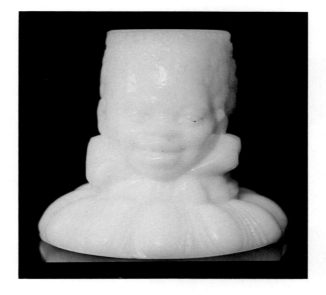

Plate 329 - Minstrel Boy figural, 2⅞" tall. Originally thought to be an inkwell, a second version has been found with a stippled "scratching section" on the front below the chin. We probably have both an inkwell and a match holder. *$125.00 – 195.00 depending on paint.*

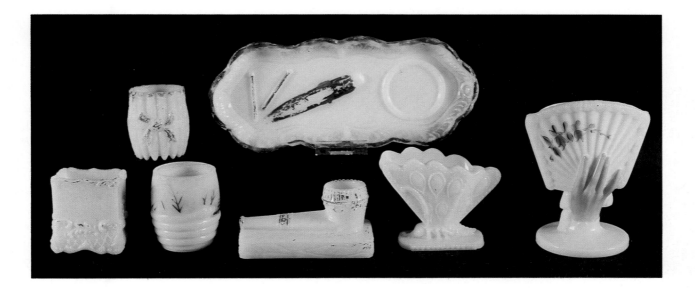

Plate 330 - Top: Bunch of Cigars match holder. Matching 8½" long tray with the legend "Ash Receiver" embossed along with a large, raised cigar. Made by Eagle Glass Company, 1899. *$55.00 – 65.00 set.*
Bottom (l to r): 2¼" rectangular match or toothpick holder with raised scrollwork. *$15.00 – 20.00.* 2½" barrel-shaped holder with snake figure twining around and painted foliage. *$25.00 – 30.00.* 4¾" long Pipe match holder on base covered with raised tobacco leaves, Eagle Glass, 1899. *$30.00 – 35.00.* Butterfly match, 2¾" tall. Eagle Glass Company about 1899. *$30.00 – 35.00.* Hand and Fan match holder, 4½" tall. Lovely hand with flesh-colored paint holds decorated fan. *$35.00 – 45.00.*

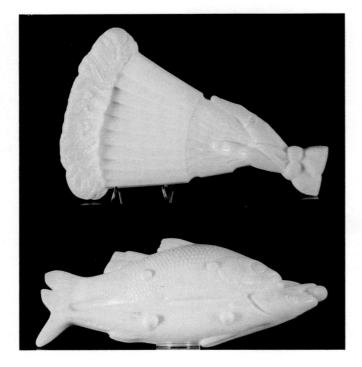

Plate 331 - Hand with Fan tray, 9¼" long, by Atterbury. On the first finger of the hand is a ring that originally was set with a red glass stone. The fan has a feathered edge and fringed tassels. *$75.00 – 80.00.* Dual Fish pickle, 11" long. Shown is the bottom of the piece with the two bodies forming a divided top surface. Patent June 4, 1872, is marked on topside. Atterbury. Elusive. *$80.00 – 85.00.*

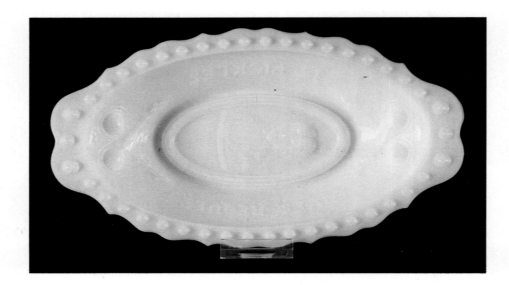

Plate 332 - Actress pickle dish, 9¼" long. Around the dish is the legend "Love's Request is Pickles." Made around 1879, and attributed to both the Crystal Glass Company and the LaBelle Glass Company, both of Bridgeport, OH, and Riverside Glass Works of Brilliant, OH. Most recently, however, it has been discovered as part of the Opera set made by Adams & Co. of Pittsburgh. A scallop shell was incorporated into most designs in this set, which traditionally was a sign of theater people. Reproduced in milk glass by Imperial Glass and most recently by Boyd's Crystal Art Glass. *$35.00 – 40.00.*

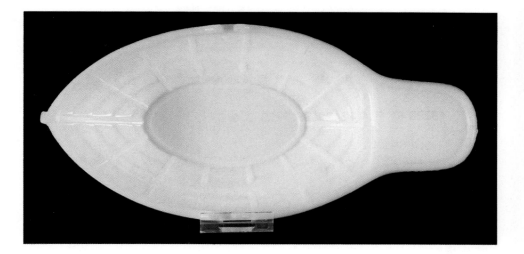

Plate 333 - Boat pickle dish, 9½" long. Inside view shows oars resting along the sides. *$40.00 – 50.00.*

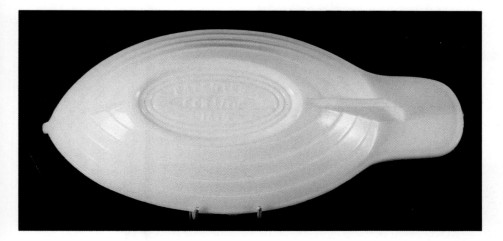

Plate 334 - Outside view of Boat pickle. Says "Pickle" on each side of front point. Marked "Patented Feb. 17, 1874." Shown in 1874 and 1881 Atterbury catalogs. Found also in clear and blue, and in a somewhat smaller size.

Plate 335 - Partitioned 9½" x 9" Apple relish by Imperial Glass, 1951–52. *$25.00 – 30.00.* Fire King turquoise blue three-part relish, 11 x 7¾", with gold trim, 1957–58. *$10.00 – 12.00.*

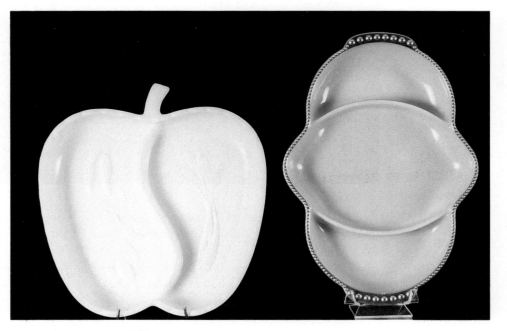

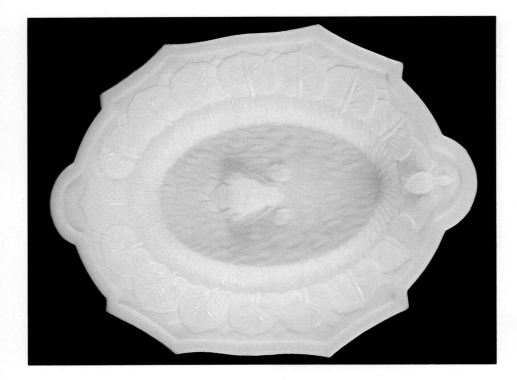

Plate 336 - Retriever platter. 9¾" x 13¼". A very popular and well-loved piece, although not too rare. Notice the lily pad border design and the dog swimming through the water after the wounded duck. All in all a beautiful piece of mold work. *$75.00 – 90.00.*

Plate 337 - Rock of Ages, 13" bread tray in crystal with milk glass center. Around the crystal edge is says: "Give Us This Day Our Daily Bread." Under the center medallion is "Pat. Nov. 23, 1875." On the cross is inscribed: "Simply to Thy Cross I Cling." "Rock of Ages" is imprinted under the figures. By Atterbury. Also in all milk glass (Pat. Dec 7, 1875) and in transparent blue and clear with blue insert. The central milk glass medallion is made separately from the crystal and somehow fused (glued?) in. *$150.00 – 165.00.*

Plate 338 - Diamond Grille, 12" bread plate. An Atterbury product shown in their 1874 catalog. Around the edges is the legend: "Give us this day our daily bread." *$45.00 – 50.00.*

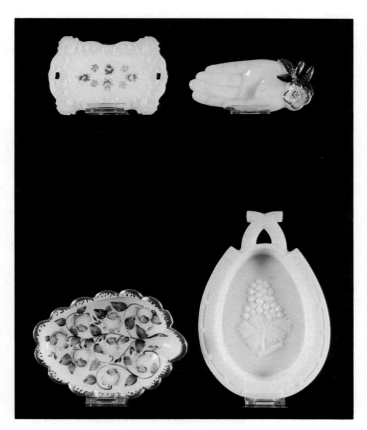

Plate 339 - TOP: 11½" x 10½", Big Leaf dish by Fenton Art Glass, 1955. *$20.00 – 25.00.* Lady and Fan, 7" dish. A beautifully sculpted "topless" lady reclining on an open fan. Fiery opalescent edges. *$45.00 – 50.00.*
BOTTOM: Child and Shell tray, 8¾" x. 6¾". Called by several names including Moses in Bulrushes. Deeply and beautifully sculptured. Be careful though, it was reproduced in recent years as a soap dish for Avon. *$80.00 – 90.00.* 8½" x 8" Small Leaf by Fenton Art Glass. *$15.00 – 20.00.*

Plate 340 - TOP: 5" x 3½" Lion Face or Monkey Face pin tray by Kemple. Says "Hand-Painted" on back, which means it was probably decorated by Lornita Glass. *$12.00 – 17.00.* 5" x 2½", Helping Hand flower pin tray by McKee during the Depression era. *$15.00 – 20.00.*
BOTTOM: 6¼" x 4½" shell dish with beautiful hand-painted roses by Cambridge Glass. Back is very sculptured in shell pattern. *$35.00 – 40.00.* Horseshoe and Grapes, 7¾" x 5½" tray by Imperial Glass, 1950's. *$15.00 – 20.00.*

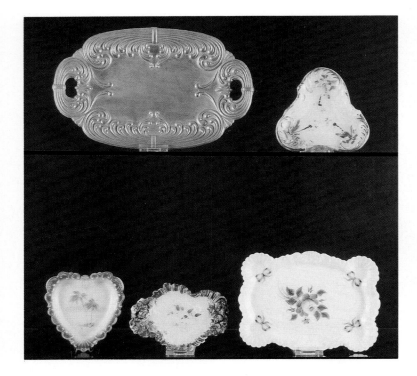

Plate 341 - TOP: Heavy Scroll, 11½" x 7" dresser tray. This one is completely covered in gold paint. *$20.00 – 25.00.* 5½" Rounded Triangle pin tray with flowers and gold. *$8.00 – 10.00.*

Bottom: Heart shaped 4¾" x 4¼" pin tray by Westmoreland in the Palm Tree pattern. *$10.00 – 12.00.* 6" x 4¼" pin tray with straight and stick pins embossed in the center. *$15.00 – 12.00.* 8¼" x 6" tray hand painted by Louise Plues in the Roses and Bows pattern for Phil Rosso in 1992. Old Westmoreland mold now marked with the "R" inside a keystone which is the mark for Rosso. *$12.00 – 15.00.*

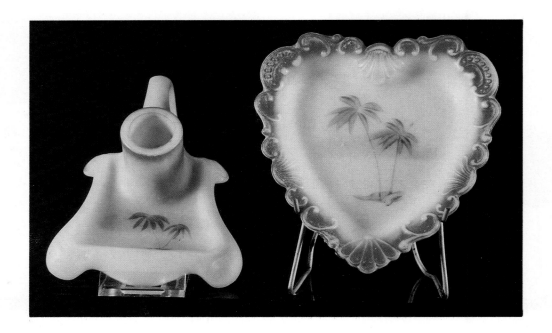

Plate 342 - More in the Palm Tree decorated set by Westmoreland Specialty Co. Candle is 3¾" at widest. Tray is 4¾" long. Quite number of items were included in this set:
#36 Short blown wide base vase. #27 Taller blown vase. #209 Pen tray (packed 20 doz. to a barrel). #214 Heart tray (shown). #215 Diamond tray. #216 Club tray. #219 Match holder or toothpick. #222 Spade tray. #235 Candle holder (shown). #275 square jewel box. #282 Child's mug. #294 Sugar bowl. #295 Creamer. #344 Coaster. #346 Large round ashtray. #451 Oval covered box. #703 Hatchet. All originally retailed from twelve to fifteen cents each! *N.P.A. for all items.*

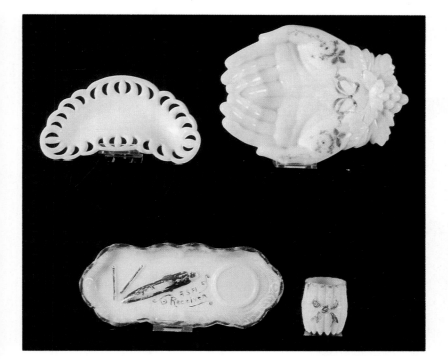

Plate 343 - TOP: Lacey Edge, 6¼" bone dish. $30.00 – 35.00. Westmoreland's Queen Victoria's Hands tray. This design was patented in 1875 by George Hatch and the English pieces carry a registry mark. Atterbury made the piece in 1881 and called it a "Card Holder" (for calling cards). Made in opal, pink opaque, and amber. Westmoreland Specialty Company introduced it in the late 1930's and made it until their closing in 1985. Also found in green milk, almond, coral, and blue milk. This particular piece carries the Roses & Bows decor. $45.00 – 50.00.

BOTTOM: Here we have the ash receiver about 1899. Also pictured elsewhere in this book. $55.00 – 60.00 set.

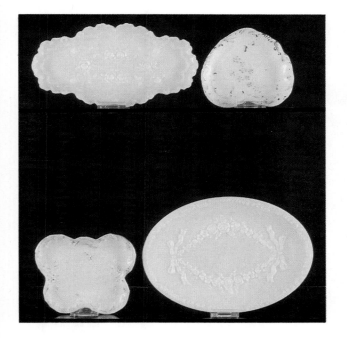

Plate 344 - TOP: Versailles pin tray, 9⅜" x 5". By Dithridge. $20.00 – 22.00. Heart-shaped pin tray, 5⅛" x 4⅞". $8.00 – 10.00.

BOTTOM: Five Loops or Butterfly shape 5⅝" x 4¾" pin tray. $10.00 – 12.00. Rose Garden tray, 6¾" x 9⅝". $12.00 – 15.00.

Plate 345 - TOP: Shape and edges of this 9⅜" x 5" tray are the same as Versailles, but instead of rose garlands, this has five-petaled daisy-like flowers in chains. Dithridge. $20.00 – 22.00. Deep blue, 8⅞" x 4½" tray with Scroll Edge. Shown in Butler Brothers 1905 catalog in a set consisting of two large toilet bottles, one large and one smaller tray, covered puff box, and jewel box. Sold at $.69 a set! $20.00 – 25.00.

BOTTOM: Summer Flowers comb and brush tray, 12½" x 8½". Flowers are embossed and then painted. $25.00 – 30.00.

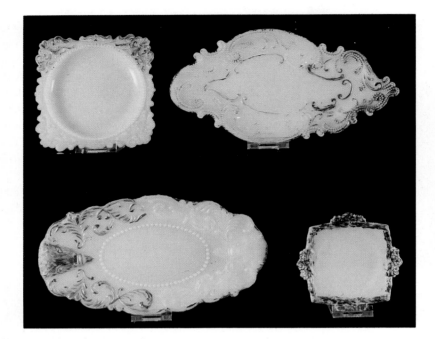

Plate 346 - TOP: 4½" square Fleur de Lis & Scroll, beaded circle center. $7.00 – 10.00. 8½" Fine Beaded tray. The little beads on this tray are wonderfully fiery! $12.00 – 15.00.
BOTTOM: 8½" Buffalo Head tray marked "M." $35.00 – 40.00. 4" square Leaf & Branch pin dish. The gold on these pieces has been enhanced to show pattern more clearly. $6.00 – 10.00.

Plate 347 - Beautiful butterfly-shaped 5½" x 4" pin tray with hand-painted floral spray and lavish gold. $15.00 – 20.00.

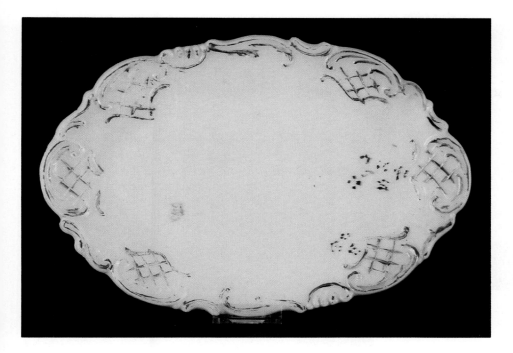

Plate 348 - Crosshatch comb and brush tray, 10" x 6¾". *$20.00 – 25.00.*

Plate 349 - Bottom view of Crosshatch comb and brush tray showing relief advertising message: "Souvenir of Freed Furniture and Carpet Co." Trays are not unusual, but finding one with this permanent (not painted) advertising is difficult at best.

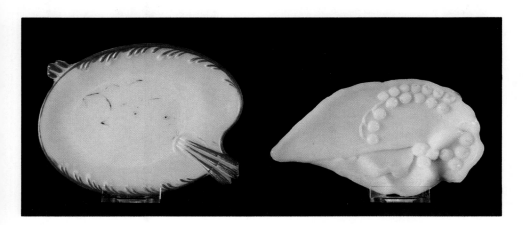

Plate 350 - Artist's Palette, 5¾" at widest point. Decorated with red paint and evidently had a central decoration also, now worn off. *$20.00 – 25.00.* Leaf with highly sculpted lily of the valley flowers. Makers unknown. *$8.00 – 12.00.*

Plate 351 - Wagon Wheel dresser tray, 7⅜" x 10¼". Also found in a larger size decorated with "Happy Easter." *$15.00 – 20.00.*

Plate 352 - **TOP:** Very heavy, 6½" x 10" Grape Cluster tray by Imperial Glass, 1951 – 1952. *$20.00 – 25.00.* 10¼" x 7" Sunflower Tray. *$30.00 – 35.00.*
BOTTOM: 10" x 8" comb & brush tray marked McKee. Venetian pattern. Belknap calls it Chrysanthemum (57), Millard calls it Dahlia Corner (38). *$30.00 – 35.00.* 10" x 7¾" dresser tray with embossed leaves scattered. *$15.00 – 20.00.*

Plate 353 - Here we have three out of a set of four Trivet ashtrays made by Imperial Glass, 1950–1964. *$35.00 – 40.00, set of four.*

Plate 354 - An assortment of dresser trays made in abundance by a number of glasshouses from around 1880–1915. TOP: 9¾" long with lovely hand-painted roses in the center and much gold-covered scroll-work. *$15.00 – 18.00.*

BOTTOM: 6¼" diameter, handled scroll tray. *$8.00 – 10.00.* 5½" oval Grape pattern tray sometimes found with Four-sided Grape shakers on it. See Shaker section of this book. *$10.00 – 12.00.*

Plate 355 - 11⅛" x 7⅜" tray. Belknap calls it Monkey Face Tray. Or could it be a lion? I vote for lion... Originator uncertain, but made later in two sizes by Kemple Glass. *$25.00 – 30.00.*

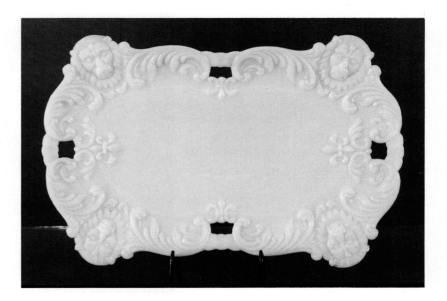

Plate 356 - Souvenir ashtray, 5⅝" wide, 7¼" long. Depicts four monks around a wine cask. Legend is "Souvenir of Deckerville, Michigan." There is an eagle embossed on one end and crossed flags on the other. Notice that the mold did not fill entirely on the right end just above the flags and also on the base for the flags. They didn't care in those days — they just went ahead and painted it anyway! *$45.00 – 50.00.*

Plate 357 - Ashtrays — some folks believe with all the furor over smoking, ashtrays will one day disappear...well, we'll see.
TOP: 3⅞" diameter, Indian Head tray. *$20.00 – 25.00.* 4⅜" diameter, Straw Hat or Skimmer by Westmoreland. Mold now owned by Summit Art Glass and made in cobalt and carnival and maybe more. *$25.00 – 30.00.*
BOTTOM: Bare Foot, 4¾" long. Unmarked. *$12.00 – 15.00.* 5½" long Banjo, also no markings. *$10.00 – 12.00.*

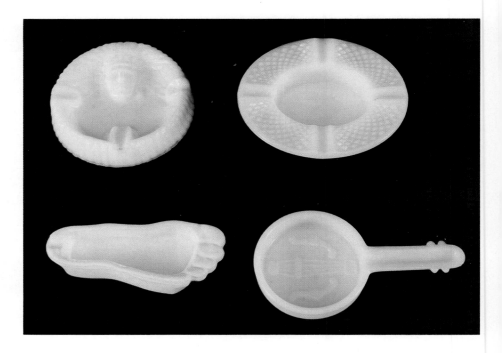

Plate 358 - Delicate little bridge set done in a very opalescent glass. Average 3¼" diameter and come with several floral decorations. At first thought to be Westmoreland, but second thoughts have come up on that. *$25.00 – 30.00 set.*

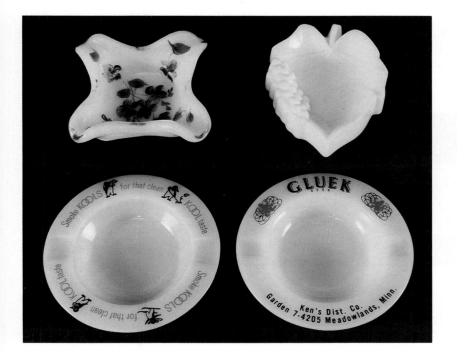

Plate 359 - TOP: 5¼" diagonal heavy, hand-painted ashtray in the Regent line by Consolidated Glass. *$15.00 – 20.00.* 4¾" Grape Leaf ashtray by Imperial Glass, 1951–1969 and again in 1977–1979. *$8.00 – 10.00.*
BOTTOM: Two advertising, 5¼" diameter ashtrays, maker unknown. *$5.00 – 7.00.*

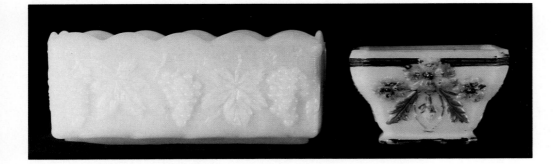

Plate 360 - Rectangular, 8" x 3½", Grape pattern planter in Fire King by Anchor Hocking. 1960's. *$4.00 – 6.00*. Square planter bowl with corners cut at an angle. 4⅜" square, maker unknown. *$10.00 – 12.00*.

Plate 361 - Old King Cole and friends on a 3¼" tall, 5" long planter. Little Bo Peep decoration, 3½" tall, 4" long. Jack & Jill, 3½" tall, 3⅛" long. All by Sowerby of England. *Range $75.00 – 125.00*.

Plate 362 - Open satchel, 3¼" tall, 3¾" long. Marked and registered between 1876–1880. Rectangular "Birds Nest" posy holder. 2½" tall, 6¼" long. Design has four "Sunbonnet-type" girls looking at a birds nest, accompanied by a sheep and a frog. John Sowerby illustrated children's books in a Kate Greenaway style, which certainly shows up on this piece. Vase or planter, 3" tall, 4⅝" long. Shows a mother with baby on her knee sitting in a window with drapes and brick sill. Legend says "Ma Mammy, Dance a Baby." End panels depict a crying toddler, maybe jealous of the new baby? All have Sowerby Peacock mark. *$75.00 – 125.00*.

Plate 363 - Assortment of Sowerby pieces. 4½" vase showing on various panels, man with fan, priest with book, lady with ceremonial piece, and man alone. Hexagonal handled basket, 3¼" tall. Registry mark. Rather squashed basket, 2½" tall. No mark. Footed tumbler, 3⅜" high. Shows man offering flowers to lady and cupid flying nearby. All have Peacock mark but the squashy basket. *$75.00 – 125.00.*

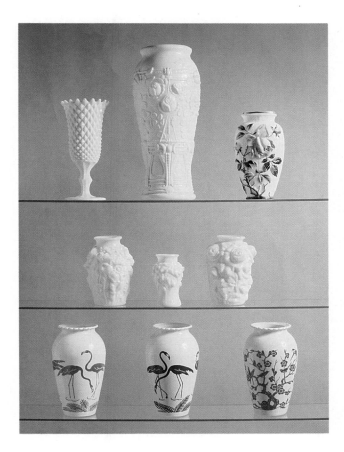

Plate 364 - 1ST ROW: Sawtooth pedestal vase. *$10.00 – 12.00.* Westmoreland pickle jar vase, 14" tall, early 1920's. *$75.00 – 100.00.* Bristol type hand-painted with splashy flowers. *$30.00 – 35.00.*
2ND ROW: Gaudy Roses vases in several sizes and shapes. These have blown-out roses and flowers that really "stand out." Some molds made later by Imperial, 1955–1968. *$40.00 – 45.00.*
3RD ROW: Several different decorations of Anchor Hocking vases, 1940's–1950's. *$8.00 – 10.00.*

Plate 365 - 9" blue vase with blown-out scrollwork. Turn of the century. *$30.00 – 35.00.* 5⅜" tall Admiral Nelson vase. Contains portrait of Nelson on one side and roses and vines on the other. Around Admiral Nelson's portrait is "21 Oct. 1805–21 Oct. 1905." An English centennial piece. *$35.00 – 40.00.*

Plate 366 - l to r: 3⅜" squared urn shape vase. Modern, maker unknown. $5.00 – 7.00. 4¾" Hobnail bud vase by Fenton Art Glass. $15.00 – 20.00. 5⅛" Horse and Foliage vase by L. E. Smith for Mary Walrath, about 1981, found in many colors. $15.00 – 20.00. 3¾" vase, Raised Grape clusters. Modern. Maker unknown. $5.00 – 7.00.

Plate 367 - TOP: Westmoreland Lily of the Valley vase, 6", with the top spread out to form a different shape than usually found. $25.00 – 30.00. 5¾" vase in the Con-Cora line by Consolidated and decorated by Fay Forsythe. $20.00 – 25.00.
BOTTOM: Westmoreland, 6½" Three Swans vase. $30.00 – 35.00. Gaudy Roses, 5¼" vase blown out and deeply sculptured roses are crammed together to form this vase. Shown in Butler Brothers 1905 catalog. $20.00 – 25.00.

Plate 368 - Mephistopheles, 9½" vase. Squared shape. Alternate panels have embossed roses. Vallerysthal. $60.00 – 80.00.

Plate 369 - Lamp shaped vase in the Grape pattern, 7¼" tall. By Imperial Glass, 1953–1960. *$20.00 – 25.00.* Lamp shaped vase in Hobnail pattern by Imperial Glass, 1955–1960. *$25.00 – 30.00.*

Plate 370 - Flame vase, 9" tall by Dithridge. Shown in Butler Brothers 1910 catalog. *$25.00 – 30.00.* 4¼" tall vase or perhaps toothbrush holder. Maker unknown. *$20.00 – 25.00.*

Plate 371 - Westmoreland Lily of the Valley, 7½" tall vase. *$25.00 – 30.00.* 6½", hand holding Hobnail cornucopia by Fenton Art Glass. *$30.00 – 35.00.* 6½", Imperial Glass Grape pattern vase, 1950–1969. *$25.00 – 30.00.*

Plate 372 - A group of Fostoria's Art Decorated vases ranging from 5" to 8" tall. Sprayed with background color, shaded, and then stenciled. Early 1900's –1920's. *$25.00 – 30.00. $40.00 – 45.00 with Indians.*

Plate 373 - 4½", bulbous vase by Fostoria. Turn of the century through 1920's. *$15.00 – 20.00.* 7¼" vase with splashy blown-out daffodil type flower covering side. *$50.00 – 55.00.* Dutch mother and child, 5¼" vase. Rare, especially with paint. *$30.00 – 35.00.* Jack in the Pulpit vase by Terry Crider. Flared top has applied clear red edge while the body is decorated with green glass strings. Early 1980's. *$40.00 – 45.00.*

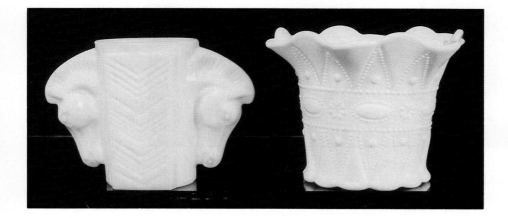

Plate 374 - Double Horse Head vase, 3¾" tall. Maker unknown. *$10.00 – 12.00.* Beaded Jewel or Lace & Dewdrop, 3½" x 4¾" vase with crimped top. By Kemple Glass. *$15.00 – 20.00.*

Plate 375 - Hand holding cornucopia or horn. Early 1900's. *$45.00 – 50.00.* Loganberry, 9" vase by Imperial Glass, 1950–1979. *$35.00 – 40.00.* 8½" Pyramid with Flowers vase. Raised, hand-painted roses decorate the sides. Early 1900's. *$25.00 – 30.00.*

Plate 376 - Grille & Scroll, 8½" vase, shown in Butler Brothers 1912 catalog. *$20.00 – 25.00.* Blown-out scrollwork vase, 8¾" tall. Shown in Butler Brothers 1910–1912 catalog. Probably Dithridge. *$20.00 – 25.00.* Also blue.

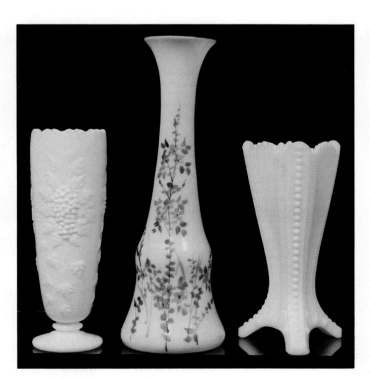

Plate 377 - Vintage Grape, 9" vase by L. E. Smith. 1970's. *$15.00 – 20.00.* Bristol type, 13½" vase. Blown and hand-painted. *$35.00 – 40.00.* Tri Panel, 9" vase by U.S. Glass. Shown in undated catalog. *$15.00 – 20.00.*

Plate 378 - Scroll and Daisy, 9" vase. Blown and hand decorated. 1905 catalog. *$20.00 – 25.00.* Bristol-type beauty, 10¼" tall. *$35.00 – 40.00.* 8½" Fostoria, Indian on Horseback. Art Decorated line from early 1900 to 1920's. *$45.00 – 50.00.*

Plate 379 - Bristol-type, 10" vase with hand-painted foliage and black edge and base bands. *$35.00 – 40.00.* Zipper & Jewel, 7" vase, maker unknown. *$12.00 – 15.00.* Another Bristol-type, 10" with beautiful hand-painted grosbeak and pink flowering branches. *$35.00 – 40.00.*

Plate 380 - 6", Cornucopia vase from Westmoreland's 1933 line. *$30.00 – 35.00.* 3¾" hat-shaped vase by Fenton Art Glass. Has amber crest, hand-painted flowers, and gold. *$30.00 – 35.00.* 3" Swan Song vase, Depression era, 1939, MacBeth Evans Co. *$12.00 – 15.00.*

Plate 381 - Corn vase, 4¼" tall. Maker unknown. Turn of the century. *$20.00 – 25.00.* Bud vase, 5¾" tall, fairly recent florist type vase. *$5.00 – 7.00.* Beads, Stars and Scroll, 6½" vase. Early 1900's. *$10.00 – 12.00.* 3¾", Hand with cornucopia by Fenton Art Glass. *$25.00 – 30.00.*

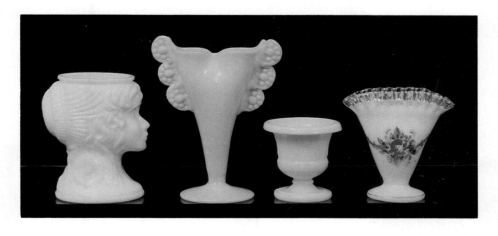

Plate 382 - Lady Head, 5" tall. Florist's ware about 1980. *$18.00 – 20.00.* Double opening, 6½" vase. This is a strange piece, perhaps a glass worker's whimsey. Has applied solid handles and the top is pinched in to form division. *$12.00 – 15.00.* Bianca, 3¼" urn by MacBeth Evans during the Depression era. *$10.00 – 12.00.* Fan vase, 4¼" tall with hand-painted rose bouquet and crystal ruffle edge that has been overpainted with gold. By Fenton Art Glass. *$25.00 – 30.00.*

Plate 383 - Flattened Sphere, 7" tall, 8" diameter with beautiful hand-painted floral bouquet. Marked decorated by Charlton. *$25.00 – 30.00.*

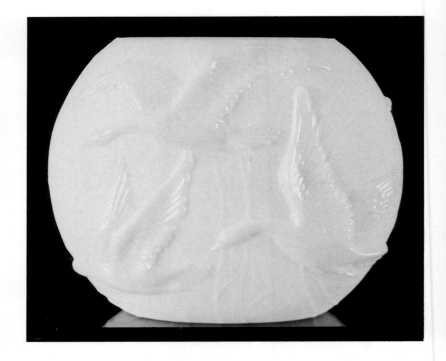

Plate 384 - Regent Line by Consolidated, 10" tall. Hand-painted with pinecones and needles. 1950's–1960's. *$30.00 – 35.00.*

Plate 385 - Wild Geese vase, 9¾" tall, 11½" wide. By Consolidated. *$135.00 – 140.00.*

Plate 386 - Regent line, 10" vase by Consolidated. Hand-painted with lovely violets. 1950's–1960's. *$30.00 – 35.00.*

Plate 387 - Con-Cora line, 12" vase by Consolidated. Hand-painted with lovely violets. 1950's–1960's. *$45.00 – 50.00.*

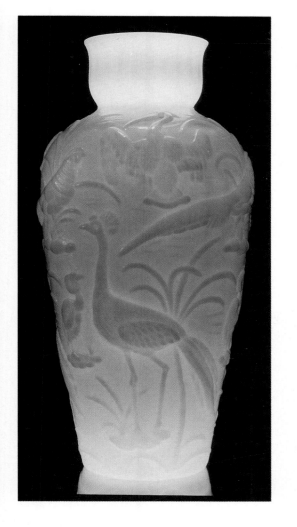

Plate 389 - Two Regent line vases by Consolidated. Both have hand-painted violets. 6½" tall. *$25.00 – 30.00.* 9¼" tall. *$25.00 – 30.00.*

Plate 388 - Bird vase, 15½" tall by Consolidated. *$130.00 – 145.00.*

Plate 390 - Regent line, 9½" tall vase by Consolidated. Hand-painted by Mary Livitski, 1956. *$30.00 – 35.00.*

Plate 391 - Regent line, 5¾" tall vase by Consolidated. 1950's–1960's. *$25.00 – 30.00.*

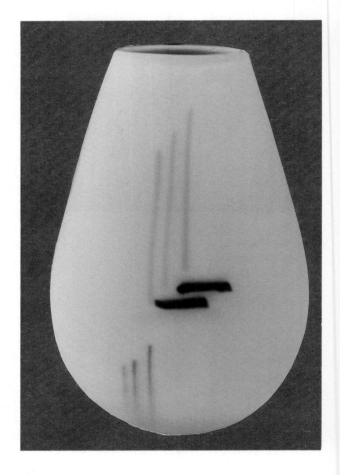

Plate 392 - 10" vase in satin finish milk with soft line decor in pastel colors. By Pairpoint, 1989. *$50.00 – 55.00.*

Plate 393 - Three sleighs by Fostoria in 3", 4¼", and 6" sizes. Made in mid- 1950's. *3", $30.00; 4¼", $35.00; 6", $40.00.*

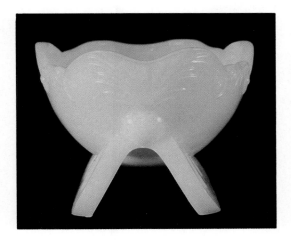

Plate 394 - Close-up of the front view of Fostoria sleighs. Notice the plume effect spreading to either side and the ball-like protrusion just above the front runners.

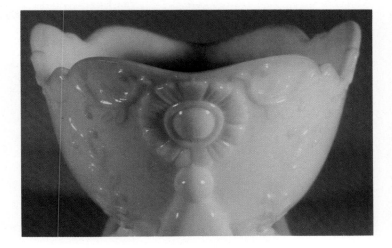

Plate 395 - Close-up of the front view of Westmoreland sleighs. Note the large daisy-like embossing just above the front runners. Also, Westmoreland sleighs have beading on the short runner supports, while Fostoria sleighs have entirely smooth runners.

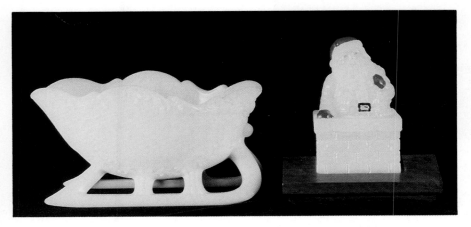

Plate 396 - Large, 9¼" long sleigh by Westmoreland. *$65.00 – 70.00.* Santa on Chimney by Fenton Art Glass. Pearlized finish. Wooden "roof" base is separate. A light can be placed inside the 3¼" square chimney. Without base: 5½" tall. Produced 1988. *$35.00, retail.*

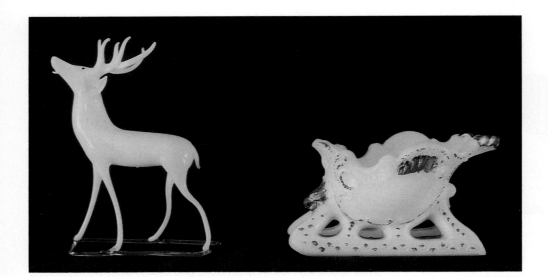

Plate 397 - German, blown reindeer on clear base. 4¾" tall. Scarce. *$75.00 – 95.00*. Rare Eagle Head sleigh. Belknap calls it a salt. 2⅝" tall, 4¾" long. Note the eagle head on the front just between the runners. Rare. *$50.00 – 60.00*.

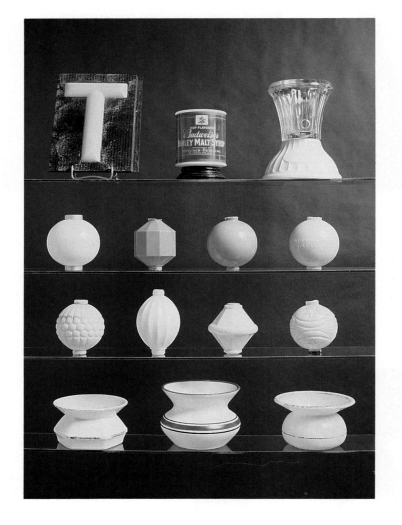

Plate 398 - 1ST ROW: Letter "T," probably from an old movie house marquee. In old signs, the spaces were filled with tin pieces that locked together and had cut-out letters. The letters often were in milk glass so that the bulbs behind them could shine through and illuminate the "coming attraction." Usually about 8½" to 9" tall. *N.P.A.* Top and base for Malt Shoppe type drink mixer. *N.P.A.*

2ND & 3RD ROWS: Lightening Rod Balls. These were made in various shades of milk glass and in various patterns such as Moon & Star, about 1900–1927. Distributed by Lightening Rod companies and made by several manufacturers such as Thompson Lightening Rod Co., Hawkeye Lighting Rod Co., and Cole Brothers Lightening Rod Company. *$65.00 – 75.00*.

4TH ROW: Various shapes and sizes of Spittoons. (Aren't you glad those days are gone?) *$30.00 – 35.00*.

Plate 399 - Ladies spittoon. 5⅜" tall, 7¼" diameter. Worn hand-painted floral decorations. *$30.00 – 35.00.*

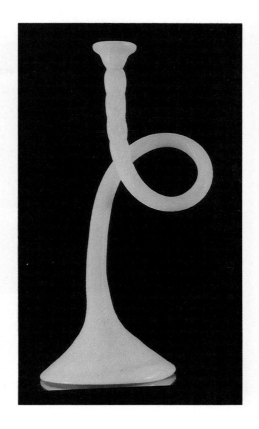

Plate 400 - An unusual glass bugle measuring 9" long with the bell being 3⅝" in diameter. Made by the glass blowers offhand work and it can really give a toot! Probably European. *N.P.A.*

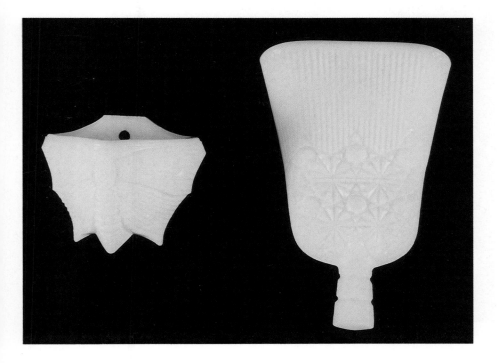

Plate 401 - Alpha Butterfly wall pocket, 4" wide. Maker unknown but probably early 1900's. *$35.00 – 40.00.* Whiskbroom wall pocket, 7½" long, by Imperial Glass. *$35.00 – 40.00.*

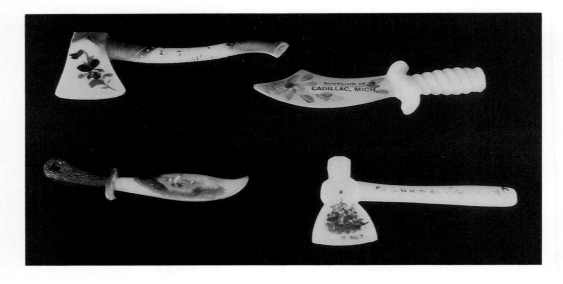

Plate 402 - **Top:** *7"* Axe. Souvenir piece with hand painting and gold. *$15.00 – 20.00.* 7⅛" long Scimitar, "Souvenir of Cadillac, Michigan." Made by U.S. Glass. *$20.00 – 25.00.* **BOTTOM:** 6½" long Sword with hand-painted boating scene on side of blade, and "Souvenir of Wilson, New York" on the back. *$25.00 – 30.00.*

Shingling Hatchet (according to Bill the tool buff). Hand-painted souvenir piece, 6¼" long. Worn enough to be unreadable. Shown in an old Cambridge Nearcut catalog, 1902–1924. *$18.00 – 22.00.*

Plate 403 - **Top:** 6½" x 6¼" Easel by Dithridge about 1900. Shown as Easter Easel in "China, Glass & Lamps" trade journal. *$35.00 – 40.00.* 5" bell with hand-painted cardinal by Westmoreland. *$18.00 – 22.00.* **BOTTOM:** 3½" stein with hand-painted scene. Top says "Field Artillary RGT No. 11, Cassel, 1907–09." Bottom is marked "Original BMF Schnapps Krugerl, made in West Germany." This interested me particularly because my paternal grandfather came from Cassel, Germany. *$30.00 – 35.00.* 3¾" playing card holder. Very worn and darkened. Dutch Windmill scene barely visible. *$20.00 – 25.00.* Train desk plaque, 4¼" x 2¾" by Fenton. Numbered 128 out of 5000. Hand-painted by Carol Shaffer. 1986. *$50.00 – 55.00.*

Plate 404 - TOP: Two 2½"
tall, 3¾" diameter Uncle
Sam hats. The hat on the
left is the old Westmore-
land Specialty hat. *$45.00
– 50.00, old.* On the right is
a new version made in the
1990's for Phil Rosso of
PA. Note the color differences: on the old hat, the
background of the star
band is painted blue
while on the new one, just
a few *stars* are blue. On
the old hat, the raised
vertical stripes are red,
but on the new version
only every other inset
stripe is red. *Currently
available.*
BOTTOM: Here we have
two versions of the Hom-
burg hat. The hat on the

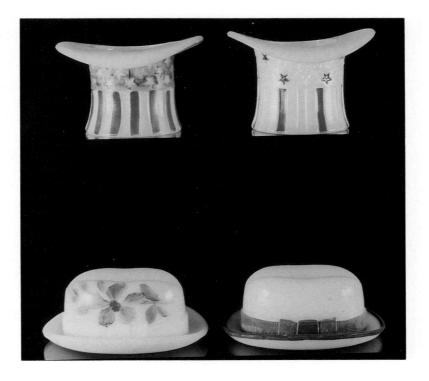

left is quite opalescent and hand-painted with flowers. *$25.00 – 30.00.* The one on the right has a sedate
gray grosgrain type band and brim edge. Made by U.S. Glass at Tiffin, 1924–1936. *$20.00 – 25.00.* The
lavender flower pattern on the left hat will be found on a number of U.S. Glass, Tiffin items.

Plate 405 - TOP: Tramp
Shoe, 3" tall. A well-worn
high top shoe with the
tramp's toes sticking out.
1890 originally. Kemple
reproduced. *$40.00 –
45.00.* 4" Coal Scuttle,
marked "Souvenir Mani-
tou Beach, Devil's Lake,
Mich." Produced by
Kemple and U.S. Glass.
$20.00 – 25.00. 2¾" tooth-
pick with allover floral
embossing. *$10.00 – 12.00.*
BOTTOM: 4" x 6½" footed
dish shaped like a scoop.
Millard calls it a "master
salt" but I'm afraid it is
rather large and rather
shallow for that. Butler
Brothers catalogs early

1900's. *$35.00 – 40.00.* Daisy & Button, 4¼" baby shoe by Fenton Art Glass. This early one is quite
opalescent — later ones are more dead white. Also made in many colors for many years. *$25.00 – 30.00.*

Plate 406 - TOP: 4¼" diameter, three-section egg holder with metal center handle. What else could it be? *$35.00 – 40.00.* 2⅞" hanging burnt match holder. Gillinder's 1900 catalog described it as "Made in opal glass, gold finished letters and brass chain." This hung on the gaslight fixture. *$30.00 – 35.00.* Three Bees or Bees on a Basket toothpick. Three variations are found, as shown, with a handle on the back top, and with handles on each side. Those with two side handles have been found as Sowerby's #213, however, no positive American manufacturer has been found. Seen in purple slag as well. Bees on the milk glass shown are gold with blue wings. *$30.00 – 35.00.*

BOTTOM: 6¼" long Canoe, usually found as souvenir piece. U.S. Glass, Tiffin, Ohio, 1924–36. *$15.00 – 20.00.* 3¼" tall mustard jar with hinged cover and hand-painted decor. *$15.00 – 20.00.* 3½" tall blue candle pot. Sometimes used in the mid 19th century with a wire hanger or tin lantern for hanging on Christmas Trees. They held water, with a layer of oil on top and a wick. Came in white, blue opaque, and a number of transparent colors and varying shapes. *$35.00 – 40.00.*

Plate 407 - Lovely, 9" lighthouse or Cabin Fairy light. Top piece sets on "brick" base. By Vallerysthal. *$225.00 – 250.00.*

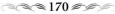

Plate 408 - Lilac-decorated Plum Crest basket by Fenton. 8¼" diameter. Signed by Bill Fenton and numbered. 1993. *$65.00, current retail.* Lace Edge basket by Imperial Glass. 8¾" long, 1956–1960. *$35.00 – 40.00.*

Plate 409 - l to r: Westmoreland, #602 egg cup, 3½" tall. *$15.00 – 20.00.* Westmoreland, #603 Chick emerging from egg cup, 3⅛" tall. *$15.00 – 20.00.* Opalex, France, egg cup 2¼" tall. *$8.00 – 10.00.* Swan salt, 3½" to top of neck, 4½" long. L. E. Smith. *$12.00 – 15.00.*

Plate 410 - An assortment of mainly Japanese-made Christmas light bulbs. Milk glass with hand-painted colors. There are many different variants available and appeal to both milk glass and Christmas collectors. *Wide price range dependant on subject.*

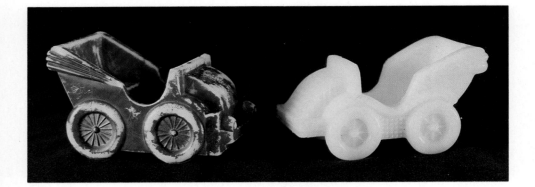

Plate 411 - A pair of Automobile figurals. 4¾" long, 3" tall. 4⅞" long, 2¾" tall. Notice the red car has headlights while the other does not. "Bill the Car Buff" says the red one is about a 1900–1905 model! In Butler Brothers 1906 catalog in crystal. $100.00 – 145.00.

Plate 412 - Horse and Cart, 9⅜" long, 4⅛" tall (cart). Sometimes called Donkey and Cart. By K. R. Haley Glass Company. Some were made with two ashtrays resembling hay that fit on top of the cart. (These I have never seen.) Crystal and milk glass. Recently reproduced in Mexico and Taiwan in crystal and milk glass. Also found in a smaller size. $30.00 – 35.00.

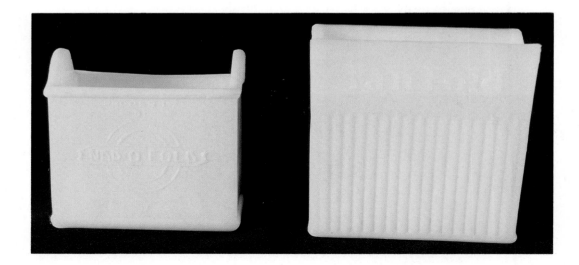

Plate 413 - Napkin holders. 4" tall, 4⅛" long. Says "Nar-O-Fold, Property of National Paper Napkin Co., Trade Mark; Chicago, Reg. U.S.A." $40.00 – 50.00. 4⅜" tall, 4⅝" long. Marked "Fan Fold" on one side and "Diana Mfg. Co, Green Bay, Wis." on other side. $40.00 – 50.00.

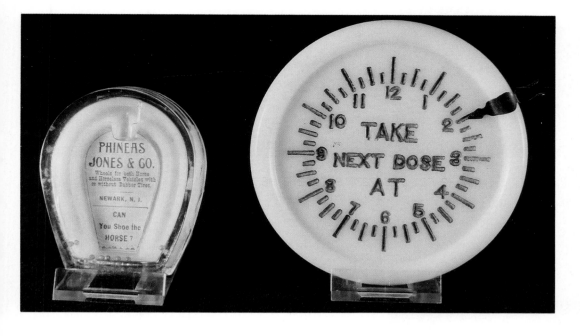

Plate 414 - Horseshoe game. 3" long. Back is marked "Pat. Oct 12, 1897." On front is "Phineas Jones & Co., Wheels for both horse and horseless vehicles with or without rubber tires, Newark, N.J." and "Can you shoe the horse?" The idea is to get the little moving beads into the nail holes on the shoe. Bill says it's a "tricky little son-of-a-gun." *$50.00 – 60.00.* Dosage Reminder. 4" diameter. Has an adjustable metal pointer to remind you when the next dose of medicine is due. On the back is "Acme Tumbler Cover and Dose Indicator, Sharon Mfg. Co., Philad, Pa. Pat. Applied For." Also found with "PATENTED NOV. 17th, 1896," and still another version will have U.S.A. above the patent date. Evidently the cover was sold boxed by itself and you were to use it with whatever tumbler you had on hand that it would fit. *$45.00 – 50.00.*

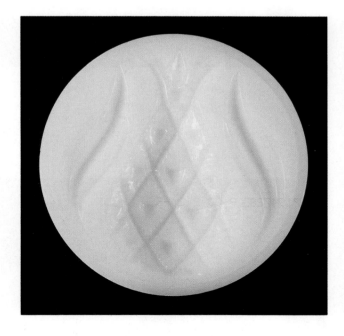

Plate 415 - Butter press. 4½" diameter. Top is decorated with hand-painted flowers while the underside is a Pineapple. It looks to this old farm girl like the press should fit right into a 2 lb. butter crock. You press the mold into the butter, leaving a pineapple on the top to "fancy it up." *$30.00 – 35.00.*

Plate 416 - Underside of butter press.

Plate 417 - Watering can, 2⅛" tall. Perhaps a toothpick or match holder. *$30.00 – 35.00.* Baby shoe, 2⅛" tall. This is a darling little shoe with gold-edged eyelets for lacing and a "worn" look. Very thin and porcelain-like. Decorated by Lornita Glass. *$35.00 – 40.00.* Sock darner. 5¾" long. Blown darning egg takes us back to the days when every housewife had a basketful of socks to darn. *$40.00 – 45.00.*

Plate 418 - Inkwell made to resemble an old-time lap desk. 3⅛" wide, 4" long. The well on the lower right for dipping the pen is removable. This is a charming little piece, hand decorated and with great mold work. Scarce. Perhaps French. *$75.00 – 90.00.*

Plate 419 - Old Oaken Bucket, 3½" tall. West Virginia Specialty Co. *$10.00 – 12.00.* Cradle, 5¼" long. Type of piece known as florist's ware with a bit more quality than usually found. Probably 1960's–70's. *$10.00 – 12.00.* Liberty Bell, 3½" tall with metal clapper. Legend says "Proclaim Liberty in Philad. by order of" On the other side is: "Pass & Stow Philad. M.D.C.C.L.I.I." Confused? Me too! *$20.00 – 25.00.*

Plate 420 - Horseshoe picture frame, 7" tall. An Atterbury product found in an 1881 catalog. Made in milk glass, clambroth, and other colors. Around the shoe is "Good Luck" while the tab just above the base section says "JUSTICE FOR ALL." *$100.00 – 120.00.* Skillet, 4¾" long, souvenir of New Orleans. U.S. Glass. *$45.00 – 55.00.*

Plate 421 - TOP: Easter basket, 4¼" long. Chicken head on one side and mean-looking rabbit on the other. Probably originally with wire bail handle. Same hen and rabbit we found on an old Easter egg; probably late 1800's or early 1900's. *$25.00 – 30.00.* Bird cage water cup. 3⅛" tall. Has embossed eagle and shield. *$10.00 – 12.00.*
BOTTOM: Child's compote or salt dip. Vallerysthal. *$10.00 – 15.00.* Horseshoe dish, 3" x 2½". *$10.00 – 12.00.* Turtle salt dip, 4½" long. (Shown upside down.) Vallerysthal, PV sticker, early 1900's. *$35.00 – 45.00.*

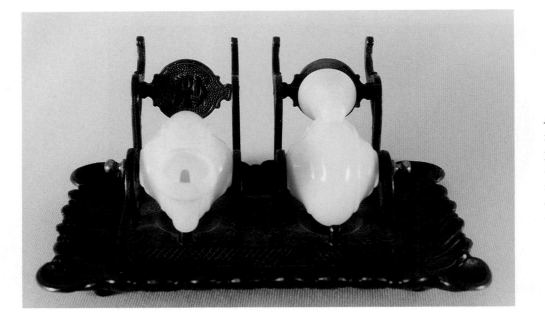

Plate 422 - Here we have a metal and white milk glass desk piece. The tray measures 8¾" x 5¾". The milk glass ink bottles rotate (shown with one up and one down) to use ink. Maker unknown. *$180.00 – 190.00.*

Plate 423 - Puss 'N Boot candy container by Westmoreland Specialty. 4" long. Marked "Souvenir of Breckenridge, Michigan." Milk glass was made at the turn of the century. Later in 1970's it was produced again in Softmist blue and green. Difficult to find. *$80.00 – 90.00.*

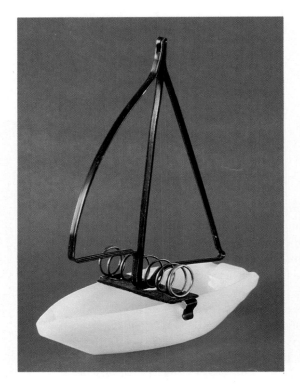

Plate 424 - Sailboat ashtray with metal sails. 6¼" long. Marked "Made in USA Pat. D124322." Your cigarette fit into the metal spring and if left burning, it would put itself out when the coals reached the spring. *$20.00 – 25.00.*

Plate 425 - Easter eggs. Plain, 2¾" egg box. *$8.00 – 10.00.* 6" blown egg with embossed "Easter Greetings" and allover scattered hand-painted flowers. *$35.00 – 40.00.* Chick emerging from egg. 3⅜" long. "Easter" painted on. Late 1800's. *$45.00 – 50.00.*

Plate 426 - 6" blown-out egg with cross, hand-painted flowers, and word "Easter." *$35.00 – 40.00.* 5" egg with embossed scroll, flowers and "Easter." *$30.00 – 35.00.*

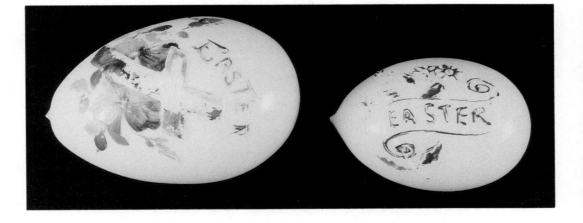

Plate 427 - Chick emerging from egg, 2½" long. *$40.00 – 45.00.* 4" egg with Easter and leaves embossed and gold touched. *$30.00 – 35.00.* Easter and full chick figure, 4" long. *$25.00 – 30.00.* All blown eggs, made by many companies around 1899, including National Glass, Gillinder, Eagle.

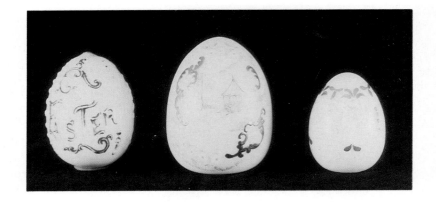

Plate 428 - These three eggs have flat spots on the bases so they will stand upright. Scrolled egg, 3¾" with raised "Easter" on one side and "Greetings" on the other. *$25.00 – 30.00.* Eggs made by Fenton Art Glass in 1991. Larger pearlized egg has gazebo and weeping cherry tree. *$60.00, current retail.* Smaller has pastel flowers. *$50.00, current retail.* This was Fenton's first time using real gold trim.

Plate 429 - 5" Easter basket egg with word "Easter" above the basket. *$25.00 – 30.00.* 6" egg has hand-painted forget-me-not wreath. Satin

finish. *$30.00 – 35.00.* 2⅜" molded solid egg with chick peeking out by Mosser Glass, 1993. *Currently Available.* 4" blown egg with chick emerging also has flat base for display. Gillinder & Sons, about 1889, and U.S. Glass about 10 years later. *$40.00 – 45.00.*

Plate 430 - Blown Easter eggs were a specialty of Eagle Glass, but were produced by many glasshouses during the late 1800's and early 1900's. Ornately scrolled egg with a rabbit head on the opposite side. Also has a flat base to keep it from rolling. *$35.00 – 40.00.* 6½" Horseshoe trimmed with hand-painted flowers and word "Easter." *$30.00 – 35.00.* 4¼" homely, swirl-decorated egg. Cold painted, manufactured this way, or did somebody do it in their home? *$5.00 – 7.00.*

Plate 432 - Clock, 6½" x 4½". "Davies" in shield on front. Pat. May 15, 1877. *$200.00 – 225.00.*

Plate 431 - Clock, 8" tall. Has a cherub peeking out above the clock face. Maker unknown, however, is seen with "Pat. June 12, June 13, 1900." *$250.00 – 275.00.*

Plate 433 - Satin milk glass clock, 5¾" tall. Base is 4¼" x 6½". A draped cherub stands on either side. The clock mechanism is by New Haven Clock Co. Maker unknown. *$225.00 – 250.00.*

Plate 434 - Here we have McKee's Wren Hut and bracket. Hut is 6" tall. Bracket extends 4" from vertical surface. *$75.00 – 80.00.* One rarely finds the bracket with this piece. The hut will be found with a green roof also. There is a snap-on tin bottom for cleaning the hut. The idea was to be able to watch the family of birds from your window. Unfortunately, nobody took into consideration that inside a solid glass piece such as this, the temperature in summer could reach 130 degrees! A reward was offered to anyone who would send McKee a photo of birds using their hut, but it was never claimed. 1930's.

Plate 435 - Grape snack tray with cup well and cup by Indiana Glass. Tray, 8¼" x 10". Cup, 3" tall. *$8.00 – 12.00, set.* 1960's–1970's.

How many of you can remember the days when gasoline was twenty-five cents a gallon and the pumps were topped with big milk glass globes, Shells, Crowns, and Eagles? Back in the 1920's, 30's and 40's most gas pumps sported the globes, mainly used for advertising, but also handy to keep rain, snow, and dirt out of the pumps. By the 1950's, the globes began to disappear. Companies began changing the style of the pumps to flat tops, and the glass globes were expensive to replace.

The globes vary in shape and size as well as material. Very early globes from the 1920's or before were made of globular-shaped milk glass with the company name painted or etched on the glass. Some of the early 15" and 16½" globes had two metal rims into which the glass disks fit, one on each side. Later the trend went toward a plastic body containing two 13½" glass lenses. Finally, the interesting old globes vanished entirely. Today, collectors hunt for the White Eagle, the Standard Oil Crown, and logos featuring any of the small independent companies such as Aviation Gas and White Rose that flourished for a time and then disappeared. These gas station globes are a double collectible, hunted by milk glass collectors as well as auto buffs.

Plate 436 - Texaco Sky Chief gas pump globe. *$495.00 – 500.00.*

Plate 437 - Gas pump globes without glass or plastic advertising insert looked like this. *$150.00 – 200.00.*

Plate 438 - Sinclair Power-X gas pump globe. *$250.00 – 300.00.*

Plate 439 - Standard Oil of Indiana crown shape gas pump globe. The Standard Crown with raised lettering are 1920's, one-piece globes. Those made in the 1950's have no raised letters. And why doesn't it surprise me to learn that even gas pump globes are now being reproduced. *$1200.00+ for old.*

GLASS COMPANY HISTORIES

AKRO AGATE COMPANY

Akro Agate started in Akron, OH, in 1911 by George Renkin, Gilbert Marsh, and Horace Hill. They moved to Clarksburg, WV, in 1914, where they began manufacturing their own glass. Their only product was marbles until 1932, when they branched out into children's dishes, and flower containers. Akro went out of business in 1951. Their trademark was a crow flying through the letter "A." The crow has a marble in each claw and one in his beak, although usually the marks are so small it is difficult to detect these without a magnifying glass. Some pieces have "Made in U.S.A." on them, and a few will have a mold number.

ATTERBURY & COMPANY

The White House Works was established in Pittsburgh, PA, in 1859, by Hale, Atterbury & Co. By 1865–67 the firm name was Atterbury & Co., owned by James S. and Thomas B. Atterbury. In 1893, the firm became Atterbury Glass Company with the sons of James and Thomas managing.

James Seamen Atterbury and Thomas Bakewell Atterbury were grandsons of Job Atterbury and Sarah Bakewell Atterbury, sister of Benjamin Bakewell, founder of Bakewell, Page and Bakewell. Beginning and ending dates for the company are uncertain, as various references give different dates. However, from the beginning, they were noted for fine tableware including milk white, opaque blue, opaque green, and opaque lavender flint glass; plain and colored glass; lamps; fancy colored bar bottles; gas and kerosene globes. They exhibited and glassware at the 1876 Centennial Exposition, and received an award for lime glass lamps, chimneys, and globes.

Many design and invention patents were issued to Atterbury. Especially in covered animal dishes, their designs and products were outstanding. Advertised were "white rabbits with imported pink glass eyes and blue and dappled hens with ruby eyes made in Bohemia." Glass eyes cost the buyer extra. Most Atterbury animal dish covers are smooth on the underside surface that touches the base, unlike the products of Kemple, for instance, where that surface is usually finely stippled. Atterbury ceased business about 1903.

BOYD'S CRYSTAL ART GLASS, INC.

This family operation was founded in 1978 by Bernard C. Boyd and his son Bernard F. Boyd in the old Degenhart factory building in Cambridge, OH. They acquired 50 Degenhart molds then, and have since produced many original Boyd molds. A number of old Imperial Glass molds have also been added to their stock. The plant is currently owned and operated by Bernard F. Boyd, his wife Sue, and their son John. Bernard C. passed away in 1988.

Every five years, the Boyd mark is changed to help the collector date his pieces. Trademarks are: 1978–1983— B inside a diamond; 1983–1988— B inside a diamond with a bar underneath; 1988–1993— B inside a diamond with a bar at top and bottom of the diamond.

CAMBRIDGE GLASS COMPANY

The Cambridge Glass Company was incorporated first in 1873 with eight incorporators. Evidently, however, they failed to sell enough stock to finance the company. In 1901, another groups of men applied for a charter, only to find that a Cambridge Glass Company already existed, as the old charter had never been cancelled by the state. This group of incorporators also owned the National Glass Company of Pennsylvania. Officials of National Glass appointed Arthur J. Bennett to manage the new factory in Ohio. By 1907, National was facing bankruptcy, whereupon Mr. Bennett purchased the company. After a number of "up and down" years, Cambridge became known as one of the makers of really fine glass in the country, manufacturing tableware, stemware, tumblers, giftware, and novelties in many designs. Production ceased on June 17, 1954.

Cambridge's production of milk glass was confined mainly to the years 1951 and 1952. Items made in milk glass are as follows:

W 54 – 55 Jug and tumblers	W93 12 oz. Mug
W60 Jug	W94 3" Swan
W61 Sugar and creamer	W95 4½" Swan
W62 Sugar and creamer	W96 6½" Swan
W63 Sugar and creamer	W97 8½" Swan
W65 Goblet	W98 4½" Swan candle
W66 Sherbet	W118 Deviled egg plate
W67 Tumbler	W119 Heron figure flower holder
W68 Tumbler	W120 Girl figure
W71 Decanter	W121 Scotty book ends
W85 Puff box and lid	W123 3" Urn
W86 Honey dish and lid	W124 4½" Vase
W87 Urn with lid	W125 3½" Vase
W88 Candlestick	W126 5" Vase
W89 Candy box with lid	W127 6" Vase
W90 Three ounce oil	W127 Pigeon book ends
W91 Three-light candle	W128 7½" Vase
W92 3½" Cornucopia	W129 12" Vase

CHALLINOR, TAYLOR & CO., LTD.

This was founded by David Challinor in Pittsburgh, PA. After working for a number of glasshouses including Bakewall & Pears where he was one of the few making silvered glass, Challinor became partners with Edward Dithridge, and went in business under the name of Dithridge & Company. This lasted about seven years. After this, he formed a partnership with Edward Hogan and purchased the Pittsburgh Glass Manufacturing Company in 1864. The company was called Challinor, Hogan and Company and their main product was lamps. In 1885, David Challinor and his new partner David Taylor transferred the factory to Tarentum, PA, to a site along the Allegheny River, being now known as Challinor, Taylor & Co. In 1891 the plant became part of U.S. Glass Company, known as Plant C. The facility burned shortly after that and was never rebuilt.

David Challinor received his early training at Bakewell & Pears, along with one of the Atterburys, which may explain in part why the products of these two firms are so similar. In June of 1886, Challinor patented the manufacture of "mosaic glass" or what collectors now call "slag." Challinor's mosaic was very sharp and clean and not as blended as English ware. Opaque white, blue, and green along with much transparent, tinted, and art glass were products of this glasshouse. In 1891 the very popular "Farm Yard Assortment" was introduced, which included the covered hen, rooster, and Mother Eagle on basket base; the Block Swan; Wavy Base Duck; and Open Block Fish pickle. This assortment was also produced in transparent colors and painted crystal, along with milk glass.

COUDERSPORT TILE & ORNAMENTAL GLASS CO.

This company originated Feb. 5, 1900, in Coudersport, PA. They produced glass tiles and a variety of plain and fancy glassware. The company used several names during their production years: Webb Patent Tile Co., Coudersport Tile & Glass Co., Joseph Webb Glass Works, and Barstow Glass Company. Fire destroyed the plant in 1904.

Shards have been found at the factory site of white and blue milk glass; pink, green, and custard translucent glass; and a pink and white slag type. The milk glass Hen on Rush Base is now attributed to Coudersport as well as Cane Woven, Stag & Holly, Fleur-de-Lis in Scroll, and Endless Vine, among other patterns. No catalogs have been found for this company which makes proof of production rather "iffy."

DITHRIDGE & COMPANY

Dithridge and Company was located in New Brighton, PA. In 1857, Edward Dithridge was a glass blower employed by Fort Pitt Glass Works. By the mid 1860's Dithridge purchased the plant! Now there's the American dream for you! Upon his death in 1873, his son, Edward D. Dithridge, Jr. continued the plant operation as Dithridge & Co. In 1881, he purchased the Union Flint Glass factory where he manufactured mainly lamp parts under the name Dithridge Flint Glass Works – Dithridge Chimney Company. In 1887 he moved to New Brighton. In the late 1880's the craze for opal glass began, at which point the plant began to make crystal and milk glass tableware and novelties, plus opalescent and colored glass decorated with enamels. The plant closed in 1901.

DUNCAN & MILLER GLASS COMPANY

The history of Duncan & Miller is a varied one. In 1866 Ripley and Co. began production in Pittsburgh, PA, at 10th and Washington Streets. The company consisted of Daniel C. Ripley, George Duncan, Thomas Coffin, John and Jacob Strickel, and Nicholas Kunzler. They made flint glass tableware, bar goods, cut, engraved, and pressed glass. In 1874, the company became George Duncan & Sons, being George Duncan Sr., George Duncan, Jr., James E. Duncan, and Augustus H. Heisey. Around 1886 or shortly after, the company became Duncan & Heisey (James E. Duncan and Augustus Heisey). In 1891 they joined U.S. Glass and in 1892 fire destroyed the plant and dissolved the association with U.S. Glass. A new plant was opened in Washington, PA. In 1900 they incorporated, with officers and owners being Mrs. Anna Duncan, James E. Duncan, Andrew P. Duncan, Harry Duncan, and J. Ernest Miller. The new company was named the Duncan and Miller Glass Company.

After many successful years, the plant closed in 1955. Some molds and equipment were sold to U.S. Glass in Tiffin, OH, who produced ware under the "Duncan Miller Division" name. Milk glass was made until World War II when some of the necessary ingredients were no longer available. Fire destroyed the building in 1956.

EAGLE GLASS & MANUFACTURING CO.

Eagle Glass was founded by four Paull brothers: James, H. W., S. O., and Joseph in Wellsburg, WV, in 1894. They specialized in lamps, globes, decorated opal items, novelties. Glass jars, druggist bottles, nest eggs, kerosene lamps and shades were also produced. During 1897 – 1898 they had the largest line of opal novelties on the market. Their first product, and one that continued for many years, was the glass liners for metal caps on fruit jars. The company as such ended in 1924. After that time the word "glass" was dropped from the title and metal items were manufactured such as oil and gas containers, safety cans and oilers, still under the third and fourth generation members of the Paull family.

FENTON ART GLASS COMPANY

Frank Leslie Fenton began this company in Martins Ferry, OH, in 1905. The plant decorated glass made by other glasshouses. Fenton opened their own glasshouse in Williamstown, WV, in about 1907. Family members were Frank, John, Charles, Bob, and Jim Fenton. They are makers of a large variety of art glass, mainly by hand work, and are still in operation today. Frank Fenton claims Fenton has made almost every one of their hundreds and hundreds of molds in milk glass at one time or another.

FLACCUS BROTHERS CO. - E.C. FLACCUS CO.

This company began as E.C. Flaccus Company in Wheeling, WV. It was also known as George Flaccus & Sons, which was a food-related business begun around 1877. They were makers of catsup, mustard, mincemeat, vinegar, and preserves. Flaccus designed milk glass packer's containers, which were then manufactured by other glasshouses for them. There was a cousin, Charles Flaccus, in Tarentum, PA, who made glass containers and undoubtedly some of the ones used for condiments came from his plant also. By 1898 there was a split among the Flaccus brothers, and after that time, exact dates of production and closure are cloudy.

FOSTORIA GLASS COMPANY

Fostoria Glass Co. was founded by L. B. Martin in 1887 at Fostoria, OH. They moved to Moundsville, WV, in 1891. They were absorbed by the Lancaster-Colony Organization in 1983, and the doors closed in 1986.

Fostoria was a maker of fine, hand-made glassware of all types. To milk glass collectors, they are most noted for their pink and aqua milk glass made in a few items in the late 1950's as well as for their lines of milk white glass produced in the 1960's. Interest is also picking up in their "Art Decorated" ware produced between 1900 and 1910.

GIBSON GLASS

Charlie Gibson started in the glass industry in West Virginia about 1950, working for Bischoff and then Blenko. By the 1960's he left the glass business to concentrate on the ministry, but in 1976, he worked for a time for Joe St. Clair Glass in Indiana. Later on, Charlie opened a shop in his brother's garage. He stayed there about a year and finally opened his own glasshouse in Milton, WV, in the mid 1980's.

Gibson glass makes a myriad of bird, Easter egg, and animal novelties as well as table sets, lamps, and cruets. In recent years, he has introduced a line of very popular large collector's marbles in various slags and sulphides.

GILLINDER & SONS

William T. Gillinder founded Franklin Flint Glass Works in Philadelphia in 1861. The company became Gillinder & Sons in 1867 (sons James and Frederick), and by 1876 was one of the largest in the U.S.A. The pressed glass department moved to Greensburg, PA, in 1888 and in 1891 became Plant G when absorbed by U.S. Glass Company and ceased production of tableware.

Gillinder set up a factory at the Centennial Exposition site in 1876, where they demonstrated the manufacture of glass, doing blowing, pressing, engraving, cutting, etching, and acid finishing. They also made a vast array of Victorian trinkets now so dear to the heart of collectors. The star was the Liberty Bell pattern.

Three third generation Gillinders opened a new plant at Port Jervis, NJ, called Gillinder Brothers, Inc. The two Gillinder plants operated until 1930 when the Philadelphia plant went out of business.

HOBBS, BROCKUNIER & COMPANY

This company was located in Wheeling, WV, from 1845 – 1890. It was established by John L. Hobbs and James B. Barnes who left the New England Glass Company and bought Punkett and Miller's South Wheeling Glass Works, naming it Hobbs, Barnes & Company. Later, they were joined by sons John H. Hobbs and James F. Barnes. Their first products were jars, lamp chimneys, and flint pattern glass. By 1854 another larger factory was built across the Ohio River at Martens Ferry. In 1863, the sons, plus Charles

Brockunier, founded Hobbs, Brockunier & Co. William Leighton, Sr., former superintendent of New England Glass Company took charge of production. His experiments with lime glass introduced a new era in glassmaking. An award for lime glass tableware was awarded them at the Centennial Exposition. Various types of art glass were also manufactured including Peachblow and pressed Amberina. They became part of U.S. Glass in 1891 and closed shortly thereafter.

HOCKING — ANCHOR HOCKING

This company began in Lancaster, OH, in 1905, making mainly hand-done items. By the mid 1920's they were making table and lamp products as well and in 1928, they were advertising automatic pressed tableware in addition to their booming container business.

During the early years, they assumed Lancaster Glass Company, Standard Glass Company, and Monongah Glass Company, among others. In 1969 the name was changed to Anchor Hocking Corporation. They are still in business today, operating twenty-some plants and advertising itself as the largest manufacturers of glass tableware in the world.

IMPERIAL GLASS COMPANY

Imperial Glass Company was organized by an investor group in 1901. The first glass was produced in 1904. Bankruptcy was declared in 1929, but the company continued under receivership, and with the help of an order that came in from Quaker Oats in 1931 for a premium piece, Imperial stayed in business until 1984. Imperial acquired Central Glass Works of Wheeling, WV, in 1940, and bought molds from Cambridge Glass Co. and A. H. Heisey Corporation in 1958.

Milk glass production began in the early 1930's, growing to nearly 600 line items in the 1950's. The famous "I over G" trademark was introduced on February 1, 1951. Also in 1951, twenty-two items were introduced from the Belknap Collection; these were produced from 1955 to 1958 and discontinued completely by 1968. "Doeskin" was a satin finish milk glass introduced about 1950, and sold at high prices for the time. Imperial also did some hand decorated milk glass pieces. The company was sold to Lenox, Incorporated in 1973, at which time the mark was changed to LIG. They closed in 1984.

INDIANA GLASS COMPANY

Indiana Glass was founded in Dunkirk, IN, in 1907 by Frank W. Merry, plant superintendent, and Henry Batsch, among others. They leased the property and assets of Beatty-Brady Glass Company from the National Glass Company. In 1909, Indiana Glass was incorporated and purchased the Beatty-Brady assets and plant. Frank W. Merry was elected president; he died in 1931.

As late as 1959 the officers and board of directors of Indiana Glass Company still included the family names of Merry and Batsch. Indiana made both hand and machine-made tableware.

Currently, the plant operates as a subsidiary of the Lancaster-Colony Corporation. They have made milk glass from the 1950's onward and still produce it today.

INDIANA TUMBLER & GOBLET CO.

This company was founded in 1896, in Greentown, IN, by David C. Jenkins, who was a former apprentice at McKee Glass Co. They first made rather undistinguished bar goods. In 1899, nineteen companies formed the National Glass Company. At Indiana Tumbler & Goblet, Jacob Rosenthal was director. The formulas for chocolate glassware are credited to this talented glass chemist. Charles Beam, their first designer, left in 1899, and was replaced by Frank Jackson. This artistic duo is credited with many if IT&G's novel designs. The plant was destroyed by fire in 1903.

The war heroes around 1898 were Admiral Dewey and Admiral Sampson. Naturally, IT&G hopped on the band wagon and made the Dewey pattern and the Sampson pattern. Sampson did not catch the public fancy until the name was changed to Teardrop and Tassel. Beautiful tableware sets were made in opaque white, some chocolate, and various transparent colors— Nile green being the most rare. Dewey is rare in opaque white and easily found in transparent colors, some chocolate, and Nile Green opaque.

Charles Beam designed the Dolphin dish and the two styles of Cat on the Hamper— the flat, square version being harder to locate than the tall one— either would be a real find in opaque white. The tall hamper version has been reproduced by Summit Art Glass and is signed with a V inside a circle. The Dolphin has been re-produced by Kemple and later by St. Clair. The Cactus pattern was popular in 1900, but evidently housewives were tiring of milk glass during that period and little was made. Cactus in milk glass has been heavily produced by Fenton Art Glass mainly in shapes and sizes not originally made.

JEANNETTE GLASS COMPANY

It began as a bottle plant in Jeannette, PA, at the turn of the century. They opened as a glass house in 1961 in the old McKee factory building. They were makers of much table and kitchenware in many colors, plus iridescent glass and opaque colors. Their opaque green was called Jadite and the opaque light blue was named Delfite. These were used mainly for kitchenware, but some tableware was also made. Pieces today are very scarce and unique. They are perhaps best known to milk glass collectors for the pink opaque called Shell Pink issued in 1968. In the 1960's some of the items from this line were made in milk white. Jeannette closed in 1983. Their mark was a J inside a square, but not everything was marked by any means.

KANAWA GLASS COMPANY

Kanawa Glass was founded in 1955, in Dunbar, WV. It was purchased by Raymond Dereume Glass Company of Punxsutawney, PA, in July of 1987. Kanawa's gift line was discontinued at that time, but Dereume sold remaining Kanawa ware until it was sold out. Kanawa was the maker of many novelty pieces plus pitchers and vases. Many of them were milk glass with colored glass overlays.

KEMPLE GLASS WORKS

Kemple Glass Works was founded by John E. Kemple in 1945. John was a fifth generation glassmaker who worked in various glass factories from age eleven until his death. He and his wife, Geraldine, opened their own plant in East Palestine, OH, making only milk glass. The Kemples owned a large collection of old glass formulae. When Thatcher Glass Company of Jeannette, PA, purchased the McKee Glass Company in 1951, they sold a number of McKee molds to Kemple. When fire destroyed the Kemple plant in 1956, they moved to Kenova, WV, and resumed production. Here they produced colored glass as well as milk glass, using over seven hundred molds purchased from many different glasshouses and mold brokers. Their product was advertised as being "Authentic Reproductions in Milk Glass - Made in the Original Molds."

Kemple glass will often be found nicely decorated. The first of this decorating was done by Mrs. Kemple herself. Soon, however, the demand for decorated items became too much for one person and the decorating was "farmed out" to several people. Mr. Pete Zarilla of Rochester, PA, painted scenery; a Mr. Wilson of East Palestine did the decal work; while Hans Meyers, Rochester, PA, did boxes and trays. During 1958 – 59 Mr. Zimmerman was head of the decorating shop at Kenova with a staff of three. Some Kemple products will be found marked with a K inside a circle, or sometimes with the entire name written out, but most pieces were unmarked.

John Kemple died in 1970, and the factory equipment and molds were sold to the Wheaton Company of Millville, NJ.

McKEE AND BROTHERS

In 1850, Fred and James McKee built a glass factory in Pittsburgh, PA, called S. McKee & Co. In 1888 they moved to a little village in Pennsylvania, and virtually founded the town of Jeannette, PA, named after the wife of the founder, H. Sellers McKee. By 1899 they became a part of the National Glass Company. 1903 found them operating as McKee Glass Co. In 1951 they became the McKee Division of Thatcher Glass Co., and in 1961, they were purchased by Jeannette Glass Corporation. Milk glass was produced from 1930 – 1940 and it is said that the opaques kept the company in business during the depression. Mark is McK inside a circle.

MOSSER GLASS COMPANY

Located on Route 22 East, Cambridge, OH, this plant was founded about 1964 by Tom Mosser. They are makers of much pressed novelty and tableware pieces. Most items are marked with an M or an M inside a circle. Currently in business.

NATIONAL GLASS COMPANY

Founded in 1899, the driving force behind National Glass was A. Hart McKee of the McKee and Brothers Glass Company. National Glass was, like U.S. Glass, a combination of nineteen glass factories. Factory personnel included W.A.B. Dalzell, Harry Northwood, Addison Thompson, H. C. Fry, D. C. Jenkins, Jr., and Al Dugan.

National erected a working glass factory at the Pan-American Exposition in 1901, which gave the new company a lot of publicity. The Exposition glasshouse had an eight-pot furnace, a raised visitor's gallery surrounded the working area, and a three hundred foot counter offered their wares for sale. A number of milk glass pieces were made at the Exposition including the Buffalo paperweight and a trunk with the legend "Put Me Off At Buffalo."

National declared bankruptcy in 1904, amid speculation that the costs of appearing at the Exposition contributed to their difficulties.

The National Glass Company included: as of Sept 4, 1899:

Rochester Tumbler Co, Rochester, PA
McKee Brothers, Pittsburgh, PA
Crystal Glass Company, Bridgeport, OH
Indiana Goblet & Tumbler, Greentown, IN
Model Flint Glass Co., Albany, IN
Cumblerland Glass Co., Cumberland, MD
Greensburg Glass Co., Greensburg, PA
Riverside Glass Co., Wellsville, WV
Robinson Glass Co., Zanesville, OH
Royal Glass Co., Marietta, OH
Central Glass Co., Summitville, IN

In November of 1899 the following were added:

Northwood Co., Indiana, PA
Keystone Tumbler Co., Rochester, PA
Dalzell, Gilmore & Leighton Co., Findlay, OH
Ohio Flint Glass Co., Lancaster, OH
West Virginia Glass Co., Martin's Ferry, OH
Canton Glass Co., Marion, IN
Beatty-Brody Glass Co., Dunkirk, IN
Fairmont Glass Co., Cumberland, MD

OLDE VIRGINIA GLASS

This separate line was introduced by Fenton Art Glass in 1960. It was marked with a green and white paper label reading "Olde Virginia Glass Handmade" and showed a colonial couple. First produced in milk glass Thumbprint pattern were:

Covered Compote	Chip and Dip Set	Hanging planter
Lavabo	Bud Vase	Footed Nut Dish
8½" Basket	6½" Oval Basket	Footed Cake Plate
Oval Candy Box	Round Bowl	Shakers
10" Planter	Candleholder	Epergne

In 1962, the Thumbprint line added a creamer and covered sugar, bud vase, 10" Hobnail epergne, and other items in transparent colors.

1967 – 1968 they introduced Desert Tree (Cactus) pattern in amber and milk glass. Cactus was made in the regular Fenton line in 1959.
Desert Tree included:

Cruet	8", 10" Bowls	Compote
Epergne Set	Goblet	Bonbon
7", 9" and 10" Baskets	Candleholder	Sugar
5" and 7" Vases	6" Fan Vase	Creamer
¼lb. Butter dish	Student Lamp	Candy Jar
Bud Vase	Shakers	

Fine Cut, Block, and Daisy and Button patterns were added in 1969, in many pieces.
Fine Cut & Block:

Footed Bowl	Footed Nut Dish
7" Bowl	Swung Vase
7" Basket	4½" Vase
Candle Bowl	Candy Box

Daisy and Button included:

Sugar	9", 7", 10½" Bowls	Bell
Creamer	5", 6", 8", 10½" Baskets	Candleholder
Shakers	Kitten Slipper	Hat
Oval Bowl	8" Fan Vase	Bootee

In 1970 the OVG logo was added to glass pieces. Before this, everything was marked with just a paper label. The Pelican ashtray and Bird ashtray were added in 1970.
The Candle bowl with candle and flower ring was added in 1973.

A special group of milk glass items produced for A. L. Randall and Company's special sale was as follows:

Hobnail Footed Bowl	7" Ribbed Basket
5½" Bowl	6" Ribbed Bud Vase
4½" Ribbed Bowl	7" Ribbed Vase
6" Bowl	

The whole Olde Virginia line was discontinued in 1979.

PLUM GLASS COMPANY

This company was started in 1986–87 in Plum, PA, by brother and sister, John and Annie Bondich. John was a twenty-eight year employee of Westmoreland Glass Company. Sisters Zora and Helen, and brother George joined in the partnership. The family built a factory behind their home in Plum. The equipment and molds were purchased from Westmoreland Glass. The plant produces pressed glass only and the specialty is milk glass. At first, Plum made their glass with no markings except for a paper label, leaving the Westmoreland mark intact. This is what will give collectors of Westmoreland the most trouble because the molds and formulae used are the same as those used by Westmoreland. After awhile, Plum began marking the glass using a PG inside a Keystone *along with* the old Westmoreland mark. If the item has two pieces, such as covered dishes, usually only the base will be marked by Plum.

SOWERBY & COMPANY

Sowerby and Company, Ellison Glass Works was located on East Street, Gateshead-on-Tyne, England. It was founded by John Sowerby in 1763, and was originally called The New Stourbridge Glass Works. John was succeeded by his son, John George Sowerby, who changed the name to Sowerby and Company. After his death, John George's son-in-law continued the business as Sowerby's Ellison Glassworks, Ltd.

Beginning in the late 1870's, Sowerby produced much press-molded glass and registered many new designs. By 1882, they were known as the largest pressed glass works in the world, with 700 to 1,000 employees. They could turn out 1100 – 1200 tumblers per seven hour shift.

Registry marks are often pressed on the base of the pieces. Many opaque colors were produced including Jet (opaque black), Opal or Blanc de Lait (opaque white), Gold (opaque yellow), Turquoise (opaque light blue), and Patent Queen's Ware (a pale opaque cream), plus purple, green, and greenish-black slags and the rare opaque terra-cotta and opaque olive green. Vitro-Porcelain was the name Sowerby's used for their opaque glasswares.

I understand that John Sowerby was also an illustrator for children's books, which is why some Sowerby pieces have figures resembling Kate Greenaway or Tasha Tudor characters. Most Sowerby pieces carry their distinctive "Peacock Head" trade mark.

TIFFIN GLASS

Established in 1888 in Tiffin, Ohio. Became Factory R when they joined U.S. Glass in 1892. Tiffin employees purchased the plant in 1963, and continued until 1966, when it was sold to Continental Can Company. They in turn sold to Interpace in 1969, and in 1980 the doors closed. They were makers of very high-quality table, bar, and decorative glassware. They did not produce too much milk glass, but what they did make was beautiful.

U.S. GLASS COMPANY

In 1891, eighteen glass companies merged to form U.S. Glass. In 1894 they built a new glass factory along the Monongahelia River in the Township of Port Vue, PA. The town that sprung up around the plant was, in 1902, incorporated as the Borough of Glassport. The company manufactured a huge line of pressed and blown glass in all colors and treatments. After the merger of 1891, patterns made were referred to by the letter which represented the factory, as listed:

* Adams & Co., Pittsburgh, PA – A
* Bryce Brothers, Pittsburgh, PA – B
  Challinor, Taylor & Co., Tarentum, PA – C
  George Duncan & Sons, Pittsburgh, PA – D
  Richards & Hartley, Tarentum, PA – E
* Ripley & Co., Pittsburgh, PA – F
  Gillinder & Sons, Wheeling, WV – G
  Hobbs Glass Co., Wheeling, WV – H
  Columbia Glass Co., Findlay, Ohio – J
* King Glass Co., Pittsburgh, PA – K
  O'Hara Glass Co., Pittsburgh, PA – L
  Bellaire Goblet Co., Findlay, OH – M
  Nickel Plate Glass Co., Fostoria, OH – N
  Central Glass Co., Wheeling, WV – O
* Doyle & Co, Pittsburgh, PA – M
* A.J. Beatty & Sons, Tiffin, OH – R
  A.J. Beatty & Sons, Steubenville, OH – S
  Novelty Glass Co., Fostoria, OH (leased) – T
  New Factory, Gas City, IN – U

*Only factories with an asterisk before the name were still in business after 1900.

Officers of the company were: President, Daniel C. Ripley; Vice President, Wm. C. King; Secretary, Andrew Bryce; Manager of Commercial Department, A. H. Heisey; Treasurer, John Stevenson.

VALLERYSTHAL & PORTIEUX

In 1833, the Baron of Klinglin took over an existing glass plant at Plaine-de Walsch. Five years later, the factory was transferred to Val de Vallery. Extensive construction was done and the first oven was lit on November 4, 1838. It is reported that the name Vallerysthal originated somewhere in the family name of the Chevalier Charles Cordier de Vallery. The plant could be called a small village, having ovens, sand washing facilities, drying ovens, warehouses, a window glass workshop, a water wheel for glass cutting, and ovens for oxidizing bones and calcifying lime. A six-pot furnace was later constructed. There were living quarters for the cashier and director, an administration building, a school with lodgings for women teachers, servant's lodgings, housing for horses, and a chapel. By 1841 about 250 persons were employed. They produced mainly clear and colored crystal glass without lead. By 1874, they were decorating glass by the acid etch method.

In 1870, Germany annexed Alsace-Lorraine where Vallerysthal was located, making service to French customers who could no longer purchase directly from Vallerysthal impossible. To alleviate this, a partnership was formed in 1872 between Vallerysthal and the Portieux factory in the Vosages area. In 1891–92, a railroad between Sarrebourg and Vallerysthal was built and a new prosperity began. By 1931 Vallerysthal employed 960 people and the director was Joseph Stenger. During the World War II years, production was down with only one furnace operating.

In 1970, Vallerysthal and Portieux, along with a group of other glasshouses became members of the "French Crystal Society." However, the competition from mechanically produced glass and imports took their toll and in 1977 the Vallerysthal plant closed. In 1986, the "Cristallerie De Vallerysthal" opened on the old site, where they still make novelties for the tourist trade. Portieux also operated under new management in 1986 and continues on today. The round paper label bearing "P.V. France" is thought to indicate Portieux-Vallerysthal. This was used on items for export from 1890 – 1970. Square gold labels with Portieux-France in black, along with drawings of glass pieces can be found. Current Portieux exports used a round gold label with Portieux-France in black. The embossed S.V. sometimes found on glass are also thought to be Vallerysthal products, made for an importer. Some milk glass pieces are still being produced and since a number of the old molds are still preserved, who knows what new issues may surface in the years to come.

WESTMORELAND GLASS COMPANY

Westmoreland was located in Grapeville, PA, and originally known as Westmoreland Specialty Company from 1889 – 1923. The Specialty Glass Co, East Liverpool, OH, moved to Grapeville in 1889, and built a glass plant. It was sold to the West brothers in the early 1890's, backed financially by Ira Brainard. Brainard bought half of the business in 1920. In 1937, the Brainard family bought the entire company with James Brainard as president. The plant closed in 1985, after nearly one hundred years of producing fine milk glass and colored glass.

Marks were as follows:
W inside a keystone, 1910 – 1929
Letters WG stacked over each other began in the late 1940's
About 1982 the mark was WESTMORELAND spelled out in a circle with a strange-looking W in the center that looks more like three vertical, hooked lines.
Several styles of paper labels were also used through the years.

L.G. WRIGHT COMPANY

L.G. Wright has been located in New Martinsville, WV, from the 1960's through the present time. This is actually a glass brokerage house and mold owner, not a glass manufacturer. Various glasshouses have made items for L. G. Wright from the molds owned by them. Their products are generally not marked. However, the pieces they make (with the exception of the Cambridge turkey) are usually not identical to the earlier pieces. Dates are removed, or bases changed; colors are generally different from the original production or the shape slightly altered.

Their catalogs contain many antique glass reproductions along with many vases, lamps, and cracker jars. They also include items in china, pottery, and metalware.

THE BIG LINES

It appears that the majority of milk glass pieces being offered for sale in the malls and markets today are products of Westmoreland Glass, Fenton Art Glass, or Imperial Glass. All three of these glasshouses produced huge lines of milk glass dinnerware. Most collectors call this "new" or, as in the case of Fenton, "current production" milk glass. Mr. Frank Fenton once remarked to us that he believed every shape or mold Fenton produces was made in milk glass at one time or another.

Westmoreland began their big milk glass line of Paneled Grape in the 1940's. It has been discovered that Paneled Grape was first designed and made by Kokomo Glass in Kokomo, Indiana, at the turn of the century. It was then taken over by Jenkins Glass. Did Westmoreland purchase these molds or simply make their own? No one

knows. English Hobnail began in the 1920's; Old Quilt at the turn of the century; Beaded Grape in the 1950's. Looking at these dates, some will say these lines are not "new," but when you consider that most items were produced in the same molds until the closing in 1985, they cannot very well be classified as "old" either. (Maybe whether you think of them as old or new depends on how old you are yourself!)

Imperial Glass's production of milk glass began in the early 1950's. Production of Fenton's Hobnail started up in 1940 and their Silvercrest line just a couple of years later.

The following catalog pages will acquaint you with the hundreds of pieces that made up "the big lines" plus a sampling of milk glass production from other companies.

3465W FOOTED CAKE PLATE
Size...10" Dia., 4¾" H.
Individually Gift Boxed
6/Master—22 lbs.

3479W FOOTED FRUIT BOWL
Size...9¼" Dia., 6¾" High
Individually Gift Boxed
6/Master—21 lbs.

cameo
GLASSWARE
by JEANNETTE

*Exquisite Traditional Styling
in Gleaming Milk White*

These seven unusual pressed patterns offer new volume in popularly-priced milk white glassware. Each item bears the distinctive finish and color of CAMEO by Jeannette. Individual blue-colored gift box.

3401W WEDDING BOWL with COVER
Size...4½" L., 4"½ W., 8" H.
Individually Gift Boxed
6/Master—16 lbs.

3412W WEDDING BOWL with COVER
Size...4" L., 4" W., 6½" H.
Individually Gift Boxed
6/Master—9 lbs.

3125W AZTEC ROSE BOWL
Size...6½" Dia., 2½" H.
Individually Gift Boxed
6/Master—10 lbs.

275W GONDOLA BOWL
Size...17½" L., 6" W., 4½" H.
Individually Gift Boxed
6/Master—26 lbs.

3435W LOMBARDI BOWL
Size...10¼" L., 6¾" W., 5⅜" H.
Individually Gift Boxed
6/Master—27 lbs.

THE JEANNETTE GLASS COMPANY
JEANNETTE, PENNSYLVANIA

367-AC-5

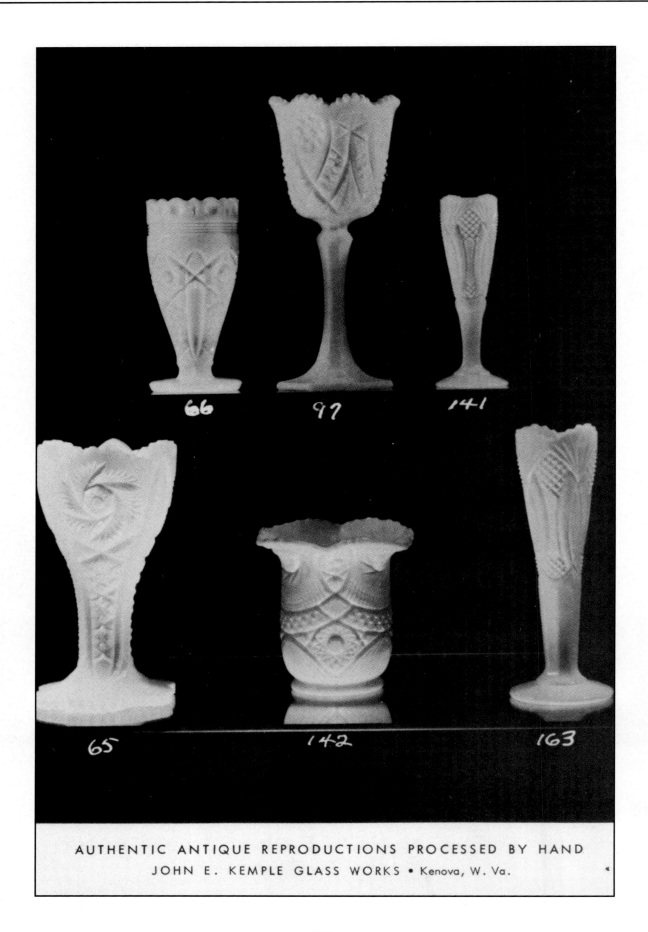

AUTHENTIC ANTIQUE REPRODUCTIONS PROCESSED BY HAND
JOHN E. KEMPLE GLASS WORKS • Kenova, W. Va.

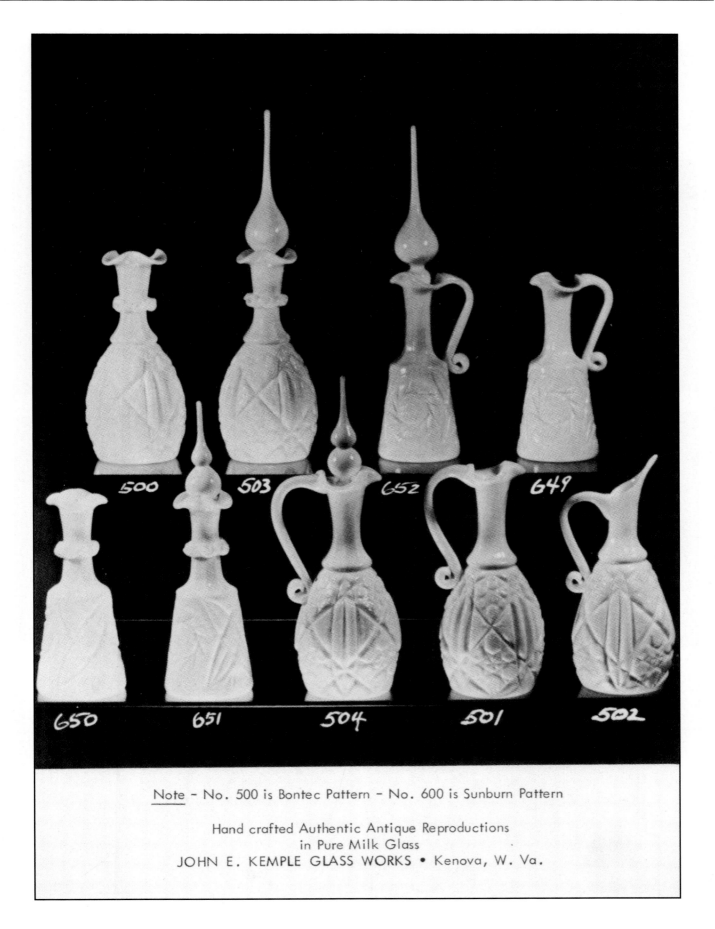

Note – No. 500 is Bontec Pattern – No. 600 is Sunburn Pattern

Hand crafted Authentic Antique Reproductions
in Pure Milk Glass
JOHN E. KEMPLE GLASS WORKS • Kenova, W. Va.

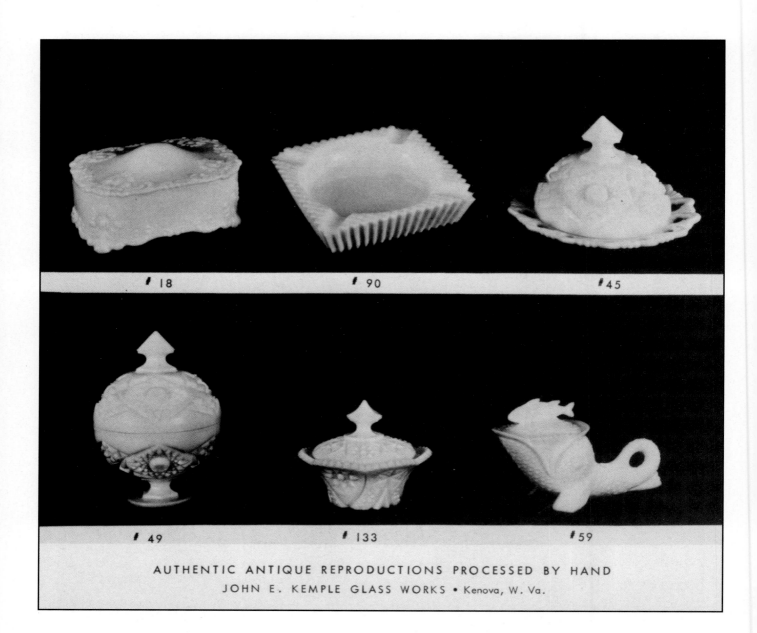

#18   #90   #45

#49   #133   #59

AUTHENTIC ANTIQUE REPRODUCTIONS PROCESSED BY HAND
JOHN E. KEMPLE GLASS WORKS • Kenova, W. Va.

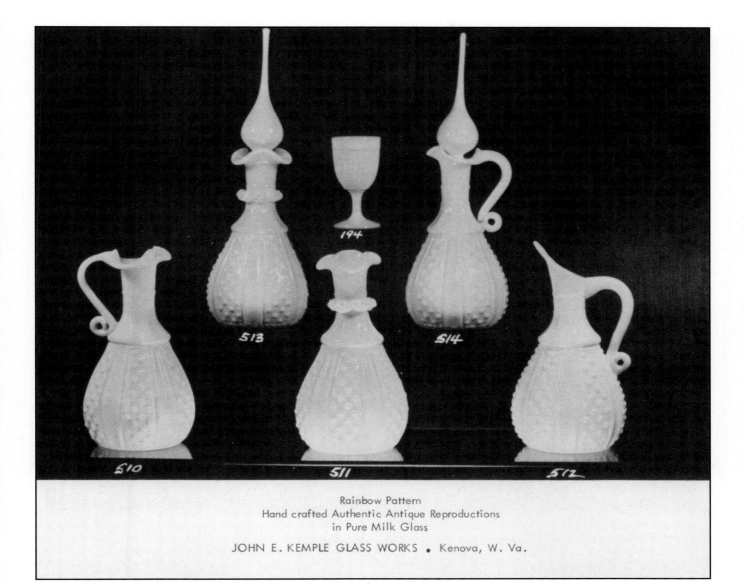

Rainbow Pattern
Hand crafted Authentic Antique Reproductions
in Pure Milk Glass

JOHN E. KEMPLE GLASS WORKS . Kenova, W. Va.

CATALOG No. 500

Westmoreland's Handmade "Old Quilt" Pattern

America's Finest Handmade Milk Glass

WESTMORELAND GLASS COMPANY
GRAPEVILLE, PENNSYLVANIA

Handmade Glassware of Quality
SINCE 1889

Westmoreland's Handmade, Quaint "Old Quilt" Milk Glass Collection

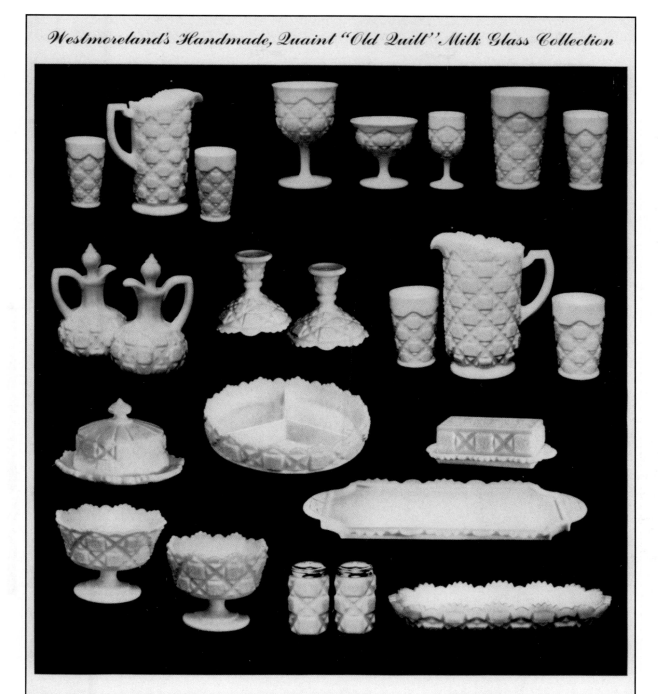

TOP ROW: *No. 500/9 pc. "Old Quilt", Juice Set.* Consists of: 8-5 oz. Juice Glasses, and 1-1 pt. Jug. Jug is 7½ inches tall.

No. 500/1 pt. "Old Quilt", Juice Jug.

No. 500/8 oz. "Old Quilt", Goblet.

No. 500 "Old Quilt", Low Foot Sherbet.

No. 500/2 oz. "Old Quilt", Wine Glass.

No. 500/11 oz. "Old Quilt", Ice Tea.

No. 500/5 oz. "Old Quilt", Juice Glass.

SECOND ROW: *No. 500/6 oz. "Old Quilt", Oil and Vinegar Cruets, with stoppers.*

No. 500/4" "Old Quilt", Candlesticks.

No. 500/9 oz. "Old Quilt", Tumbler.

No. 500/9 pc. "Old Quilt", Beverage Set. Consists of: 8-9 oz. Tumblers and 1-3 pt. Jug. Jug is 8½ inches tall.

No. 500/3 pt. "Old Quilt", Beverage Jug.

THIRD ROW: *No. 500 "Old Quilt", Covered Cheese Dish.* Grandmother's Butter Dish.

No. 500/9" "Old Quilt", Relish Dish, 3-part.

No. 500/¼ lb. "Old Quilt" Covered Butter Dish, Quarter Pound, Oblong.

BOTTOM ROW: *No. 500/5" "Old Quilt", Mayonnaise, Bell Shape, Footed.*

No. 500/4½" "Old Quilt", Mayonnaise, Round Shape, Footed.

No. 500 "Old Quilt", Salt with Chrome Top.

No. 500 "Old Quilt", Pepper, Chrome Top.

No. 500/13"x6" "Old Quilt", Oval Tray. A utility tray for vanity or dresser. Also used with No. 500 Condiment and Dresser Sets.

No. 500/10" "Old Quilt", Pickle Dish. A lovely container for flower arranging.

Westmoreland's Handmade, Quaint "Old Quilt" Milk Glass Collection

TOP ROW: *No. 500 "Old Quilt", Sugar and Cream Set*, Individual. Creamer is 3½" tall.

No. 500/6" "Old Quilt", Plate, Bread and Butter.

No. 500/8½" "Old Quilt", Plate, Salad.

No. 500/10½" "Old Quilt", Plate, Dinner.

No. 500/3 oz. "Old Quilt", Pitcher, Syrup, Individual, 3¼ inches tall.

No. 500/3½" "Old Quilt", Cocktail, Fruit.

SECOND ROW: *No. 500/5½" "Old Quilt", Nappy, Bell Shape.*

No. 500/4½" "Old Quilt", Nappy, Round.

No. 500/8" "Old Quilt", Nappy, Round.

No. 500 "Old Quilt", Cup (Flared) and Saucer. Tea or Coffee.

THIRD ROW: *No. 500 "Old Quilt", Sugar and Cream Set, Open.* Sugar is 4 inches tall.

No. 500/4" "Old Quilt", Nappy, Round.

No. 500 "Old Quilt", Spoonholder.

No. 500 "Old Quilt", Sugar, Covered and Creamer Set. Sugar with cover is 6½" tall.

BOTTOM ROW: *No. 500/5 pc. "Old Quilt", Condiment Set.* Consists of: 1-13"x6" Oval Tray; 1-Salt and 1-Pepper with chrome tops; 1-6 oz. Oil Cruet; 1-6 oz. Vinegar Cruet.

No. 500/10½" "Old Quilt", Bowl, Round, 4¼ inches tall. A lovely low bowl suitable for fruit or floral centerpieces.

Westmoreland's Handmade, Quaint "Old Quilt" Milk Glass Collection

TOP ROW: No. 500/5" "Old Quilt", Compote and Cover, Low Foot. For honey, candy or nuts. One of Westmoreland's early pieces.

No. 500 "Old Quilt", Sweetmeat and Cover, High Foot. 6½" high. A very popular gift item. For condiments, preserves and for flower arranging, too.

No. 500/4 pc. "Old Quilt", Dresser Set. Consists of: 1-4½" Puff Box and Cover; 2-5 oz. Toilet Bottles; 1-13"x6" Oval Tray.

SECOND ROW: No. 500/10 pc. "Old Quilt", Waffle Set. Consists of: 1-1 pt. Beverage

Jug; 1-6" Plate, B & B; 4-3 oz. Syrup Pitchers; 4-Saucers. Just the thing for Sunday Brunch, with waffles or crepes with syrup. Adds pleasure to informal entertaining.

No. 500/6" "Old Quilt", Bowl, Cupped, Footed. A novel bowl for original flower arrangements. One of Westmoreland's first "Old Quilt" originals.

BOTTOM ROW: No. 500/4½" "Old Quilt", Puff Box and Cover. Also used as Covered Jelly and for table service.
No. 500/3½" "Old Quilt", Box and Cover,

Square, 5½ inches tall. A Westmoreland original which has many uses.

No. 500/5 oz. "Old Quilt", Toilet Bottles.

No. 500/14"/15 pc. "Old Quilt", Punch Set. Consists of: 1-8 qt. Bell Shape Punch Bowl; 1-Pedestal; 12-Punch Cups; 1-1800 Milk Glass Ladle. (Red Plastic Hooks shown in the photograph are not included with the Punch Set. Should be purchased extra.)

No. 500 "Old Quilt", Punch Cup. Cups are available separately in any quantity.

Westmoreland's Handmade, Quaint "Old Quilt" Milk Glass Collection

TOP ROW: *No. 500/9" "Old Quilt", Bowl, Crimped, Footed.* For fruits or flowers.

No. 500/11" "Old Quilt", Salver, Cake, Footed. Quaint "Old Quilt" Pattern is underneath in this lovely Westmoreland original.

No. 500/9" "Old Quilt", Bowl, Bell, Footed. A most attractive small bowl for console or small table.

SECOND ROW: *No. 500/7" "Old Quilt", Bowl, Cupped, Footed.* A well shaped bowl for old fashioned flowers, or fruits.

No. 500/11" "Old Quilt", Bowl, Banana, Footed. An exquisite bowl with many uses.
No. 500/6½" "Old Quilt", Ash Tray, Square. King Size.

THIRD ROW: *No. 500/5"x4" "Old Quilt", Cigarette Box and Cover, King Size.*
No. 500/3 pc. "Old Quilt" Cigarette Set. Consists of: 1-King Size Cigarette Box and cover; and 2-4" "Old Quilt" Ash Trays, as shown directly below.
No. 500/9" "Old Quilt", Bowl, Shallow, Round, Footed. Makes a perfect low centerpiece.

FOURTH ROW: *No. 500/12" "Old Quilt", Salver, Skirted, Footed.* One of Westmoreland's most popular cake salvers.

No. 500/4" "Old Quilt", Ash Tray, Square.

No. 500/9" "Old Quilt", Bowl, Shallow, Round. A 2¼" high bowl with many uses.

BOTTOM ROW: *No. 500/12" "Old Quilt", Bowl, Lipped.* 4 inches high. An original.

No. 500/13" "Old Quilt", Bowl, Flared. Flanked by "Old Quilt" Candlesticks, this low bowl makes a lovely console set.

Westmoreland's Handmade, Quaint "Old Quilt" Milk Glass Collection

TOP ROW: *No. 500/9" "Old Quilt" Vase, Bell.* Classic in its simplicity.

No. 500/7½" "Old Quilt", Bowl, Round, Footed.

No. 500/9" "Old Quilt", Vase, Fan Shape, Footed. A delight for the home flower arranger. A Westmoreland original.

CENTER: *No. 500/6½" "Old Quilt", Celery Vase, Tall.* From a very old original mould.

BOTTOM ROW: *No. 500/9" "Old Quilt", Vase, Bell, Footed.* A popular Westmoreland original.

No. 500/6½" "Old Quilt", Jardiniere, Straight, Footed. Holds standard size pots.

No. 500/6½" "Old Quilt", Jardiniere, *Cupped, Footed.* This shape is excellent for short-stemmed garden flowers.

No. 500 "Old Quilt", Sugar and Cover. Has long been popular as Covered Candy Jar. Also available in floral or gold decoration.

No. 500/14" "Old Quilt", Vase, Swung. (Due to hand forming, height of this vase will vary.) For long stem roses, mums and other tall flowers.

WESTMORELAND GLASS COMPANY

GRAPEVILLE, PENNSYLVANIA

Handmade Glassware of Quality

SINCE 1889

THE WESTMORELAND GLASS COMPANY was founded October 1889. Without interruption it has continued to produce fine glass entirely by hand, and by the same meticulous methods which were employed more than two generations ago.

We are solely manufacturers of handmade glassware and sell only through our authorized dealers, for which reason we are unable to quote prices or sell to the consumer direct.

Westmoreland's Handmade Milk Glass Reproductions are identified as *reproductions* by the "WG" monogram imbedded inconspicuously in the glass. They are offered to the public through appointed retail outlets as reproductions. Some are from very old molds which have been in use by Westmoreland since the late 1800's.

This brochure illustrates Westmoreland's Handmade "Paneled Grape" Milk Glass Collection. The most comprehensive selection of a single handmade milk glass pattern available.

Since all Westmoreland Glassware is entirely handmade, the sizes given in this brochure can only be approximate and may vary a trifle from the sizes shown. This is because of hand shaping or due to other manual operations.

WESTMORELAND GLASS COMPANY
Grapeville, Pennsylvania

Westmoreland's Handmade "Paneled Grape" Milk Glass Collection

Top Row: No. 1881/2/11½". "Paneled Grape" Vase, Bell, Tall. Exquisitely sculptured all-over grape design.

No. 1881/2/11½". "Paneled Grape" Vase, Straight, Tall. (Not illustrated.)

No. 1881/9". "Paneled Grape" Vase, Bell. Grapes and leaves in bold relief.

No. 1881/9½". "Paneled Grape" Vase, Straight.

No. 1881/12 oz. "Paneled Grape" Ice Tea.

No. 1881/1 qt. "Paneled Grape" Quart Jug.

No. 1881/9 pc. "Paneled Grape Beverage Set: Consists of 1-1 quart Jug, and 8-12 oz. Ice Teas.

Second Row: 1881/8 oz. "Paneled Grape" Goblet. A long time Westmoreland favorite.

No. 1881. "Paneled Grape" Sherbet, Low Foot.

No. 1881 "Paneled Grape" Sherbet, High Foot. (Shown on Page 5, opposite).

No. 1881/3 oz. "Paneled Grape" Cocktail.

No. 1881/2 oz. "Paneled Grape" Wine. Also makes attractive cigarette holder.

No. 1881. "Paneled Grape" Parfait.

No. 1881/6 oz. "Paneled Grape" Cocktail, Old Fashioned.

No. 1881/4". "Paneled Grape" Candlesticks.

Third Row: No. 1881/5". "Paneled Grape" Nappy, Bell.

No. 1881/4½". "Paneled Grape" Nappy, Round.

No. 1881/5". "Paneled Grape" Nappy, Round, Handled.

Bottom Row: No. 1881. "Paneled Grape" Open Sugar.

No. 1881. "Paneled Grape" Creamer, 6½ oz.

No. 1881. "Paneled Grape" Candy Jar and Cover.

No. 1881/7". "Paneled Grape" Compote and Cover, Footed.

No. 1881. "Paneled Grape" Salt, with chrome top.

No. 1881. "Paneled Grape" Pepper, with chrome top.

No. 1881/2 oz. "Paneled Grape" Oil or Vinegar Cruet.

Westmoreland's Handmade "Paneled Grape" Milk Glass Collection

Top Row: *No. 1881/5 oz. Juice.*
No. 1881/1 pt. "Paneled Grape" Pint Jug.
No. 1881/9 pc. "Paneled Grape" Juice Set. Consists of 1 pint Jug and eight 5 oz. Juice Tumblers.
No. 1881/8 oz. "Paneled Grape" Tumbler.
No. 1881/9". Three-part Relish Dish.
No. 1881/3 pc. Appetizer Set. Consists of 1-9" Relish Dish, 1 Round Fruit Cocktail, and 1 No. 1837 Milk Glass Ladle.
Second Row: *No. 1881/9". Nappy, Shallow, Round, 2" high.*

No. 1881/4½". "Paneled Grape" Jelly and Cover. Suitable for Condiments and Nuts.
No. 1881/6½". Chocolate Box and Cover.
No. 1881/7". Cheese and Cover.
Third Row: *No. 1881/6". "Paneled Grape" Vase, footed.* A very popular small vase.
No. 1881. "Paneled Grape" High foot Sherbet.
No. 1881/4½". Fruit Cocktail, Bell Shape.
No. 1881/3½". Fruit Cocktail, Round Shape.
No. 1881/5½". "Paneled Grape" Saucer for Round and Bell Shape Fruit Cocktails.
No. 1881/3 pc. Mayonnaise Set. Consists of

1 Round Fruit Cocktail, 1 Saucer, and 1 No. 1837 Milk Glass Ladle.
Fourth Row: *No. 1881/5". "Paneled Grape" Jardiniere, footed.*
No. 1881/6½". "Paneled Grape" Jardiniere, footed. (Also available with 22 kt. gold decoration.)
No. 1881/5". Candle Holder, Colonial, Handled.
No. 1881/1. "Paneled Grape" Sugar and Cover. Lacy edge design on Bowl serves as Spoon Holder.
No. 1881/1. "Paneled Grape" Creamer.

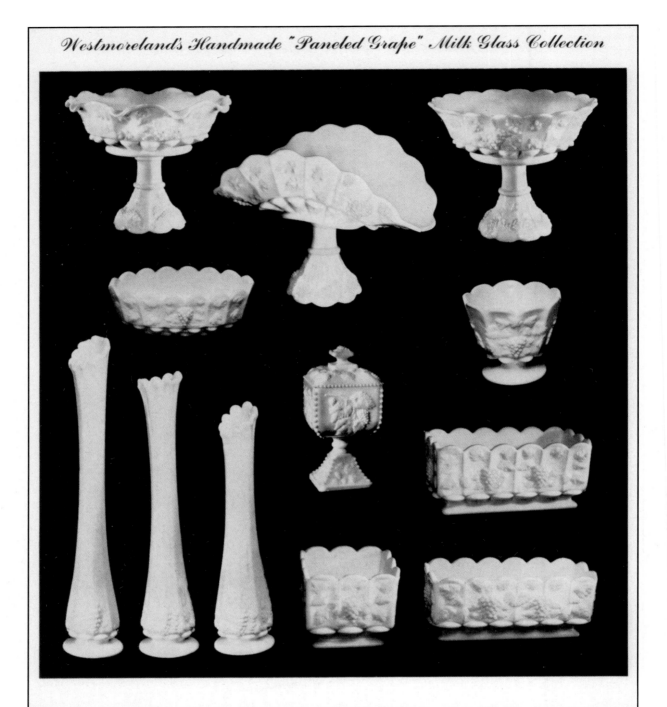

Westmoreland's Handmade "Paneled Grape" Milk Glass Collection

Top Row: *No. 1881/9". "Paneled Grape" Bowl, Lipped, Footed.*

No. 1881/12". "Paneled Grape" Bowl, Banana, Footed.

No. 1881/9½". "Paneled Grape" Bowl, Bell, Footed.

Second Row: *No. 1881/6½". "Paneled Grape" Dish, Oval. A very useful and attractive small bowl.*

No. 1881/4". "Paneled Grape" Mayonnaise, Footed.

Third Row: *No. 1884/7". "Beaded Grape" Square Bowl, Footed, with Cover.*

No. 1881/5"x9". "Paneled Grape" Planter, Oblong. (This item also available with 22 kt. gold decoration: No. 1881/5"x9"/915 Planter, Oblong.)

Bottom Row: *No. 1881/18". "Paneled Grape" Swung Vase.*

No. 1881/16". "Paneled Grape" Swung Vase.

No. 1881/14". "Paneled Grape" Swung Vase. (Note: All hand swung vases vary in height

due to off-hand operations. Sizes given are approximated.)

No. 1881/4½". "Paneled Grape" Planter, Square. Matches No. 1881/5"x9" oblong planter above. (Also available in 22 kt. No. 915 gold decoration.)

No. 1881/3"x8½". "Paneled Grape" Planter, Window, Oblong. This narrow planter was designed for window ledges. (Also available in 22 kt. gold decoration: No. 1881/3"x8½" 915 Planter, Window.)

Westmoreland's "Paneled Grape" and "Beaded Grape" Items

Top Row: No. 1881/9". "Paneled Grape" Bowl, shallow, footed. 6 inches high.
No. 1881/12x6½". "Paneled Grape" Oblong Bowl, 3⅛" high.
No. 1884/5". "Beaded Grape" Honey and Cover.

Second Row: No. 1881/7". "Paneled Grape" Round Nappy.
No. 1881/11". Cake Salver, round, footed, skirted, 4¾" high.
No. 1881/9½". "Paneled Grape" Bowl, Bell Shape.

Third Row: No. 1881/8½". "Paneled Grape" Round Bowl.
No. 1881/10". "Paneled Grape" Cake Salver, footed, 4½" high.
No. 1881/8". "Paneled Grape" Cupped Bowl.
Fourth Row: No. 1881/9". "Paneled Grape" Bowl, Lipped.
No. 1884/4". "Beaded Grape" Ash Tray.
No. 1881/7". "Paneled Grape" Salad Plate, depressed center.
Fifth Row: No. 1884/5". "Beaded Grape" Ash Tray.

No. 1884/4x6". "Beaded Grape" King Size Cigarette Box and Cover.
No. 1881/10" appx. "Paneled Grape" Bud Vase. Because these vases are hand swung the height varies.
No. 1881/12". "Paneled Grape" Lipped Bowl. Illustrated on separate 5" base.
No. 1881/5". "Paneled Grape" Bowl Base for 12" Lipped Bowl. Also used as base for 12½" Bell Bowl, 10½" Round Bowl, and for 3 pc. Epergne Sets. Can also be used inverted.
No. 1881/1/10". "Paneled Grape" Bell Nappy.

Westmoreland's Handmade "Paneled Grape" Milk Glass Collection

Top Row: *No. 1881/14". "Paneled Grape" Bowl, Shallow, Round.* A beautifully sculptured bowl, with grape clusters in bold relief. Perfect for canapes, and buffet use.

No. 1881/1/14½". "Paneled Grape" Plate. This large torte plate matches the 14" shallow, round bowl.

Second Row: *No. 1881/12". "Paneled Grape" Vase, Hand Blown.* This attractive vase beautifully delineates the sculptor's art.

Perfect for long stem roses, mums, glads, and other large flowers.

No. 1881/9". "Paneled Grape" Bowl and Cover, Footed. This is a larger version of the No. 1881/7" Compote and Cover, on bottom of page 4.

No. 1881/9". "Paneled Grape" Compote, Crimped, Footed. Perfect for a small table or buffet.

Bottom Row: *No. 1881/5 oz. "Paneled Grape" Bottle, Toilet.*

No. 1881. "Paneled Grape" Puff Box and Cover.

No. 1881/13½". "Paneled Grape" Tray, Oval.

No. 1881/4 pc. "Paneled Grape" Dresser Set. Consists of: 2-5 oz. Toilet Bottles, 1-Puff Box and Cover, 1-13½" Oval Tray. This set is also available with Hand Painted "Roses and Bows." Shown on page 10.

No. 1881/9". "Paneled Grape" Tray, Oval.

Westmoreland's "Paneled Grape" and "Beaded Grape" Items

Top Row: *No. 1884/9''. "Beaded Grape" Square Bowl, footed, with Cover.*
No. 1881/6''. "Paneled Grape" Celery, Tall.
No. 1881/1/6''. "Paneled Grape" Plate.
No. 1881/1/8½''. "Paneled Grape" Plate.
No. 1881/1/10½''. "Paneled Grape" Plate.
Second Row: *No. 1884/4''. "Beaded Grape" Bowl, Square, with Cover.*
No. 1881/12½''. Bowl, Bell.
No. 1881/1/8''. Nappy, Bell.
No. 1881/10½''. Bowl, Round.

Bottom, at left: *No. 1881/13''. "Paneled Grape" Bowl, Punch, Bell Shape.*
No. 1881. "Paneled Grape" Punch Cup.
No. 1881. "Paneled Grape" Pedestal for Punch Bowl.
No. 1881/13''/15 pc. "Paneled Grape" Punch Set: 1-13'' Punch Bowl; 1 Ladle; 12 Punch Cups; 1 Pedestal.
No. 1881/13''/15 pc./915. "Paneled Grape" Punch Set, with 22 kt. gold decoration. (Not illustrated with decoration.) This truly exquisite Punch Set is same as above, but

with gold decorated leaves and grapes.
No. 1881/11''. "Paneled Grape" Punch Bowl, Round. (Not illustrated.)
No. 1881/11''/15 pc. "Paneled Grape" Punch Set. (Same as illustrated, except with 1881/11'' Round Punch Bowl.)
No. 1800. Ladle, Punch, plain milk glass.
At right: *No. 1881/6½''. "Paneled Grape" Basket, oval, handled.*
No. 1881. "Paneled Grape" Cup and Saucer.
No. 1881/¼ lb. Butter and Cover.

Westmoreland's Hand Painted "Paneled Grape" and "Beaded Grape" Items

Top Row: *No. 1881/7"/32. "Paneled Grape" Compote and Cover, with Hand Painted "Roses and Bows." This popular compote has many uses. Ideal for candy, nuts, and preserves.*

No. 1881/4 pc./32. "Paneled Grape" Dresser Set with Hand Painted "Roses and Bows." Consists of: 2-5 oz. Toilet Bottles, 1-Puff Box and Cover, 1-13½" Oval Tray. This set is also available without decoration.

No. 1884/7"/32. "Beaded Grape" Bowl and Cover, Square, Footed, Hand Painted "Roses and Bows."

Second Row: *No. 1881/32. "Paneled Grape" Puff Box and Cover, Hand Painted "Roses*

and Bows." Can also be used as a covered jelly.

No. 1884/4"/32. "Beaded Grape" Bowl and Cover, Square, Hand Painted "Roses and Bows."

No. 1884/4"/32. "Beaded Grape" Ash Tray, Hand Painted "Roses and Bows."

No. 1884/4"x6"/32. "Beaded Grape" Cigarette Box and Cover, Hand Painted "Roses and Bows." A "king size" cigarette box for boudoir, living room, or dinner table.

No. 1884/9"/32. "Beaded Grape" Bowl and Cover, Square, Footed, Hand Painted "Roses and Bows."

Third Row: *No. 1881/2 oz. "Paneled Grape" Oil or Vinegar. Without decoration.*

No. 1881. "Paneled Grape" Salt.

No. 1881. "Paneled Grape" Pepper.

No. 1881/9". "Paneled Grape" Tray, Oval.

No. 1881/5 pc. "Paneled Grape" Condiment Set. Without decoration. Consists of: 1-Salt, 1-Pepper, 1-2 oz. Oil, 1-2 oz. Vinegar, 1-9" Oval Tray.

No. 1884/5"/32. "Beaded Grape" Honey and Cover. Hand Painted "Roses and Bows."

Bottom Row: *No. 1881/3 lite. "Paneled Grape" Candelabra. A charming piece for use on mantle or table. Not decorated.*

No. 1881. "Paneled Grape" Sugar and Cream Set, Individual. Not decorated.

No. 1881. "Paneled Grape" Soap Tray.

Westmoreland's 22kt. Gold Decorated "Paneled Grape" and "Beaded Grape"

Top Row: *No. 1881/9½"/916. "Paneled Grape" Vase,* Straight. Decorated with 22 kt. gold bands top and bottom, as illustrated.

No. 1884/9"/915. "Beaded Grape" Bowl, footed. Leaves and grapes decorated with 22 kt. gold, gold bands on finial and base.

No. 1881/7"/915. "Paneled Grape" Compote and Cover. Decorated with 22 kt. gold.

No. 1884/4"/915. "Beaded Grape" Ash Tray. Decorated with 22 kt. gold. Also available with same decoration in No. 1884/5" size.

No. 1884/4x6"/915. "Beaded Grape" King Size Cigarette Box and Cover. Decorated in 22 kt. gold, on box and cover.

Second Row: *No. 1884/4"/915. "Beaded Grape" Square Bowl and Cover,* 5 inches high. Decorated in 22 kt. gold, as illustrated.

No. 1881/10½"/915. "Paneled Grape" Round Bowl. Decorated with 22 kt. gold, as illustrated.

Bottom Row: *No. 1881/4"/915. "Paneled Grape" Candlesticks.* Decorated with 22 kt. gold, as shown.

No. 1884/5"/915. "Beaded Grape" Honey and Cover. Decorated, as illustrated, with 22 kt. gold.

No. 1881/8". "Paneled Grape" Two-lite Candleholder. (Not decorated.) Illustration shows four Candleholders used to make a circle of candlelight. Attractive centerpiece.

Not illustrated:

No. 1881/5"/915. "Paneled Grape" Jardiniere, Cupped, Footed, with 22 kt. Gold

Decoration. (Illustrated, without decoration, on page 3.)

No. 1881/6½"/915. "Paneled Grape" Jardiniere, Footed, with 22 kt. Gold Decoration. (Illustrated, without decoration, on page 5.)

No. 1881/4½"/915. "Paneled Grape" Planter, Square, with 22 kt. Gold Decoration. (Illustrated, without decoration, on page 6.)

No. 1881/3"x8½"/915. "Paneled Grape" Planter, Window, with 22 kt. Gold Decoration. (Illustrated, without decoration, on page 6.)

No. 1881/5"x9"/915. "Paneled Grape" Planter, Oblong, with 22 kt. Gold Decoration. (Illustrated, without decoration, on page 6.)

No. 1881/13"/15 pc. "Paneled Grape" Punch Set, with 22 kt. Gold Decoration. (Illustrated, without decoration, on page 9.)

WESTMORELAND GLASS COMPANY . . . GRAPEVILLE, PENNSYLVANIA

Westmoreland's Handmade "Beaded Grape" Milk Glass Collection.

TOP ROW: *1884/9". Vase, Crimped, Footed.*
1884/4". Candlesticks.
1884/9". Bowl, Flared, Square, Footed. Bowl used with candles makes most charming buffet or console ensemble.
1881/2 oz. Wine.
1881/26 oz. Decanter, Hand Blown.

SECOND ROW: *1884/4". Bowl and Cover, Sq.*
1881/3 oz. Cocktail, Old Fashioned.

1884/6½". Ash Tray, Square, "King Size."
1884/5". Ash Tray, Square.
1884/4". Ash Tray, Square.
1884/4"x6". Cigarette Box and Cover, "King Size."

THIRD ROW: *1884/5". Bowl, Flared, Footed.*
1884/5". Bowl and Cover, Flared, Footed.
1884/5". Honey and Cover, Footed.
1884/7". Bowl and Cover, Square, Footed.

1884/6". Vase, Crimped Top, Footed.
1884/7". Bowl, Flared, Low, Square.

FOURTH ROW: *1884/7". Bowl and Cover, Flared, Low, Sq.*
1884/11". Salver, Cake, Skirted, Square, Ftd. An attractive server for petits fours, sandwiches, canapes.
1884/9". Bowl, Flared, Low, Square. Makes a most attractive centerpiece.

Milk Glass Gift Items with Hand Painted "Roses and Bows,"

1881/32
Bud Vase

229/32 Bud Vase

1874/4½"/32
Candlestick

1874/10"/32 Wedding Bowl

1884/9"/32 Bowl
and Cover, Ftd. Sq.

1943/12½"/32
Urn and Cover

51/32 Double Hands

757/32 Pansy Basket

1884/5"/32 Honey

1881/6½"/32
Oval Basket

1884/4"/32 Bowl
and Cover, Square

1881/4½"/32
Puff Box

1881/5 oz./32
Toilet Bottle

500/32
Covered Sugar

1881/7"/32
Compote and Cover

1884/5"/32
Bowl, Flared, Ftd.

1874/8"/32
Wedding Bowl

1884/7"/32 Bowl
and Cover, Sq. Ftd.

500/9"/32 Fan Vase

1881/6¼"/32
Candy Jar

500/3½"/32
Square Box and Cover

1881/4 pc./32 Dresser Set

1874/6"/32
Wedding Box

1881/6"/32
Vase, Crimped, Ftd.

500/6½"/32
Celery Vase

1923/6"/32 Bon Bon

1884/6½"/32
Ash Tray

1884/5"/32
Ash Tray

1884/4"/32
Ash Tray

1/6"/32 Shell Nappy

1884/4"x6"/32
Cigarette Box

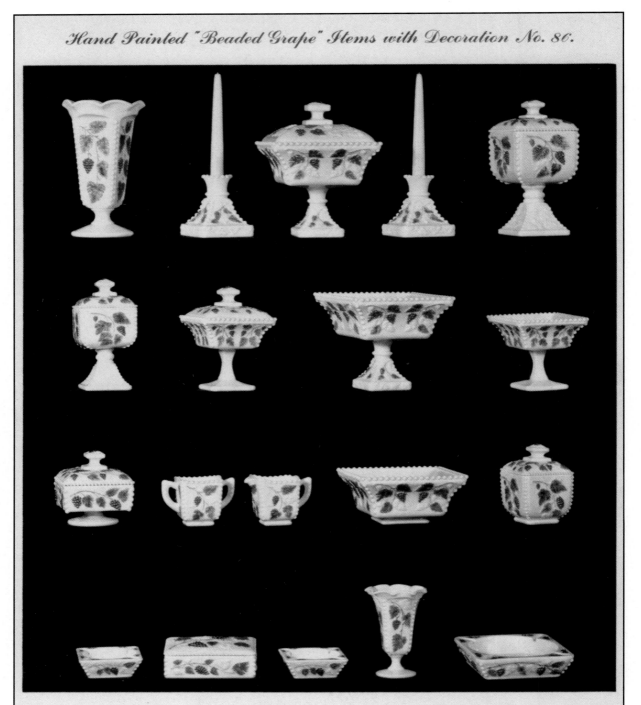

Hand Painted "Beaded Grape" Items with Decoration No. 86.

These exquisite pieces from Westmoreland's Handmade "Beaded Grape" Milk Glass Collection have been enhanced with deft touches of 22 kt. gold on grapes, with mint green leaves.

TOP ROW: 1884/9"/86. Vase, Crimped Top, Footed.
1884/4"/86. Candlesticks.
1884/7"/86. Bowl and Cover, Fld. Ftd.
1884/9"/86. Bowl and Cover, Square, Ftd.

SECOND ROW: 1884/7"/86. Bowl and Cover, Square, Ftd.
1884/5"/86. Bowl and Cover, Flared, Ftd.
1884/7"/86. Bowl, Flared, Footed.
1884/5"/86. Bowl, Flared, Footed.

THIRD ROW: 1884/5"/86. Honey and Cover, Low Foot.
1884/86. Sugar and Cream Set, Individual.
1884/7"/86. Bowl, Flared, Low, Square.
1884/4"/86. Bowl and Cover, Square.

BOTTOM ROW: 1884/4"/86. Ash Tray, Square.
1884/4"x6"/86. Cigarette Box and Cover, "King Size."
1884/3 pc./86. Cigarette Set. Consists of: 2-1884/4" Ash Trays; 1-1884/4"x6" Cigarette Box and Cover, "King Size."
1884/6"/86. Vase, Crimped Top.
1884/6½"/86. Ash Tray, Square, "King Size."

Westmoreland's Handmade "Beaded Grape" Milk Glass Collection.

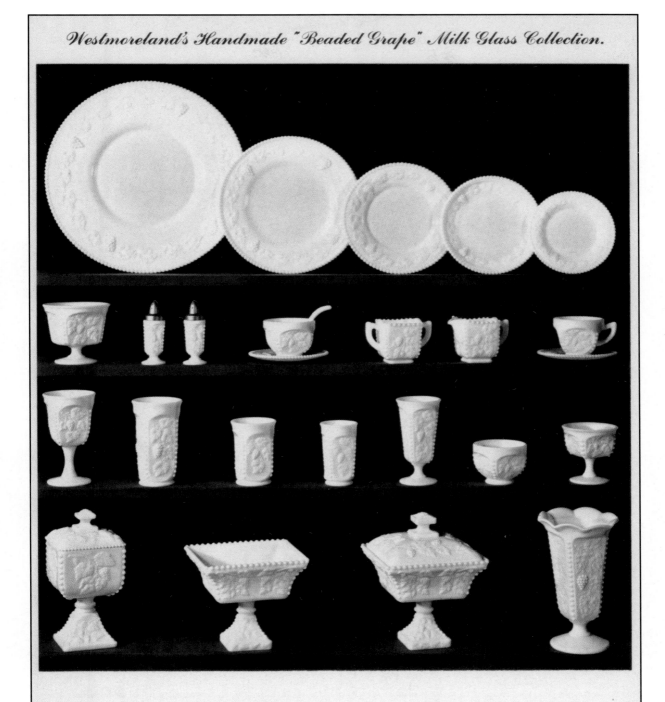

TOP ROW: *1884/15". Plate, Torte.* A delightful buffet piece for hors d'oeuvres.
1884/10½". Plate, Dinner.
1884/8½". Plate, Luncheon.
1884/7". Plate, Salad or Dessert.
1884/6". Plate, Bread and Butter.

SECOND ROW: *1884/4½". Mayonnaise, Footed.*
1884. Pepper, with Chrome Top.
1884. Salt, with Chrome Top.

1884/3 pc. Mayo Set: 1-1884, Round Fruit Cocktail; 1-1884 Saucer; 1-1837 Ladle.
1884. Cream and Sugar Set, Individual. A most charming small Sugar and Cream.
1884. Cup and Saucer.

THIRD ROW: *1884/8 oz. Goblet, Round Foot.*
1884/10 oz. Ice Tea.
1884/8 oz. Tumbler.
1884/5 oz. Juice.

1884. Parfait, Footed.
1884/3½". Cocktail, Fruit, Round.
1884. Sherbet, Low Foot, Bell Shape.

BOTTOM ROW: *1884/9". Bowl and Cover, Square, High Foot.*
1884/7". Bowl, Flared, Footed, Square.
1884/7". Bowl and Cover, Fld. Ftd. Sq.
1884/9". Vase, Bell, Footed.

Authentic Reproductions of Early Lacy-Edge Bowls

No. 1890/11". "Lattice-Edge" Bell Bowl, Footed. A popular, graceful, footed piece. No. 1890/10", "Lattice-Edge", Bowl, Cupped, Footed. (Not illustrated.) All No. 1890 footed bowls are individually packed.

No. 1890/11". "Lattice-Edge" Cake Salver, Footed. This piece is 5 inches high. It matches the 11 inch "Lattice-Edge" plates shown on pages 5 and 26. "Lattice-Edge Candlesticks are shown page 8.

No. 1890/10¼". "Lattice-Edge" Bowl, Flared, Footed. This bowl measures 6½ inches high. Used in combination with "Lattice-Edge" 4 inch Candlesticks it makes an attractive console set or a table centerpiece.

Top: No. 1890/8½". "Lattice-Edge" Bowl, Round. This open-end Lattice design has long had Collector's preference. Bottom: No. 1890/11½". "Lattice-Edge" Bowl, Flared. Hand decorated, page 25.

Top: No. 1891/8½". "Spoke and Rim" Bowl, Round, Footed. For flowers or fruit. Bottom: No. 1891/10½". "Spoke and Rim" Bowl Straight Edge, Round, Footed. With hand painted rose design shown on page 25.

Top: No. 1891/10". "Spoke and Rim" Bowl, Bell Shape, Footed. 3½ inches high. Bottom: No. 1891/11". "Spoke and Rim" Bowl, Flared, Footed. 2¾ inches high. 1891/10". "Spoke and Rim" Plate on page 5.

Westmoreland's Handmade "Paneled Grape" Milk Glass Collection

Top Row: No. 1881/14″/3 pc. "Paneled Grape" Epergne Set. Consists of: 1-14″ Flared Epergne Bowl, 1-5″ Bowl Base, and 1-8½″ Epergne Vase, Bell Shaped.

No. 1881/14″/2 pc. "Paneled Grape" Epergne Set. (Not illustrated.) Same as above but without Bowl Base.

No. 1881/5″ "Paneled Grape" Jardiniere, Cupped, Footed. (Also available with 22 kt. gold decoration.)

No. 1881/9″/2 pc. "Paneled Grape Epergne Set. Consists of: 1-9″ Epergne Lipped Bowl, and 1-8½″ Epergne Vase, Bell.

Center: No. 1881/6½″. "Paneled Grape" Jardiniere, Cupped, Footed. (Other "Paneled Grape" 5″ and 6½″ Jardinieres are illustrated on page 5.)

No. 1881/3 pc. "Paneled Grape" Canape Set. Consists of: 1-12½″ Canape Tray, Round; 1-3½″ Cocktail, Round, Fruit, and 1-1837 Ladle.

Bottom Row: No. 1881/4″ "Paneled Grape" Rose Bowl, Cupped, Footed.

No. 1881. "Paneled Grape" Sauce Boat.

No. 1881. "Paneled Grape" Sauce Boat Tray.

No. 1881/12″/3 pc. "Paneled Grape" Epergne Set. Consists of: 1-12″ Epergne Lipped Bowl, 1-5″ Bowl Base, and 1-8½″ Epergne Vase, Bell.

No. 1881/12″/2 pc. "Paneled Grape" Epergne Set. (Not illustrated.) Same as above, but without Bowl Base.

Fenton

7425 SC
7 ½" Bowl

7227 SC
7" Bowl

7271 SC
Candleholder

7316 SC
Shallow Bowl

5824 SC
Banana Bowl

7324 SC
Ftd. Banana Bowl

7224 SC
10" Bowl

7223 SC
13" Bowl

5823 SC
11" Bowl

FENTON
Silver Crest
PETTICOAT
GLASS

7427 SC
Ftd. Bowl

Handcrafted to exacting standards of beauty, Silver Crest Petticoat Glass is made only by Fenton. For the customer who insists on something extra in the way of beauty, show her Fenton Petticoat.

7474 SC
6" Candleholder

7321 SC
11 ½" DC Bowl

7474 SC
6" Candleholder

FENTON HANDMADE
Silver Crest
PETTICOAT GLASS

Here's a "party perfect" glass hand-fashioned exclusively by Fenton. Its sparkling-fresh beauty will do nice things for your shop and your sales.

7222 SC
Low Dessert

7303 SC
Chip 'n Dip

7201 SC
Sugar & Cream

7296 SC
2 Tier Tidbit

7295 SC
3 Tier Tidbit

7403 SC
Shrimp 'n Dip
with Toothpick

7203 SC
Mayonnaise Set

7428 SC
8" Bonbon

7225 SC
5½" Bonbon

7294 SC
2 Tier Tidbit

7291 SC
Sandwich Tray

7394 SC
2 Tier Tidbit

7262 SC
12" Vase

7258 SC
8" DC Vase

7305 SC
5 pc. Epergne Set

7308 SC
4 pc. Epergne Set

7217 SC
8½" Plate

7211 SC
12½" Plate

7356 SC
6¼" DC Vase

7254 SC
4½" Vase

7354 SC
4½" DC Vase

7210 SC
10½" Plate

7216 SC
16" Torte Plate

7451 SC
6" Vase

7156 SC
6" DC Vase

FENTON HANDMADE

Peach Crest

PETTICOAT GLASS

Fenton Peach Crest, with its beautiful ruby overlay encased in milk glass, is truly an artistic piece of workmanship.

When your customers want to see something unusually exquisite, Fenton Peach Crest is the glass to show them.

7224 PC
10" Bowl

7156 PC
6" DC Vase

7157 PC
6" Vase Tulip

7166 PC
6" Jug

7237 PC
7" Basket

7227 PC
7" Bowl

7223 PC
13" Bowl

7233 SC
13" Basket

7234 SC
12" Basket

7336 SC
6½" Hdl. Basket

7237 SC
7" Basket

7228 SC
Ftd. Comport

7329 SC
Low Ftd. Comport

7229 SC
Ftd. Nut Dish or Sherbet

7213 SC
Ftd. Cakeplate

7429 SC
Ftd. Comport DC

7430 SC
Ftd. Comport Flared

7334 SC
Divided Relish

7333 SC
Handled Relish

5813 SC
Low Ftd. Cakeplate

Silver Crest in Spanish Lace

3510 SC
11" Ftd. Cakeplate

3580 SC
Ftd. Candy Box

3508 SC
Salt & Pepper Set

Fenton
Hobnail
America's Favorite
Handmade Glass Pattern

Fenton
Handmade Hobnail Baskets

3637 MI
7" Basket

3734 MI
12" Basket

3736 MI
6½" Basket

3837 MI
7" Basket

3830 MI
10" Basket

3638 MI
8½" Basket

3735 MI
5½" Basket

3834 MI
4½" Basket

Hobnail

A Tradition of Its Own

Trends and colors come and go, but Fenton Hobnail continues to be the most popular, best selling glass pattern of all time.

1975 marks the 36th anniversary of the introduction of Hobnail to our line. Its tremendous sales appeal has been an important part of the Fenton success story — and, of course, important to you in consistent retail sales.

Fenton makes the finest Milk Glass anywhere and the best selling pattern — Hobnail. Frequent additions to the fast selling Hobnail pattern keep it alive and fresh. This year is no exception. If you display Fenton Hobnail, it will sell.

3723 MI
Ftd. Bowl

3728 MI
Comport

3938 MI
12" Bowl

3926 MI
6" Bonbon

3639 MI
8" Bowl

3627 MI
Ftd. Peanut Dish

3920 MI
Ftd. Comport

3724 MI
8½" Bowl

3727 MI
Bowl

3706 MI
Handled Bonbon

3937 MI
7" Bonbon

3731 MI
10" Ftd. Bowl

3621 MI
9" Ftd. Oval Bowl

3635 MI
3 Toed Bowl

3620 MI
Low Banana Bowl

3716 MI
8" Bonbon

Fenton

3750 MI
6″ Vase

3752 MI
11″ Vase

3699 MI
Square Planter

3954 MI
7″ Vase

3956 MI
6¼″ Vase

3697 MI
8½″ Planter

3854 MI
4½″ Vase

Vases, Planters and Bowls

No one in hand made glass can match the versatility and the variety in Fenton vases, planters and bowls — from the unusual Epergnes to the smallest vase.

3799 MI
10″ Planter

3958 MI
8″ Vase

3898 MI
Jardiniere
(Takes a 4″ Clay Pot)

3704 MI
2 Pc. Epergne Set

3655 MI
5″ Vase

3850 MI
5″ Vase

3657 MI
7″ Vase

6

3704 MI
2 Piece Epergne

3867 MI
Lavabo

3701 MI
4 Piece Epergne

3801 MI
Miniature
4 Pc. Epergne

3992 MI
Boot

3690 MI
9½" Planter

3927 MI
7" Bowl

3654 MI
3 Toed Vase

3625 MI
8" Oval Bowl

3668 CB
Candy Box

Our Newest...

3668 CA
Candy Box

3668 MI
Candy Box

3668 CG
Candy Box

3600 MI
Cov'd Jam or Candy

3784 MI
Ftd. Candy Box

3700 MI
Cov'd Slipper

3786 MI
Oval Candy Box

Fenton Candy Boxes

Every year Fenton candy boxes are on our "best sellers" list. Carry a wide selection for your customers . . . they really do sell.

3980 MI
Ftd. Candy Jar

3885 MI
Ftd. Candy Box

3780 MI
Wedding Jar

3688 MI
Candy Jar

3984 MI
Candy Box

3880 MI
Candy Jar

3802 MI
Candy Box

3886 MI
Candy Box

8

3764 MI
54 oz. Jug

3740 MI
12" Relish

3906 MI
Sugar and Cream

3703 MI
Chip 'n Dip

3977 MI
Cov'd Butter

3913 MI
Ftd. Cakeplate

3902 MI
Cov'd Sugar & Cream

3762 MI
12 oz. Pitcher

3606 MI
Cov'd Sugar & Cream

3777 MI
Cov'd Butter

3609 MI
Salt & Pepper

3802 MI
Cov'd Butter Bowl

3601 MI
Cov'd Jam Jar

3605 MI
Cov'd Mustard

3822 MI
Relish

10

Handmade Hobnail Milk Glass

One could almost say that Fenton Hobnail Milk Glass has become an institution, for never has a glass pattern met with such enduring popularity. Your customers are buying more and more of this traditionally styled glassware each year.

Fenton Hobnail has proved outstandingly successful because it is as beautiful as it is authentic in its Early American styling.

This period, reflected in so many traditionally decorated homes today, is constantly growing in favor, for the graciousness and warmth of its beauty is timeless.

3794 MI
2 Tier Tidbit

3664 MI
70 oz. Ice Lip Jug

3602 MI
Kitchen Salt & Pepper

3806 MI
Salt & Pepper

3803 MI
Mayonnaise Set

3806 BW
Salt & Pepper

3709 MI
2 Tier Server

3917 MI
Sugar & Cream Set

3607 MI
Handled Divided Relish

3630 MI
Ice Cream or Nut Dish

3633 MI
Oval Nut Dish

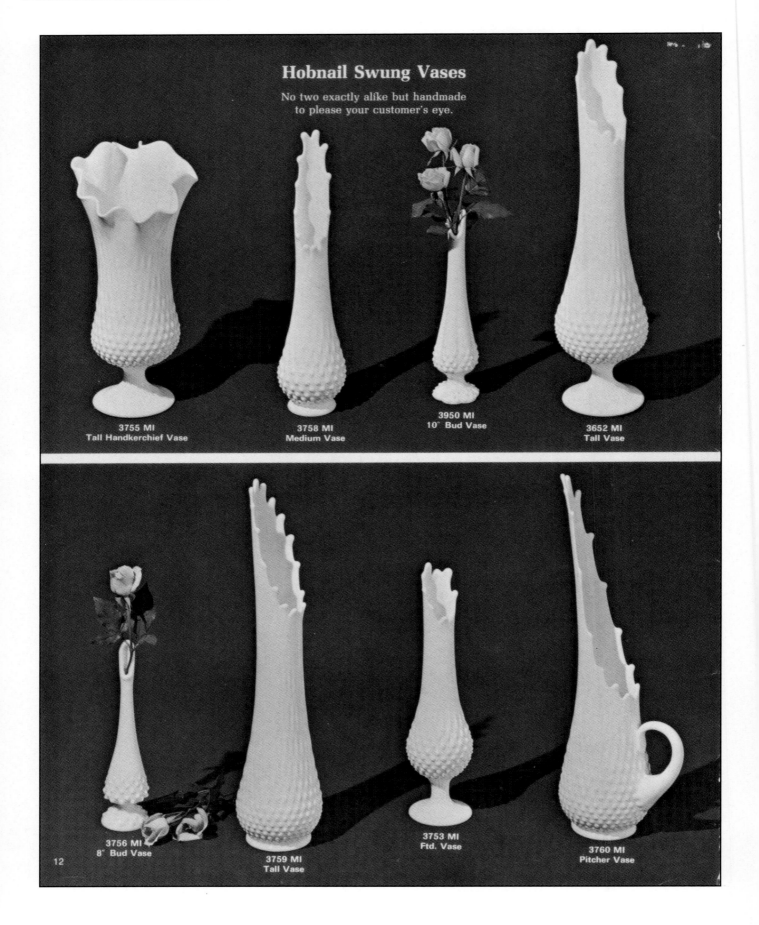

Hobnail Swung Vases

No two exactly alike but handmade
to please your customer's eye.

3755 MI
Tall Handkerchief Vase

3758 MI
Medium Vase

3950 MI
10" Bud Vase

3652 MI
Tall Vase

3756 MI
8" Bud Vase

3759 MI
Tall Vase

3753 MI
Ftd. Vase

3760 MI
Pitcher Vase

12

Fenton

Our oldest, most popular pattern....

3720 MI
Banana Bowl

3916 MI
Oil & Vinegar

3624 MI
10½" Bowl

3924 MI
9" Bowl

3629 MI
Ftd. Nut Dish

3640 MI
8" Oval Pickle Dish

3733 MI
Heart Relish

397 M
Basket 10"
Grape

Kanawha

393 M
Vase 9"
Grape

395 M
Vase 8½"
Hob Nail

399 M
Basket 9½"
Grape

394 M
Pitcher 9"
Grape

396 M
Pitcher 8½"
Hob Nail

403 M
Pitcher 6½"
Grape

401 M
Vase 6½"
Grape

Page 5

Kanawha

385 M
Pitcher 7"
Grape

806 M
Candy Jar 8"
Moon & Star

869 M
Rooster 9½"

919 M
Candle Holder 5"
Hob Nail

925 M
Bowl 6½"
Hob Nail

818 M
Goblet 9 oz.
Figured

287 M
Basket 7"
Grape

924 M
Nut Bowl 5"
Hob Nail

388 M
Vase 5¾"
Hob Nail

315 M
Vase 5"
Diamond Dot

880 M
Vase 10"
Hob Nail

888 M
Vase 11"
Figured

881 M
Goblet 12-oz.
Hob Nail

811 M
Toothpick 2¼" Scroll

911 M
Toothpick 2½"
Strawberry

829 M
Slipper 6"
Rose

810 M
Slipper 5½"
Daisy & Button

296 M
Basket 7"
Hob Nail

882 M
Compote 6"
Hob Nail

Milk Glass

922 M
Basket 7½"
Hob Nail

905 M
Hen On Nest 7½"

291 M
Cruet 6"
Hob Nail

885 M
Ash Tray 6½"
Hob Nail

86 M
Vase 14"
Hob Nail

386 M
Pitcher 5½"
Grape

915 M
Candy Jar 9½"
Hob Nail

298 M
Bowl 6"
Hob Nail

297 M
Handled Bowl 6½"
Hob Nail

917 M
Sugar & Cream
Hob Nail

917 M
Sugar & Cream
Hob Nail

330 M
Basket 8"
Grape

290 M
Salt & Pepper 5"
Hob Nail

324 M
Basket 8"
Diamond Dot

81 M
Pitcher 12"
Hob Nail

382 M
Pitcher 3¾"
Grape

367 M
Pitcher 4"
Grape

921 M
Vase 16"
Hob Nail

Page 7

FOSTORIA GLASS COMPANY

1121/ 388

1121/ 389

1200/ 146

1200/ 155

1200/ 677

1200/ 792

1300/ 149

886/ 281

886/ 544

2056/ 713

2056/ 714

2056/ 715

2056/ 162

2056/ 763

2056/ 799

2056/ 804

2183/ 202

2183/ 248

2412/ 300

2412/ 354

2412/ 387

2513/ 155

2513/ 676

2519/ 357

2595/ 672

2676/ 422

2679/ 580

2682/ 412

2693/ 162

2700/ 743

2700/ 747

2714/ 287

2720/ 718

2710/ 300

2710/ 501

2710/ 686
2710/ 687
2710/ 688
2710/ 697

2710/ 502

2712/ 179

2712/ 186

2712/ 311

2712/ 354

2712/ 355

2712/ 450

2712/ 452

2712/ 499

2712/ 550

2712/ 592

2712/ 686   2712/ 687
2712/ 688   2712/ 697

2712/ 799

2713/ 2

2713/ 11

2713/ 63

2713/ 162

2713/ 179

2713/ 183

2713/ 300

2713/ 311

2713/ 315

2713/ 347

2713/ 348

2713/ 385

2713/ 499

2713/ 500

2713/ 502

2713/ 550

2713/ 653

2713/ 686
2713/ 697

2713/ 687

2713/ 688

2713/ 720

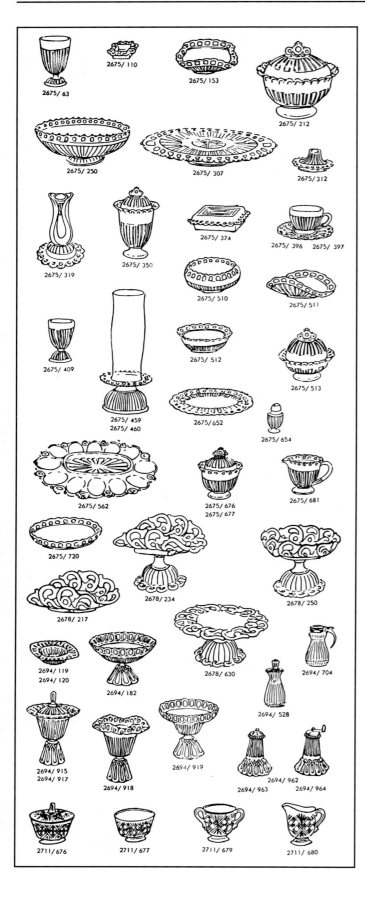

2675/ 63
2675/ 110
2675/ 153
2675/ 212
2675/ 250
2675/ 307
2675/ 312
2675/ 319
2675/ 350
2675/ 374
2675/ 396
2675/ 397
2675/ 409
2675/ 510
2675/ 511
2675/ 512
2675/ 513
2675/ 459
2675/ 460
2675/ 652
2675/ 654
2675/ 562
2675/ 676
2675/ 677
2675/ 681
2675/ 720
2678/ 234
2678/ 250
2678/ 217
2694/ 119
2694/ 120
2678/ 630
2694/ 182
2694/ 704
2694/ 528
2694/ 915
2694/ 917
2694/ 918
2694/ 919
2694/ 962
2694/ 963
2694/ 964
2711/ 676
2711/ 677
2711/ 679
2711/ 680

824/ 385
826/ 544
828/ 281
829/ 580
830/ 587
831/ 276
827/ 842
834/ 454
832/ 287
833/ 293
835/ 70
1229/ 676
1229/ 677
1229/ 710
1229/ 757
1229/ 814
1704/ 64
1704/ 76
1704/ 297
1704/ 377
1704/ 450
1704/ 451
1704/ 452
1704/ 501
1704/ 528
1704/ 457
1704/ 502
1704/ 652
1704/ 676
1704/ 615
1704/ 680
1704/ 605
1704/ 606
2620/ 2
2620/ 8
2620/ 64
2620/ 89
2620/ 192
2620/ 216
2620/ 241
2620/ 502
2620/ 314
2620/ 459
2620/ 679
2620/ 681

63-64

THE L.E.

Smith Glass

COMPANY

"*Over a Half Century of Fine Handcrafted Glass*"

WESTMORELAND COUNTY

MOUNT PLEASANT, PENNSYLVANIA

MILK

CRYSTAL

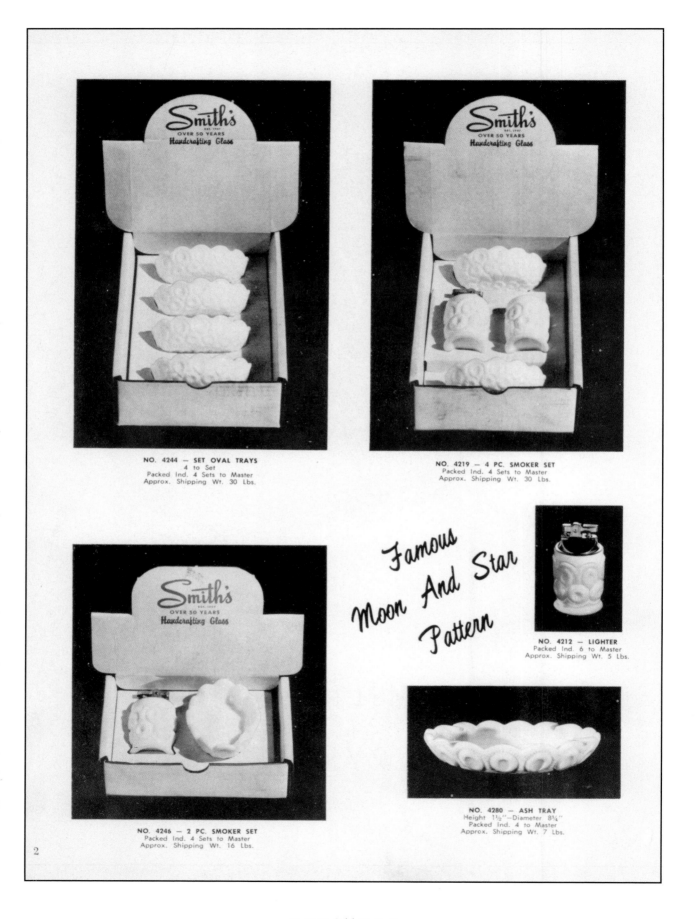

NO. 4244 — SET OVAL TRAYS
4 to Set
Packed Ind. 4 Sets to Master
Approx. Shipping Wt. 30 Lbs.

NO. 4219 — 4 PC. SMOKER SET
Packed Ind. 4 Sets to Master
Approx. Shipping Wt. 30 Lbs.

Famous Moon And Star Pattern

NO. 4212 — LIGHTER
Packed Ind. 6 to Master
Approx. Shipping Wt. 5 Lbs.

NO. 4246 — 2 PC. SMOKER SET
Packed Ind. 4 Sets to Master
Approx. Shipping Wt. 16 Lbs.

NO. 4280 — ASH TRAY
Height 1½"—Diameter 8¼"
Packed Ind. 4 to Master
Approx. Shipping Wt. 7 Lbs.

2

NO. 9961 — VASE
Height 9″—Width 3¼″
Packed Ind. 6 to Master
Approx. Shipping Wt. 14 Lbs.

NO. 9931 — BUD VASE
Height 6½″—Diameter 2½″
Packed 6 to Carton
Approx. Shipping Wt. 8 Lbs.

NO. 9952 - GOBLET
Height 6″ - Width 3¼″
Packed Ind. 6 to Master
Approx. Shipping Wt. 10 Lbs.

NO. 9951 - CRIMPED COMPOTE
Height 5¼″ - Diameter 5¼″
Packed Ind. 6 to Master
Approx. Shipping Wt. 10 Lbs.

NO. 9941 - ¼ LB. BUTTER
Height 2¾″ - Width 3¾″ - Length 8¼″
Packed Ind. 6 to Master
Approx. Shipping Wt. 15 Lbs.

NO. 9911 - SALT & PEPPER
Height 2½″
Packed 6 Sets to Master
Approx. Shipping Wt. 10 Lbs.

NO. 9901 - CREAM & SUGAR
Height 2¾″ - Length 5½″
Packed 6 Sets to Master
Approx. Shipping Wt. 10 Lbs.

NO. 9922 - NAPPY
Height 4¾″ - Diameter 5¼″
Packed 12 to Carton
Approx. Shipping Wt. 10 Lbs.

Vintage Grape

NO. 9977 — CANDY JAR
Height 7½″—Width 6¼″
Packed Ind. 4 to Master
Approx. Shipping Wt. 10 Lbs.

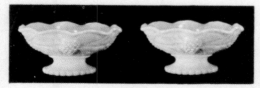

NO. 9921 - CANDLEHOLDER
Height 4¾″ - Diameter 5¼″
Packed 6 Sets to Master
Approx. Shipping Wt. 11 Lbs.

4

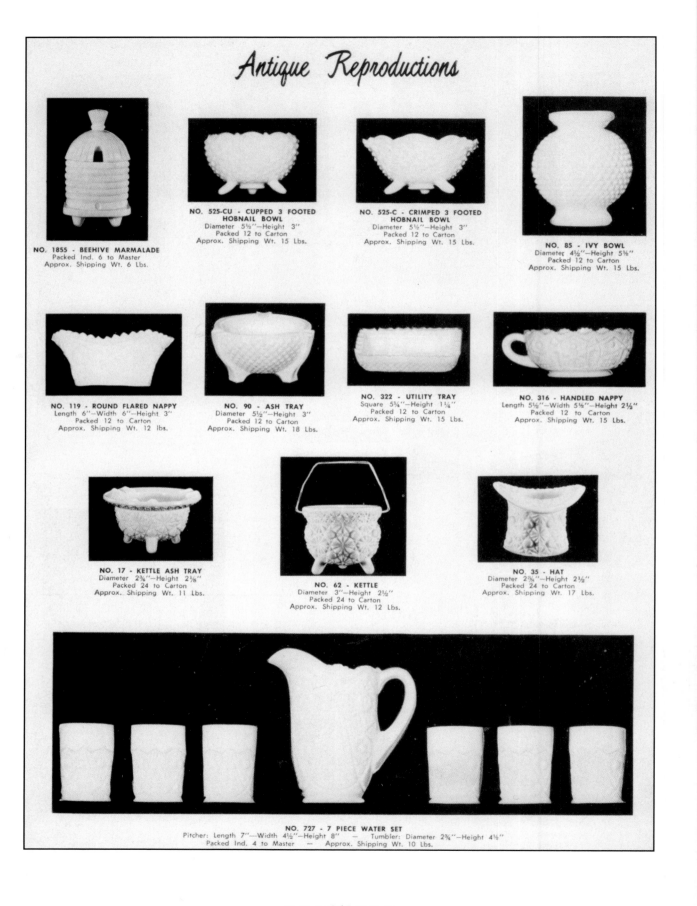

Antique Reproductions

NO. 1855 - BEEHIVE MARMALADE
Packed Ind. 6 to Master
Approx. Shipping Wt. 6 Lbs.

NO. 525-CU - CUPPED 3 FOOTED HOBNAIL BOWL
Diameter 5½"—Height 3"
Packed 12 to Carton
Approx. Shipping Wt. 15 Lbs.

NO. 525-C - CRIMPED 3 FOOTED HOBNAIL BOWL
Diameter 5½"—Height 3"
Packed 12 to Carton
Approx. Shipping Wt. 15 Lbs.

NO. 85 - IVY BOWL
Diameter 4½"—Height 5½"
Packed 12 to Carton
Approx. Shipping Wt. 15 Lbs.

NO. 119 - ROUND FLARED NAPPY
Length 6"—Width 6"—Height 3"
Packed 12 to Carton
Approx. Shipping Wt. 12 lbs.

NO. 90 - ASH TRAY
Diameter 5½"—Height 3"
Packed 12 to Carton
Approx. Shipping Wt. 18 Lbs.

NO. 322 - UTILITY TRAY
Square 5¼"—Height 1¼"
Packed 12 to Carton
Approx. Shipping Wt. 15 Lbs.

NO. 316 - HANDLED NAPPY
Length 5½"—Width 5½"—Height 2½"
Packed 12 to Carton
Approx. Shipping Wt. 15 Lbs.

NO. 17 - KETTLE ASH TRAY
Diameter 2¾"—Height 2⅛"
Packed 24 to Carton
Approx. Shipping Wt. 11 Lbs.

NO. 62 - KETTLE
Diameter 3"—Height 2½"
Packed 24 to Carton
Approx. Shipping Wt. 12 Lbs.

NO. 35 - HAT
Diameter 2¾"—Height 2½"
Packed 24 to Carton
Approx. Shipping Wt. 17 Lbs.

NO. 727 - 7 PIECE WATER SET
Pitcher: Length 7"—Width 4½"—Height 8"   —   Tumbler: Diameter 2¾"—Height 4½"
Packed Ind. 4 to Master   —   Approx. Shipping Wt. 10 Lbs.

Antique Reproductions

NO. 409 - VASE
Width 4½" - Height 9"
Packed Ind. 4 to Master
Approx. Shipping Wt. 14 Lbs.

NO. 407 - 12" FAN VASE
Length 5"-Width 2½"-Ht. 12"
Packed Ind. 4 to Master
Approx. Shipping Wt. 11 Lbs.

NO. 403 — 12" VASE
Width 4½"—Height 12"
Packed Ind. 4 to Master
Approx. Shipping Wt. 11 Lbs.

NO. 810 - URN & COVER
Height 15¾"
Packed Ind. 4 to Master
Approx. Shipping Wt. 12 Lbs.

NO. 556   CUPPED COMPOTE
Diameter 6⅜"—Height 7¼"
Packed Ind. 4 to Master
Approx. Shipping Wt. 14 Lbs.

NO. 514 - CUPPED COMPOTE
Diameter 5"—Height 6½"
Packed Ind. 6 to Master
Approx. Shipping Wt. 12 Lbs.

NO. 8 - OVAL FOOTED BOWL
Length 8½"—Width 6¼"—Height 6"
Packed Ind. 4 to Master
Approx. Shipping Wt. 14 Lbs.

NO. 551 - CRIMPED COMPOTE
Diameter 8¼"—Height 7¼"
Packed Ind. 4 to Master
Approx. Shipping Wt. 14 Lbs.

NO. 515 - CRIMPED COMPOTE
Diameter 7"—Height 6¼"
Packed Ind. 6 to Master
Approx. Shipping Wt. 12 Lbs.

NO. 373 — 9" BOWL
Width 9"—Height 3½"
Packed Ind. 4 to Master
Approx. Shipping Wt. 17 Lbs.

8

BIBLIOGRAPHY

Allison, Grace. *Kemple Glass Works 1945-1977*. Costa Mesa, CA: Shaeffer, 1977.

Belknap, E. McCamly. *Milk Glass*. New York: Crown Publishers, 1949.

Ferson, Regis F. and Mary F. *Yesterday's Milk Glass Today*. Greenburg, PA: Chas H. Henry Printing Co., 1981.

Garrison, Myrna and Bob. *Imperial's Vintage Milk Glass*. Arlington, TX: Author, 1992.

Grist, Everett. *Covered Animal Dishes*. Paducah, KY: Collector Books, 1988.

Grizel, Ruth Ann. *Westmoreland, Our Children's Heritage*. Iowa City, IA: FSJ Publishing, 1993.

Hastin, Bud & Vickie. *Avon Bottle Collector's Encyclopedia*. Las Vegas, NV: Author, 10th Edition, 1984.

Heacock, William. *Fenton Glass the First 25 Years*. Marietta, OH: Antique Publications, 1978.

Heacock, Wm. and Bickenheuser, F. *U.S. Glass from A to Z*. Marietta, OH: Antique Publications, 1978.

Jenks, Bill and Jerry Luna. *Early American Pattern Glass, 1850-1910*. Radnor, PA: Wallace-Homestead Book Co., 1990.

Kaye, Barbara Joyce. *White Gold I*. New York: Author, 1990.

————. *White Gold II*. Metuchen, NJ: Author, 1993.

Kerr, Ann. *Fostoria*. Paducah, KY: Collector Books, 1994.

Kovar, Lorraine. *The Westmoreland Story*. Marietta, OH: Antique Publications, 1991.

————. *Westmoreland Glass 1950-1984*. Marietta, OH: Antique Publications, 1991.

Krause, Gail. *The Encyclopedia of Duncan Glass*. Hicksville, NY: Exposition Press, 1976.

Lechler, Doris and Virginia O'Neill. *Children's Glass Dishes*. Nashville, TN: Nelson Publishers, 1976.

Lucas, Robert I. *Tarentum Pattern Glass*. Tarentum, PA: Author, 1981.

McDonald, Ann Gilbert. *Evolution of the Night Lamp*. Radnor, PA: Wallace-Homestead Book Co., 1979.

Metz, Alice H. *Much More Early American Pattern Glass*. Chicago, IL: Author, 1969.

Millard, T.S. *Opaque Glass*. Topeka, KS: Central Press, third edition, 1953.

Newbound, Betty. *Figurine Fact$ and Figure$*. Commerce, MI: Author, 1982.

Newbound, Betty. *Glass Collector's Almanac*. Commerce, MI: Author, 1987.

Peterson, Arthur G., Ph. D. *Glass Patents and Patterns*. DeBary, FL: Author, 1973.

Revi, Albert Christian. *American Pressed Glass and Figural Bottles*. New York: Thomas Nelson, Inc., 1973.

Schwartz, Marvin and Betsy Wade. *New York Times Book of Antiques*. New York: Galahad Books, 1972.

Smith, Frank R. and Ruth. *Miniature Lamps*. Atglen, PA: Schiffer Publishing, 1968.

Smith, Ruth. *Miniature Lamps II*. Atglen, PA: Schiffer Publishing, 1982.

Solverson, John. *Those Fascinating Little Lamps*. Marietta, OH: Antique Publications, 1988.

Warman, Edwin G. *Milk Glass Addenda*. Uniontown, PA: E. G. Warman Publishing, 1959.

Weatherman, Hazel. *Colored Glassware of the Depression Era, II*. Springfield, MO: Weatherman Glassbooks, 1974.

Welker, John and Elizabeth. *Pressed Glass in America*. Ivyland, PA: Antique Acres, 1986.

Whitmyer, Margaret & Kenn. *Bedroom and Bathroom Glassware of the Depression Years*. Paducah, KY: Collector Books, 1990.

Wills, Geoffrey. *Victorian Glass*. London: G. Bell & Sons, 1976.

Wilson, Jack D. *Pheonix Consolidated Art Glass 1928 – 1980*. Marietta, OH: Antique Publications, 1989.

Yalom, Libby. *Shoes of Glass*. Marietta, OH: Antique Publications, 1988.

National Toothpick Holder Collector's Society. *Toothpick Holders, China, Glass and Metal*. Marietta, OH: Antique Publications, 1992.

CATALOGS & ARTICLES

Edwards, Bill and Martha. *Old Virginia Glass*. (Dec/Jan 1988) Marietta, OH: Antique Publications.

Butler Brothers catalogs, 1905 – 1910.

Pittsburgh Lamp, Brass & Glass Co., undated catalog.

INDEX

Books on Antiques and Collectibles

This is only a partial listing of the books on antiques that are available from Collector Books. All books are well illustrated and contain current values. Most of the following books are available from your local book seller, antique dealer, or public library. If you are unable to locate certain titles in your area, you may order by mail from COLLECTOR BOOKS, P.O. Box 3009, Paducah, KY 42002-3009. Customers with Visa or MasterCard may phone in orders from 8:00–4:00 CST, Monday–Friday, Toll Free 1-800-626-5420. Add $2.00 for postage for the first book ordered and $0.30 for each additional book. Include item number, title, and price when ordering. Allow 14 to 21 days for delivery.

BOOKS ON GLASS AND POTTERY

1810	American Art Glass, Shuman	$29.95
1312	Blue & White Stoneware, McNerney	$9.95
1959	Blue Willow, 2nd Ed., Gaston	$14.95
3719	Coll. Glassware from the 40's, 50's, 60's, 2nd Ed., Florence	$19.95
3816	Collectible Vernon Kilns, Nelson	$24.95
3311	Collecting Yellow Ware – Id. & Value Gd., McAllister	$16.95
1373	Collector's Ency. of American Dinnerware, Cunningham	$24.95
3815	Coll. Ency. of Blue Ridge Dinnerware, Newbound	$19.95
2272	Collector's Ency. of California Pottery, Chipman	$24.95
3811	Collector's Ency. of Colorado Pottery, Carlton	$24.95
3312	Collector's Ency. of Children's Dishes, Whitmyer	$19.95
2133	Collector's Ency. of Cookie Jars, Roerig	$24.95
3723	Coll. Ency. of Cookie Jars-Volume II, Roerig	$24.95
3724	Collector's Ency. of Depression Glass, 11th Ed., Florence	$19.95
2209	Collector's Ency. of Fiesta, 7th Ed., Huxford	$19.95
1439	Collector's Ency. of Flow Blue China, Gaston	$19.95
3812	Coll. Ency. of Flow Blue China, 2nd Ed., Gaston	$24.95
3813	Collector's Ency. of Hall China, 2nd Ed., Whitmyer	$24.95
2334	Collector's Ency. of Majolica Pottery, Katz-Marks	$19.95
1358	Collector's Ency. of McCoy Pottery, Huxford	$19.95
3313	Collector's Ency. of Niloak, Gifford	$19.95
3837	Collector's Ency. of Nippon Porcelain I, Van Patten	$24.95
2089	Collector's Ency. of Nippon Porcelain II, Van Patten	$24.95
1665	Collector's Ency. of Nippon Porcelain III, Van Patten	$24.95
1447	Collector's Ency. of Noritake, 1st Series, Van Patten	$19.95
1034	Collector's Ency. of Roseville Pottery, Huxford	$19.95
1035	Collector's Ency. of Roseville Pottery, 2nd Ed., Huxford	$19.95
3314	Collector's Ency. of Van Briggle Art Pottery, Sasicki	$24.95
3433	Collector's Guide To Harker Pottery - U.S.A., Colbert	$17.95
2339	Collector's Guide to Shawnee Pottery, Vanderbilt	$19.95
1425	Cookie Jars, Westfall	$9.95
3440	Cookie Jars, Book II, Westfall	$19.95
2275	Czechoslovakian Glass & Collectibles, Barta	$16.95
3882	Elegant Glassware of the Depression Era, 6th Ed., Florence	$19.95
3725	Fostoria - Pressed, Blown & Hand Molded Shapes, Kerr	$24.95
3883	Fostoria Stemware - The Crystal for America, Long	$24.95
3886	Kitchen Glassware of the Depression Years, 5th Ed., Florence	$19.95
3889	Pocket Guide to Depression Glass, 9th Ed., Florence	$9.95
3825	Puritan Pottery, Morris	$24.95
1670	Red Wing Collectibles, DePasquale	$9.95
1440	Red Wing Stoneware, DePasquale	$9.95
1958	So. Potteries Blue Ridge Dinnerware, 3rd Ed., Newbound	$14.95
3739	Standard Carnival Glass, 4th Ed., Edwards	$24.95
3327	Watt Pottery – Identification & Value Guide, Morris	$19.95
2224	World of Salt Shakers, 2nd Ed., Lechner	$24.95

BOOKS ON DOLLS & TOYS

2079	Barbie Fashion, Vol. 1, 1959-1967, Eames	$24.95
3310	Black Dolls - 1820 - 1991 - Id. & Value Guide, Perkins	$17.95
3810	Chatty Cathy Dolls, Lewis	$15.95
1529	Collector's Ency. of Barbie Dolls, DeWein	$19.95
2338	Collector's Ency. of Disneyana, Longest & Stern	$24.95
3727	Coll. Guide to Ideal Dolls, Izen	$18.95
3822	Madame Alexander Price Guide #19, Smith	$9.95
3732	Matchbox Toys, 1948 to 1993, Johnson	$18.95

3733	Modern Collector's Dolls, 6th series, Smith	$24.95
1540	Modern Toys, 1930 - 1980, Baker	$19.95
3824	Patricia Smith's Doll Values – Antique to Modern, 10th ed	$12.95
3826	Story of Barbie, Westenhouser, No Values	$19.95
2028	Toys, Antique & Collectible, Longest	$14.95
1808	Wonder of Barbie, Manos	$9.95
1430	World of Barbie Dolls, Manos	$9.95

OTHER COLLECTIBLES

1457	American Oak Furniture, McNerney	$9.95
3716	American Oak Furniture, Book II, McNerney	$12.95
2333	Antique & Collectible Marbles, 3rd Ed., Grist	$9.95
1748	Antique Purses, Holiner	$19.95
1426	Arrowheads & Projectile Points, Hothem	$7.95
1278	Art Nouveau & Art Deco Jewelry, Baker	$9.95
1714	Black Collectibles, Gibbs	$19.95
1128	Bottle Pricing Guide, 3rd Ed., Cleveland	$7.95
3717	Christmas Collectibles, 2nd Ed., Whitmyer	$24.95
1752	Christmas Ornaments, Johnston	$19.95
3718	Collectible Aluminum, Grist	$16.95
2132	Collector's Ency. of American Furniture, Vol. I, Swedberg	$24.95
2271	Collector's Ency. of American Furniture, Vol. II, Swedberg	$24.95
3720	Coll. Ency. of American Furniture, Vol III, Swedberg	$24.95
3722	Coll. Ency. of Compacts, Carryalls & Face Powder Boxes, Mueller	$24.95
2018	Collector's Ency. of Granite Ware, Greguire	$24.95
3430	Coll. Ency. of Granite Ware, Book 2, Greguire	$24.95
1441	Collector's Guide to Post Cards, Wood	$9.95
2276	Decoys, Kangas	$24.95
1629	Doorstops – Id. & Values, Bertoia	$9.95
1716	Fifty Years of Fashion Jewelry, Baker	$19.95
3817	Flea Market Trader, 9th Ed., Huxford	$12.95
3731	Florence's Standard Baseball Card Price Gd., 6th Ed.	$9.95
3819	General Store Collectibles, Wilson	$24.95
3436	Grist's Big Book of Marbles, Everett Grist	$19.95
2278	Grist's Machine Made & Contemporary Marbles	$9.95
1424	Hatpins & Hatpin Holders, Baker	$9.95
3884	Huxford's Collectible Advertising – Id. & Value Gd., 2nd Ed	$24.95
3820	Huxford's Old Book Value Guide, 6th Ed.	$19.95
3821	Huxford's Paperback Value Guide	$19.95
1181	100 Years of Collectible Jewelry, Baker	$9.95
2216	Kitchen Antiques – 1790 - 1940, McNerney	$14.95
3887	Modern Guns – Id. & Val. Gd., 10th Ed., Quertermous	$12.95
3734	Pocket Guide to Handguns, Quertermous	$9.95
3735	Pocket Guide to Rifles, Quertermous	$9.95
3736	Pocket Guide to Shotguns, Quertermous	$9.95
2026	Railroad Collectibles, 4th Ed., Baker	$14.95
1632	Salt & Pepper Shakers, Guarnaccia	$9.95
1888	Salt & Pepper Shakers II, Guarnaccia	$14.95
2220	Salt & Pepper Shakers III, Guarnaccia	$14.95
3443	Salt & Pepper Shakers IV, Guarnaccia	$18.95
3890	Schroeder's Antiques Price Guide, 13th Ed.	$12.95
2096	Silverplated Flatware, 4th Ed., Hagan	$14.95
2348	20th Century Fashionable Plastic Jewelry, Baker	$19.95
3828	Value Guide to Advertising Memorabilia, Summers	$18.95
3830	Vintage Vanity Bags & Purses, Gerson	$24.95

Other Books
by Betty and Bill Newbound

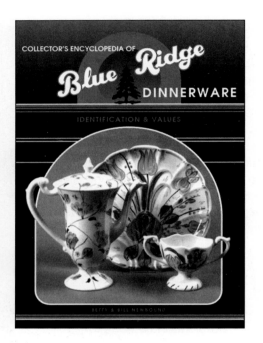

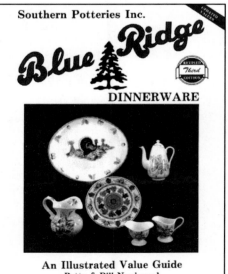